WRITERS' BLOCK
THE PARIS ANTIFASCIST CONGRESS OF 1935

# LEGENDA

LEGENDA is the Modern Humanities Research Association's book imprint for new research in the Humanities. Founded in 1995 by Malcolm Bowie and others within the University of Oxford, Legenda has always been a collaborative publishing enterprise, directly governed by scholars. The Modern Humanities Research Association (MHRA) joined this collaboration in 1998, became half-owner in 2004, in partnership with Maney Publishing and then Routledge, and has since 2016 been sole owner. Titles range from medieval texts to contemporary cinema and form a widely comparative view of the modern humanities, including works on Arabic, Catalan, English, French, German, Greek, Italian, Portuguese, Russian, Spanish, and Yiddish literature. Editorial boards and committees of more than 60 leading academic specialists work in collaboration with bodies such as the Society for French Studies, the British Comparative Literature Association and the Association of Hispanists of Great Britain & Ireland.

The MHRA encourages and promotes advanced study and research in the field of the modern humanities, especially modern European languages and literature, including English, and also cinema. It aims to break down the barriers between scholars working in different disciplines and to maintain the unity of humanistic scholarship. The Association fulfils this purpose through the publication of journals, bibliographies, monographs, critical editions, and the MHRA Style Guide, and by making grants in support of research. Membership is open to all who work in the Humanities, whether independent or in a University post, and the participation of younger colleagues entering the field is especially welcomed.

ALSO PUBLISHED BY THE ASSOCIATION

*Critical Texts*
*Tudor and Stuart Translations* • *New Translations* • *European Translations*
*MHRA Library of Medieval Welsh Literature*

*MHRA Bibliographies*
*Publications of the Modern Humanities Research Association*

*The Annual Bibliography of English Language & Literature*
*Austrian Studies*
*Modern Language Review*
*Portuguese Studies*
*The Slavonic and East European Review*
*Working Papers in the Humanities*
*The Yearbook of English Studies*

www.mhra.org.uk
www.legendabooks.com

# Writers' Block

## The Paris Antifascist Congress of 1935

❖

JACOB BOAS

*l*

**LEGENDA**

Modern Humanities Research Association

2016

Published by Legenda
an imprint of the Modern Humanities Research Association
Salisbury House, Station Road, Cambridge CB1 2LA

ISBN 978-1-78188-449-2 (HB)
ISBN 978-1-78188-450-8 (PB)

First published 2016

Copy-Editor: Dr Susan Wharton

# CONTENTS

❖

*For Pat —*
*Who Made All the Difference*

# ACKNOWLEDGEMENTS

❖

I would like to thank the following for their support, academic and otherwise: first and foremost my wife, Pat Boas to whom this book is dedicated. Longtime friend Professor Anthony d'Agostino whose expertise in Soviet and global history was indispensable. Craig Florence of Mother Foucault, Portland's most enlightened bookstore and store habitués Kyss, Tom, Will, Christine, Bob, Charles, Carrie, and A.M.; Alon Raab. Vic van de Reijt, publisher with Nijgh en Van Ditmar (Amsterdam) until his retirement, for a friendship and support dating back some 30 years. Professor Anne Hartmann and Professor Laureen Nussbaum; University of Southern California' Special Collections Archivist Michaela Ullmann, and the ever-helpful staff at the Internationaal Instituut voor Sociale Geschiedenis in Amsterdam (The International Institute for Social History). Dr Graham Nelson, Managing Editor of Legenda Books, for advice and commitment, and Dr Susan Wharton for meticulous copy-editing. Linfield College, for generous support. And, not to forget, my children Erica, Naomi, and Simon, and grandchildren Airi and Keanu.

*Writers' Block* is especially indebted to Sandra Teroni and Wolfgang Klein for *Pour la défense de la culture. Les textes du Congrès international des écrivains, Paris, juin 1935* (Dijon: Éditions Universitaires de Dijon, 2005). *Pour la défense* contains the full text of every speech, meticulously annotated, supplemented with an introduction, epilogue, author biographies, and more. All citations from the speeches are from this invaluable resource.

Translations are my own unless otherwise indicated.

J.B., March 2016

*If language is not correct, then what is said is not what is meant: if what is said is not what is meant, then what ought to be done remains undone; if this remains undone, morals and art will deteriorate, justice will go astray and people will stand about in hopeless confusion. Hence there must be no arbitrariness in what is said. This matters in everything. If left to administer a country, the first thing to do is 'to correct language'.*

CONFUCIUS

# INTRODUCTION

❖

In the early summer of 1935, 230 writers from 38 countries converged on an art deco building in the heart of Paris to consider ways and means of countering the fascist assault on the Muses. For five unseasonably hot days, between 21 and 25 June, one author after another mounted the stage of the Maison de la Mutualité to weigh in on such elusive constructs as the cultural heritage, humanism, individualism, collectivism, creativity, freedom of speech, and the role of the writer. Le Congrès international des écrivains pour la défense de la culture, also known as the antifascist Congress — respectively its official and unofficial designation — was a star-studded affair. Marquee names included the Englishmen Aldous Huxley and E. M. Forster; German exiles Bertolt Brecht and Lion Feuchtwanger; the Austrian Robert Musil and the Rumanian Dadaist Tristan Tzara. The Soviets supplied Ilya Ehrenburg and Isaak Babel; Boris Pasternak put in a cameo appearance, filling in for Maxim Gorky, who was ill (he died the following year). André Gide and André Malraux presided. Authors representing countries outside the European linguistic heartland did not go unrepresented; fascism was a global phenomenon and the Congress treated it as such. Novelists predominated, with a dusting of philosophers and historians thrown in for good measure. Political affiliations ranged from hardcore left to hardcore liberal. The delegates found themselves addressing packed houses, overwhelmingly composed of the Paris working class, reputedly the savviest on the planet.

The International Congress of Writers for the Defence of Culture was a facet of the United and Popular Fronts. Conceived by Stalin, the United and Popular Fronts established a road map for cooperation between Communists and previously shunned partners to the right; the more inclusive Popular Front became official two months after the Congress. The Soviet Union laid claim to the vanguard role the way Lenin had the Communist Party. With a landmass covering a sixth of the earth's surface, a rapidly developing industrial base and a robust counter-ideology, it seemed only natural that in the struggle against fascism the Soviets should assume the role of big brother. The Communist state on Germany's eastern flank, the fruit of 'Jewish Marxism', topped Hitler's list of countries to be wiped from the face of the earth, securing German *Lebensraum* for the next thousand years.

The siting of the Congress in the French capital was fitting. French soil had proven exceptionally fertile for growing fascist and proto-fascist movements and parties. Plagued by scandals and corruption at the highest levels of government trickling ever downward, the country seemed ripe for the plucking. Scandals were nothing new in France and tended to be taken in stride. But the Stavisky affair brought things to a boil. Stavisky — who happened to be Jewish, which only added fuel to the fire — was a notorious swindler who had made his fortune defrauding on a large scale. On the evening of 6 February 1934, 'Bloody Tuesday', the right took to the streets, determined to bring down the moderate left government of Édouard Daladier. That brought out the left and assorted defenders of the republic. For two weeks, wrote Janet Flanner in the *New Yorker*, 'the riots kept France in an unpleasant uproar'.

> For several years, every class in France has been banditized by state taxes, state politicians, state-protected swindlers; on that one night every class in Paris turned out to protest — from men in Republican derby hats down to chaps in Communist caps [...] Against horses' hooves, gunshots, and police clubs, this unpartisan mass fought in surprise, struggled with mutual courage, and was struck down without party distinction.[1]

The spectre of 'Bloody Tuesday' haunted the anti-fascist Congress no less than the spectre of Hitler.

The defeat of the right was the Popular Front in action *avant la lettre*. Yet the desiderata of the Popular Front imposed constraints. The new dynamic entailed putting aside long-standing antipathies and reservations on both sides. Concomitantly, the prestige of the Soviet Union, abetted by these very same Front politics, stood at an all-time high, both among the intelligentsia and the masses. In Paris, the Russians by and large framed the agenda, emphasizing the role and responsibility of the writer to society at large: what, how, and for whom to write. For all that, the Congress was not quite a Soviet tool; the nature of its composition, Stalin's pursuit of Front politics, and the very location itself, Paris, precluded such an outcome. In any event, the Soviets did not lack for allies inside the Mutualité, both among the public and the speakers. The Paris Congress was catnip to Stalin's new course — up to a point.

— 2 —

In the mid-1930s, years away from becoming a failed state, the Soviet Union had a significant following among Western intellectuals. Much has been made of this love affair with the world's first workers' state, condemnation compounded with abject *mea culpa*s on the part of those who once gustily sang its praises. Ultimately, Stalin's serial betrayals of the revolution hung its Western supporters out to dry. The Congress paid lip service to a united front, but the cracks could not be papered over. In many respects, 1935 was a turning point.

The Soviet imprimatur makes it impractical to separate the Paris Congress from two prior writers' congresses held in the USSR and attended by a number of Western writers instrumental in organizing the Paris sequel: Kharkov (1930) and Moscow (1934). The 'Soviet experience' runs like a red thread through the story of the Paris Congress. If *Writers' Block* were a film instead of a book, these two congresses would be the second feature of a double bill.

Among those who attended the Congresses in Kharkov or Moscow, or both,

FIG. 1. Writers' Congress for the Defence of Culture. From right to left: Paul Nizan, Henri Barbusse, Ilya Ehrenburg, Waldo Frank. (David Seymour/Magnum Photos)

FIG. 2. Writers' Congress for the Defence of Culture. Seated at the table from left to right: Paul Vaillant-Couturier, André Gide, Jean-Richard Bloch, André Malraux, speaking. In the background: poster of Maxim Gorky. (David Seymour/Magnum Photos)

either as observers or speakers, were André Malraux, Michael Gold, Klaus Mann, Jean-Richard Bloch, and Anna Seghers. These represented but a fraction of the hundreds of Western intellectuals who visited the USSR in the interwar years. Not a few headed home oozing admiration.

André Gide was an exception. The *eminence grise* of Europe's literary set between the wars visited in 1936 and returned to his upper-class flat in Paris's Rue Vaneau with a mighty bee in his bonnet. *Return from the USSR*, his one and only bestseller, amounted to a searing indictment. By this time, the infatuation with the Soviet Union was no longer what it had been even the year before, when the Soviets rather handily took control of the Paris Congress, despite rumours of mass arrests following the assassination of Sergei Kirov. The liquidation of the head of the Party organization in Leningrad on 1 December 1934 served Stalin as a pretext for an escalation of repression, culminating in the purges in the second half of the thirties.

In Paris, a genuine mobilization for the defence of culture stranded on the bedrock of irreconcilable differences spanning the entire agenda, and every effort to keep the writers within the margins of the same page collapsed on the penultimate day of the Congress. The tripwire was an invisible presence languishing in the Gulag while the Congress was in session: Victor Serge. Accused of plotting against the regime, the Belgian-born revolutionary, writer, and naturalized Soviet citizen wound up in the town of Orenburg on the Eurasian frontier, 1500 kilometres south-east of Moscow. Until then, the Soviet delegation and supporters in the Western camp had managed to keep Serge's name off the table. But the damage had been done. The Congress limped on for another day and terminated with a flurry of high-minded, if toothless, resolutions.

— 3 —

The Congress showcased dozens of prominent authors addressing a complex of issues germane to their craft and place in society at a time when much of Europe was being squeezed between forces on the right and the left. Knowing why they showed up and what they had to say is not unimportant. Their contributions are presented in the wider context of their lives. What is more, a 'collection of more or less celebrated authors' was bound to produce 'many colourful by-products,' as one delegate (Menno ter Braak) put it. And there were plenty of those. There was André Breton slapping Ilya Ehrenburg, the expulsion of the Surrealists, and the suicide of René Crevel. There was the unscripted appearance of a masked emissary bringing greetings from the German intellectual underground. There was the behind-the-scenes manoeuvring to keep the Trotskyists at bay. There was the eruption, four days into Congress, of *l'affaire Victor Serge*, setting off open warfare between Stalinists and Trotskyists, and the physical expulsion of Serge supporters who tried to crash the proceedings. There was the liberal bloc struggling to hold down the fiercely contested centre, and the two chairmen, Malraux and Gide, working up a sweat trying to keep it all from disintegrating.

— 4 —

The 1935 Congress for the defence of culture against 'the enemy of civilization' was not the only one of its kind, for in the troubled thirties the discussion of the role of the writer in politics flared up with unprecedented intensity. A similar congress, though much slimmed down, was held in London the following June. One year later, the Second International Congress for the Defence of Culture descended on Valencia, Spain. And in the summer of 1938, Paris hosted yet another such congress. None, however, quite mustered the éclat of the 1935 gathering. Its illustrious composition was one factor, but the year itself was more important. The Congress, observed Roger Shattuck, 'met in the very storm's eye of the thirties', offering 'a surprisingly clear window into that decade'.[2]

If by 'practical' we mean the failure to put a dent in the fascist onslaught on culture, then the Congress achieved little. But such a vulgar criterion is a non-starter. It is an open question whether the participants harboured any illusions on that particular score. In the meantime, beyond the walls of the Mutualité world events were spinning out of control at a dizzying clip: Hitler rearming; Spain on the brink of civil war; Mussolini set to pounce on Abyssinia; disquieting rumblings of executions in the USSR; Japan on the move in Asia. In the face of all that, what could writers really hope to accomplish?

## Notes to the Introduction

1. Janet Flanner, *Paris Was Yesterday, 1925–1939*, ed. by Irving Drutman (New York: Penguin Books, 1979), p. 112.
2. Roger Shattuck, *The Innocent Eye: On Modern Literature & the Arts* (New York: Farrar, Straus, Giroux, 1984), pp. 4, 6.

# CHAPTER I

❖

# Prologue

## I. An Age Like This

There is either proletarian revolution or fascism. In making his choice, the writer will be deciding not only the question of his place in the coming struggle, but also that of the fate of literature, the fate of art.

Karl Radek, speech at the All-Union Soviet Writers' Congress, 1934.[1]

— *1* —

Intellectuals, that is to say, men and women who write and think — writing commanding thought (Walter Benjamin) — did not have an easy time of it in the thirties of the last century. The charged ideological atmosphere of those years made it difficult to remain on the political sidelines. Even so reticent an author as André Gide broke out of his shell and tried to convince others to follow his lead. 'Some day', he told the novelist Julian Green in mid-1935, 'you won't be able to confine yourself to literature. You will be forced to choose'. Right or Left, but choose he must, Gide insisted.[2] 'The impulse of every writer,' observed George Orwell in 1938, 'is to "keep out of politics"'.

> What he wants is to be left alone so that he can go on writing books in peace. But unfortunately it is becoming obvious that this ideal is no more practical than that of the petty shop-keeper who hopes to preserve his independence in the teeth of the chain-stores. [...] It is not possible for any thinking person to live in such a society as our own without wanting to change it.[3]

In the late 1920s, French philosopher Julien Benda achieved a measure of fame with a treatise entitled *La Trahison des clercs*. In this work, the one-time Dreyfusard argued, with Cartesian precision, that intellectuals had betrayed their calling by embracing one political cause or another — nation, class, party, or race. The 'clerk' in Benda's title was someone who pursued learning for its own sake, for the pure joy of it, as in medieval times, without expectation of material reward. That lofty perch had been abandoned for the gutter of mass politics. 'Our age is indeed the age of the *intellectual of political hatreds*', averred Benda, giving the phenomenon its classic formulation (emphasis in the original).[4] The only cult intellectuals were in duty bound to serve was the cult of truth and justice, the empire of the spirit, the 'kingdom that is not of this world'. A '"clerk"', by adopting political passions, brings them the tremendous influence of his sensibility if he is an artist, of his persuasive

power if he is a thinker, and in either case his moral prestige'.[5] To France's champion
of eternal values, intellectuals were not brought into the world to strap on a helmet
and mount the political barricades.

*La Trahison des clercs* came out in 1927. Benda's hands-off manifesto caught the
attention of Wyndham Lewis. 'He accuses them [intellectuals]', wrote Lewis,
recapitulating Benda's argument,

> of going over, with all their apparatus of learning and literary magic, to the
> side of the political power-addict — the man-eater, the fire-brand: further of
> as good as accepting the standards of the philistine. [...] With all the energy at
> their disposal, a majority of the modern intellectuals have striven to excite to
> passionate action — not to exhort to reflection or moderation, not applied to
> the reason, but always to the emotions: they have pointed passionately to the
> battlefield, the barricade, the place of execution, not to the life of reason, to
> what is harmonious and beautifully ordered.[6]

Wyndham Lewis was the prototype of the kind of intellectual Benda had in mind:
a 'clerk' who had jumped the fence and entered the political arena. 'Politics', Lewis
declared,

> is for the Twentieth Century what Religion was for the Sixteenth and Seven-
> teenth. In a time so exclusively political, to stand outside politics is to invite
> difficulties: or not to identify yourself, in passionate involvement, with one or
> other of the contending parties.[7]

As for himself, the Canadian-born writer and artist rather fancied Italy's 'ice-cream
agitator' and the Austrian with the 'disarming toothbrush moustache', applauding
their resolve to be done with the 'the humbug of democratic suffrage'.

To be sure, fascist and proto-fascist movements recruited intellectuals from
one end of Europe to the other. In his introduction to René Crevel's novel
*Putting My Foot in It* (1933), Ezra Pound condemned the interwar years as an 'an
epoch of unspeakable intellectual squalor and degradation', skewered the western
democracies, and kept his eyes peeled for 'the new hope' to the east and south of
France. T. S. Eliot mused that '[w]riters should leave war and peace to practical
people', yet found much that was practical in the activities of Charles Maurras and
his monarchist Action Française.

For the most part, however, Western intellectuals tended to gravitate toward
the left, reckoning they had most to fear from men with 'open, unseeing eyes [...]
somewhere on the evolutionary path from cudgel to saber'.[8] Take Stephen Spender.
Roused to action by end-of-the world fears, the British poet reached out to the
Communist Party of Great Britain.

> Like hundreds of people, of whom I was one, the most significant happenings
> in Europe between 1933 and 1936 had been the triumph of dictatorship and
> consequent accumulation of fury. Like many others, I had watched the bases
> on which European freedoms had seemed to rest destroyed. [...] Hitler did
> more than gain political victories in Europe. He also demoralized international
> politics. [...] The intellectuals who earned themselves the label 'anti-Fascist', and
> who were reproached often for their unwarranted intrusion into politics, were
> really in the position of Emilia in the last act of *Othello* when she cries 'The
> truth must out!'[9]

Reminding himself that writing poetry was one of 'the least revolutionary' activities humans were likely to engage in, Spender went in and out as through a revolving door.[10] In the poet's own words:

> I was a member of the British Communist Party for a few weeks during the winter of 1936–1937. My membership lapsed soon after I had joined. I was never invited to join the cell in Hammersmith, where I then lived, nor did I pay any dues after my initial payment.[11]

Spender was hardly unique. In the course of the thirties, a host of intellectuals shambled toward the barricades loosely draped in a red flag. This was the meaning of the poet's observation that 'in certain circumstances whole classes of people, not in ordinary times political, may have a politically conscious role forced upon them'.[12]

Unlike Spender, Bertolt Brecht never entertained the slightest doubt where he stood politically. 'In the fight against them [fascists] nothing must be omitted', he told Walter Benjamin in 1938, displaying 'a passion he seldom shows'.

> Their intentions are not trivial. They are planning for the next thirty thousand years. Monstrous. Monstrous crimes. They hit out at everything. Every cell flinches under their blows. They stop at nothing. They deform the baby in the mother's womb.[13]

The thirties left a bad taste in the mouths of those who lived through it. It was, in the words of the poet W. H. Auden, 'a low dishonest decade'.[14] Rarely had Europe's nose been more out of joint in peacetime. The thirties was a time for choosing colours, Orwell's society writ large.

— 2 —

For many an intellectual it was not just a time for choosing political colours but also one for choosing countries. Leopold Schwarzschild, Jewish, fled Germany within months of Hitler's accession to power. In the Weimar Republic Schwarzschild made a name for himself as a journalist and resolute Nazi foe. Hitler's minions kept track of such things. In power, they went down the list of the thirty-three worst enemies of 'the Reich and the people' and circled his name.[15] Schwarzschild fled to Paris. In 1940, with the invasion of France, he found his way to the United States, where he lived between 1940 and 1949 — and metamorphosed into 'a German McCarthy'.[16]

Soon after his arrival in Paris, Schwarzschild launched a weekly émigré journal funded by Dutch sources with himself as editor. *Das Neue Tage-Buch* kept close tabs on economic, political and cultural developments in Hitler's Germany. A quick dip into Schwarzschild's contributions in the months leading up to the Paris writers' Congress convey a sense of the shockwaves precipitated by Hitler's advent to power, as well the editor's mounting frustration with Europe's democracies — with England in the forefront — for not standing up to the dictator while there was still time.

## 19 January 1935 — The Defeat
*The Third Reich has triumphed in the Saar in the grandest of styles.*

### 2 March 1935 — Challenge to Take Risks

*It is clear that Europe's postwar history received its imprint mainly from a single fact: the fact that Germany absolutely knew what it wanted while its neighbors did not. Germany wanted the destruction of the order established at Versailles. [...] Its adversaries, by contrast, teetered between the will to maintain this order and the will to somehow change it. The result of their indecision was that they were repeatedly confronted by Germany with a new fait accompli, each one of which was resignedly accepted.*

### 23 March 1935 — Germany's Military Power (After the Proclamation of Rearmament)

*If we look at this objectively, we knew from the start that the new German army existed long before it was made official and that the entire world knew it all along and did nothing about it [...] Everyone knows that with regard to the new German army nothing can be done, directly or indirectly, without unleashing a war.*

### 8 June 1935 — Africa Shakes Up Europe

*And here comes the Italian-Abyssinian business — and with it a new setback. We note that in the case of Abyssinia England once more appears to be reacting in its customary half-hearted fashion, as in the worst of times that lie behind us. [...] Mussolini wants [...] to conquer the last 'free' country in Africa. A few more helpings of this sort and Europe will once again blow up!* [17]

And blow up it did.

## II. Red Thread

— *1* —

Dammit, you come from capitalism, you come from the lands where you're a nut, a rebel, an outcast, a lone wolf, a green apple in the belly of things. Your mind has been full of Spartacus on the cross, Shelley, Karl Marx, Tolstoy, John Brown, Lenin, Byron, Gorky, 1905, 1848, 1789, 1870 — all of it, a great story. But your body has been kicked around Union Square by a bunch of Tammany cops, or it's been sick with the sight of a million white-collar scissorbills pushing through Nassau Street at lunchtime.

Just so. And then you find yourself in a dimly lit customhouse over which waves the Red Flag. A few, casual, sleepy Red soldiers lounge about, and it's Revolution, it's dull, it's normal, it's not a dream, it's the daily bread and cabbage soup of 150 million human beings. 'We will not see the Revolution in our lifetime.' I've heard this said at least 1000 times. Yet here I am in the U.S.S.R. about to see a big slice of the Revolution in my own lifetime. It comes with a great stab of joy and wonder at first. [18]

Thus Michael Gold reporting for *The New Masses*, America's premier Marxist magazine.

In November 1930, the author of *Jews without Money* was among forty non-Russian writers invited to sit in on the Second International Conference of Revolutionary and Proletarian Writers, an important milestone in the evolution of Soviet letters. Gold was part of a mix of Communists and non-Communist foreign attendees invited to Kharkov that included Anna Seghers, Egon Erwin Kisch,

Johannes Becher, Georges Sadoul, and Louis Aragon. Seghers, Kisch, Becher, and Gold identified as Communists. Sadoul and Aragon came as Surrealists and left as Communists.

Hosting a conference in the then capital of the Ukrainian Soviet Republic, where millions were about to starve to death, was no mean demonstration of power. A special train whisked the visitors from Leningrad to the site of the Congress. In Kharkov they stuffed themselves with food and drink. It is never a good idea to bite the hand that feeds you.

Six months earlier Stalin had been forced to call a halt to forced collectivization. There had been riots and other manifestations of popular discontent that threatened to get out of hand. Collectivization had left the nation 'dizzy with success', Stalin resolved. The time had come for consolidation of successes already attained and their systematic utilization 'for further advancement'.

New tracks were being laid in literature as well. Kharkov furnished an occasion for consolidation and 'further advancement' no less than the collectivization of agriculture. Stalin himself had set the literary agenda: 'Proletarian literature should be national in form and socialist in content.' A seven-step literary recovery programme was rolled out like steel. Art was a class weapon; artists were bidden to abandon 'individualism'; artistic creation was to be 'collectivized' and 'carried out according to the plans of a central staff'; the proletarian artist 'must be a dialectical materialist'. The experience of the Soviet Union in making proletarian art was the touchstone for art and literature everywhere. Proletarian authors were to assist Western writers dabbling in working-class literature overcome 'their petty bourgeois character and accept the viewpoint of the proletariat'.[19] The Communist Party would oversee it all. There never would be a 'dizzy with success' moment for Soviet writers.

Lenin proved somewhat elusive on the subject of art and literature. The founding father of the Soviet state had bigger fish to fry than chitchat about culture and the like. Zurich's Dadaists learned that their sometime conversation partner cared little for abstract art or any of the new isms. Although receptive to good literature but with little time to read, his key criterion here, as in other matters, was whether or not it advanced the proletarian cause. He had been observed dabbing his eyes at a mawkish bourgeois play starring Sarah Bernhardt. Listening to music 'made him want to talk amiable stupidities'. In poetry, he liked Pushkin, but two lines from Mayakovsky put him to sleep. Having been informed that Mayakovky's poem '150,000,000' (1920) had a print run of 5000, he was dismayed. 'Shame', he said; 1500 would have been plenty for libraries and 'the loonies'.[20] 'Art', Lenin declared,

> belongs to the people. [...] It ought to extend with deep roots into the very thick of the broad toiling masses. It ought to be intelligible to these masses and loved by them. And it ought to unify the feeling, thought and will of these masses, elevate them. It ought to arouse and develop artists among them.[21]

As for writers, Lenin laid down the following:

> Everyone is free to write and say everything he wants without the slightest limitation. Every free union (including the party) is also free to expel such members as use the party name for the propagation of anti-party views.[22]

Lenin, observed Ezra Pound, 'never wrote a sentence that has any interest in itself, but he evolved almost a new medium, a sort of expression halfway between writing and action. This was a definite creation, as the Napoleonic Code was creation'.[23]

Dogma, like nature, abhors a vacuum. Lenin's musings on culture, tearing up and dozing off, left a gaping hole to be filled. Kharkov was a promising start. Stalin supplied the next twist.

In October 1932, dozens of writers convened at Maxim Gorky's commodious dacha to talk literary politics. Reports indicate that the General Secretary arrived late and sat down in a corner, sucked on his pipe, and listened. At last, roundly toasted, 'The Boss' got up and addressed the gathering. 'Our tanks', he said,

> are worth nothing when the souls that have to drive them are made of clay. That's why I say: the production of souls is more important than that of tanks. [...] Someone here observed that writers should not sit still, that they should get to know the life in their land. Man is reshaped by life, and you have to assist in the recreation of his soul. And that is why I raise my glass to you, writers, to the engineers of the soul.[24]

— 2 —

Cameras were on hand to capture the excitement of the First All-Union Soviet Writers' Congress held in Moscow's House of the Unions between 15 August and 1 September 1934. The film's opening scene — 'The best writers of all nations come to the Congress' — features Maxim Gorky arriving by car and disappearing inside. As he makes his appearance in the Hall of Columns, the principal speakers' venue, the packed hall rises. Twenty-five hundred hands erupt in sustained rhythmic clapping. The 66-year-old author takes his seat up front alongside other writers. Dress: loose-fitting sports jacket and shirt collar, tie knotted as an afterthought. The audience sits down, ceases applauding. Gorky pulls out a handkerchief and dabs his eyes. Cameo shots of Soviet authors Alexei Tolstoi, Boris Pasternak and Ilya Ehrenburg. Other footage captures Comrade Zhdanov, Secretary of the Central Committee of the Communist Party; André Malraux, Jean-Richard Bloch, Martin Andersen Nexø, and Ernst Toller. Amid the gilded chandeliers and the twenty-eight Corinthian columns from which the Hall derived its name, the portraits of Goethe, Dante, Shakespeare, Pushkin, Tolstoy, Heine, and others preside from on high.[25]

Unsurprisingly, the largest portrait is of Gorky. His image shared the spotlight with Stalin's: 'author next to the head of state'. Outside, in the street, 'the undisputed pope of Socialistic letters' peered into the world from every third window. Stalin's literary point man was no classical Marxist and frequently fell foul of the nomenklatura. He once referred to Lenin as a 'thinking guillotine' and spent nearly the entire decade of the twenties living abroad. Stalin, recognizing the popular writer's propaganda value, was determined to hitch him to the Soviet cause. 'Gorky is a vain man. We have to tie him to the Party with cables'.[26] One cable led to the town of Nizhny Novgorod. One morning its residents woke up to find they were living in Gorky, renamed as the author's birthplace. Other cables led to parks, streets, and buildings. The world's largest plane, built with Soviet hands, plied the skies as the *Maxim Gorky* — until it crashed in 1935, killing forty-five people. Stalin had Gorky's number.

The First All-Union Congress of Soviet Writers, convened to ratify and promote the new creed of socialist realism, was an exuberant affair. Ilya Ehrenburg estimated that 25,000 Muscovites attended, overwhelmingly workers. Hundreds of writers, domestic and foreign, circulated amid the splendour of the Hall of Columns and adjacent rooms. Stalin's motto for the Kharkov Congress, 'Proletarian literature should be national in form and socialist in content', evincing impressive shelf life, had been dusted off for another tour of duty. The mood was festive. On the first day of the Congress Ehrenburg prepared 'like a girl for her first dance'.

> The opening of the Congress makes me smile in retrospect: the orchestra suddenly began to play deafening fanfares as if toasts were about to follow. People crowded the doorway to get a peek at the writers. The railwaymen lined up to the sound of a signal-whistle; pioneers blew their trumpets; women from collective farms brought huge baskets of fruit and vegetables; the Uzbeks presented Gorky with a robe and a skullcap, sailors with a model of a launch. It was all very sincere, naïve and touching and like an extraordinary kind of carnival [...].[27]

Gorky presided and delivered the opening address. The 'principal theme of European and Russian literature in the nineteenth century', Gorky stipulated, 'was personality, in antithesis to society, the state and nature'. The contemporary heroes of bourgeois literature were 'rogues, thieves, assassins and agents of the criminal police'. Bourgeois literature was at a dead end.

> I reiterate: the main and fundamental theme of pre-revolutionary literature was the tragedy of a person to whom life seemed cramped, who felt superfluous in society, sought therein a comfortable place for himself, failed to find it, and suffered, died, reconciled himself to society that was hostile to him, or sank to drunkenness and suicide.[28]

The Soviet Union was there to breathe new life into this pummelled creature. The formula was in place. In the Communist state the sole creator of culture was 'the toil of the masses'. The 'heroic work of creating a classless society' was everyone's business, from the Party leadership setting the moral tone, to the Writers' Union tasked with 'guiding all the creative working energies of the country'. The writer's job was twofold: to extol the Soviet new order, and to furnish the reader with positive role models. Superfluous people were a thing of the past. Oblomovism was dead. Gorky:

> Life is deeds, creativeness, the aim of which is the uninterrupted development of the priceless individual faculties of man, with a view to his victory over the forces of nature, for the sake of his health and longevity, for the supreme joy of living on an earth which, in conformity with the steady growth of his requirements, he wishes to mould throughout into a beautiful dwelling place for mankind, united into a single family.

Already, Gorky divulged, projects were under way 'to bring out a History of Factories and Works'.

Gorky spoke for a long time. The Dutch writer and critic Eddy du Perron, who was not present but read the speech shortly thereafter, characterized it as a combination of 'brilliant survey next to the crudest nonsense'. 'For Gorky,' Du Perron added, 'it seems that future Soviet literary geniuses can be cultivated as in a hothouse', attributing the author's faith in the creation of such prospective prodigies to his dual role as engineer of the soul and 'something resembling a minister of literature'. But then, this critic never thought much of Gorky as a writer to begin with: third-rate.[29]

The central event of the Congress, apart from Gorky's inaugural address, was Karl Radek's speech on international literature. At the time of the Congress Radek presided over the Party's International Information Bureau and enjoyed a reputation as a 'brilliant foreign policy expert'. Already, Radek boasted, the revolution had 'created hundreds of thousands of men every one of which was worthy of the chisel of Phidias or Michelangelo'.

For the occasion, Radek had concocted a rubric calculated to filter out literary impurities:

> ★  Did an author's work reflect social life?
> ★  What was the writer's attitude towards 'such great facts of historical development as the war, the October Revolution, and fascism'?
> ★  What was the author's attitude toward capitalism? Was he or she favourably disposed toward the Soviet Union?
> ★  'Socialist realism means not only knowing reality as it is, but knowing whither it is moving.' Did the author understand this?

Radek's speech, 'Contemporary World Literature and the Tasks of Proletarian Art', surveyed the period since the Great War. This was a period, he said, 'in which all tendencies of parasitism and decay in bourgeois literature have obtruded themselves in most glaring relief, in which the material collapse and decay of capitalism is being accompanied by a parallel process — the decay of world capitalist literature'.

For Radek, as for Gorky, the root of the problem was 'the idea of individualism'. Singling out Proust and Joyce, he took the knife to both. Proust's opus was like 'a mangy dog [...] endlessly licking its sores'; Joyce's *Ulysses* 'a heap of dung crawling with worms'. The new Soviet literature, Radek prophesied, would put all past efforts in the shade. 'No, we will not smother our Shakespeares', the foreign policy maven vowed,

> we will foster them. We will create a literature higher than that of the Renaissance, for it derived its models from slave-owning Greece and slave-owning Rome and expressed the interests of rising capitalism, while our literature reflects the idea of a new, socialist society.

The best of world literature, Radek terminated his discourse, 'would rally around the flag of Marx, Engels, Lenin and Stalin, because only this flag will lead humanity to victory'.[30]

Nikolai Bukharin's address, 'Poetry, Poetics and the Problems of Poetry in the U.S.S.R.', was decidedly more sophisticated. In contradistinction to Gorky and Radek, the editor of *Izvestia*, the Soviet newspaper of record, was not afraid to sound a discordant note. Acknowledging that the poetry of his day trailed the West in craftsmanship, Bukharin called for 'a marked rise in the general culture of poets and in political culture' to match the progress being made on the economic front. He further urged poets to look beyond the Russian sky. 'Those', he said, 'who really want to create "Magnitostroys of literature", having purified their ideas in regard to art, must do their best to make themselves masters of all the treasure-houses of the world's culture.'

Yury Olesha also spoke. The Soviet author of *Envy* pledged to stick to writing fiction in which moral questions predominated. Olesha's satirical novel projects a future of cheap sausages and self-peeling potatoes, but ends on the sour note of indifference.[31]

— *3* —

Bukharin's 'Magnitostroys of literature' referred to Magnitogorsk, Stalin's City of Steel on the eastern slopes of the Ural Mountains. Conceived during the First Five Year Plan, the Magnitogorsk plant was projected to 'be the biggest continuous mine-to-rolling-mill metallurgical combinat in the world'.[32] The enterprise encountered all kinds of difficulties, from shortage of skilled labour and lack of supplies to hard-to-get foodstuffs, yet was completed early in 1934, as planned. Bukharin's reference was shorthand, signalling Soviet determination to forge ahead, catch up with and overtake the West. 'Here', wrote John Scott, a twenty-year-old American transplant from Wisconsin employed by the combinat,

> at hundreds of miles from the nearest center of human activity, a gigantic plant and city had been created within five years. Even the least important of the builders, even those who worked under sentence in expiation of alleged crimes, felt that in a very real sense the city was theirs because they had helped build it.[33]

Two years after the completion of the Magnitogorsk steel plant in 1932 a book came out celebrating a feat that was on a par with, if not superior to, the enterprise in the remote southern Urals. *The Stalin Canal from the White Sea to the Baltic Sea* chronicled the construction of a waterway linking the two seas. An English translation, *Belomor*, came out in 1935.[34] Triumphing over rock, swamp and rivers, the 'fury of storms', Karelia's sub-zero temperatures and the 'dregs' of Soviet society, the White Sea canal was completed twenty months from the initial groundbreaking in 1929, testifying to the power of socialism to set nature to its hand. The project engaged thousands of prisoners, male and female, digging and blasting through 227 kilometres of rock and ice in one of our planet's most miserable climates.[35] No fewer than 120 writers were dispatched to immortalize this prodigious feat. In the end, thirty-four 'literary formulators' signed off on its content.

Upon completion of the project, Stalin himself put in an appearance, chugging down the eponymous canal in a 'little snub-nosed freighter', flanked by Kremlin luminaries. A band played. The wind kicked up. The prisoners marshalled on banks shrouded in fog strained to get a glimpse of 'the man who personified the new world to them'. *Belomor* author Mikhail Zoshchenko, 'with his hand cupped to his ear [...], tries to make out the melody played by the band. The sounds are scattered by the wind and the noise of the water spilling over the floodgate.'[36]

*Belomor*'s principal editor was Maxim Gorky. To Gorky it seemed perfectly natural that writers collaborate. If labourers working in brigades can pour cement, why not a brigade of writers working collectively on a book? An author was an economic unit no less than an industrial worker and no less exempt from central

planning and Fordism. 'We can't wait forever', insisted a leading advocate of proletarian art, 'while the professional writer tosses in his bed and gives birth to something known and useful to him alone. We assume that book production can be
planned in advance like the production of textiles and steel.'[37]

Gorky was proud of the canal workers. Their example, he asserted in a speech
lauding their achievement, had 'raised the spirits of a good hundred writers'.

> This will be of great importance. Many writers who are still undecided, and
> who will not understand many things in our construction, have received
> something through learning about your canal, something which will have a
> great effect on their work. Now there will appear in literature a spirit which
> will move it forward and bring it to the level of your great deeds. [...] You are
> now building the Moscow-Volga Canal, and many other constructions which
> will change the face and the geography of our country, and which will enrich
> it from day to day. Our writers must tell about all this. For facts appear first,
> and are then followed by their artistic reflections. And there are plenty of facts.
> [...] I congratulate you on what you have become. I congratulate the GPU on
> their splendid work. I congratulate our wise Party and its leader, the man of
> steel, Comrade Stalin![38]

This was the new direction in literature Soviet delegates came to promote, and
defend, eight months and 2500 kilometres down the road in Paris. Russian novelist
Vsevolod Ivanov felt good about having been a part of the writing team. 'In this
book', he recalled at the Paris Congress,

> we tried to relate how the Chekists re-educated the prisoners, how they dug a
> canal in rocky and frozen terrain near the White Sea. We worked with passion.
> We read to each other the pages we had written, critiqued them, corrected
> them, rewrote them. We were without pity toward one another, but at the
> same time filled with love. We were very different from one another, in taste
> and age, but we all tried to make a book of one piece, dense and powerful. As
> a first experience, it is an interesting book. It has many deficiencies and errors,
> but it is a book that to this day is very dear to me.

— 4 —

While *Belomor* presented a straightforward narrative — 'facts come first' — the
playwright Nikolai Pogodin went one better than Gorky. If Soviet engineers
could be asked to 'train the sea to flow the other way', why not draw the curtain
on a comedy set amid a heap of human misery and make people laugh? During
the construction of the Stalin Canal, Pogodin visited the White Sea prison camp
and took stock of its denizens — rogues, prostitutes, thieves, kulaks, 'wreckers',
and other 'enemies of the state'. The result was *Aristocrats: A Comedy in Four Acts*.[39]
Pogodin's comic romp through the underclass of Soviet society left audiences in
stitches while driving home its principal message: the price paid for the socialist fall
from grace and the ever-present possibility of redemption.

*Aristocrats*'s protagonist is a thug answering to the name of Kostya, also known
as The Captain; 'eighteen years in institutions of higher learning', 'ten years hard
labor, nine times married'. The very idea of clawing his way back to freedom and
playing by the rules filled The Captain with deep loathing. But the Chekists, the

Soviet secret police, are nothing if not understanding; under their patient guidance and gentle prodding, Pogodin's straw man at last 'bends with the remover to remove'. A ditty mouthed by a similarly 'reforged' prisoner captured the prison camp's reigning spirit to a T.

> 'A bandit's life I used to lead,
> A life as black as night.
> To work I thought there was no need,
> I robbed and shot on sight.
> A life like this was sure to bring
> A sentence on the new canal.
> For me it's been a second spring,
> I want to live and work and sing.
> The past is but a dreadful dream,
> A thing I must forget.
> Now tears of joy begin to stream –
> Mine aren't the only ones, I bet.'

Kostya's female counterpart is Sonya (thief, drunk, drug addict):

> [...] to hell with all this talk about moulding people's characters over again, making new people out of 'em, training 'em — it's newspaper bunk — they are just the new Soviet icons, that's all. Who do they think they'll fool? A prison's a prison — and that's all there is to it. [...] They don't understand that you can't patch up a convict's soul with sticking-plaster.

Sonya, too, eventually sees the light. In the play, as in the book, the camp was a place where honest labour was rewarded with 'good shoes and meat dinners'; where brass bands played while workers toiled; where at the day's end heavy heads sank into deep, fluffy pillows; where mothers visited well-behaved sons and bustled about the campsite in chauffeured cars; where clean living was the norm (no alcohol, no gambling, no card games); where shirkers were held up to ridicule; where you were taught to get in touch with the masses and camp violations were harshly punished — where the carrot and stick carried all before it. In The Captain's words:

> Say, pals!
> Do you feel like missing your feed?
> *Then don't work!*
> Do you want to do without tobacco?
> *Then don't work!*
> Want to lounge about this Far Northern Paradise
> Looking like poor old Adam with any Eve?
> *Then don't work!*

And here, too, as in *Belomor*, the Chekists hogged the spotlight. 'The Chekists aren't magicians', The Captain lectures engineer Sadovsky, a notorious slacker.

> Before every man they simply set a ladder and say — 'Climb it'. The higher you climb, the better life becomes. One rung. One rung gives you better boots and clothes, another — better food. Then there is the shock-brigade rung: when you get on that you forget that you are in a prison camp and you're allowed to send for your wife. But there is still a higher rung, when your entire ten-year sentence is cancelled and vanishes like a nightmare after a spree [...] the Chekists

do not wait until you make up your mind yourself to climb the ladder. They know our characters too well: some of us have to be shown how to start, others need a boost, some a good shove, while others — you, for instance — have to be given two or three hard knocks and then they're off up the ladder with violent palpitation of the heart.

In the final scene, again as in *Belomor*, the entire prison population turns out for the canal's inauguration. A prominent shock brigade leader expresses his gratitude. The Captain has the last word.

Quiet, comrades! The first steamer is passing through, from the Baltic to the White Sea. And its name, for posterity to know is 'The Chekist.' Only let's not shout 'hurrah.' Instead, let's just listen to the water singing in the locks.[40]

## III. Paris, 14–20 June

— 1 —

Friday 14 June 1935. Boulevard du Montparnasse.

Breton approaches Ehrenburg, and says, 'I've come to settle a score with you, sir.' Ehrenburg asks, 'And who are you, sir'? Breton responds, 'I am André Breton.' Ehrenburg asks, 'Who?' Breton repeats his name a number of times, each time adding an epithet against the Surrealists quoted from Ehrenburg's *Vus par un écrivain d'U.R.S.S.* published a year prior, and a slap to Ehrenburg's face. After the attack, Ehrenburg retreats, calling out: 'You're going to be sorry for that!'[41]

*Vus par un écrivain d'U.R.S.S.* portrayed Surrealists as spoiled brats for whom revolution took a backseat to theories of onanism and the pursuit of wine, women and song. Breton was furious.

This was not the first time the founder of Surrealism embraced the hoary chivalric expedient of the slap to settle a score. In 1924, Surrealists circulated the manifesto 'Did you ever slap a corpse?' The corpse was that of despised literary anachronism Anatole France, whose funeral they observed, in the words of one dismayed onlooker, with a 'noisy and most indecorous demonstration'.[42] Still, a slap aimed at a cheek, dead or alive, is child's play compared to a loaded gun firing away in a crowded street, advanced by Breton as the 'simplest Surrealistic act' (Second Manifesto of Surrealism, 1930).[43]

Breton had served in a psychiatric ward during the First World War. It was there that a shell-shocked patient of his, Jean Vaché, laid the philosophic foundation of Surrealism and supplied the definition of humour that seems to account for the juvenile high jinks that so delighted the founding father of Surrealism and his disciples: 'a sense of the theatric and joyless futility of everything when one is enlightened.'[44] Vaché committed suicide at the age of 24, overdosing on morphine.

Breton's Surrealist novel *Nadja* came out in 1927. There Breton scorns logic as 'the most hateful of prisons' and repudiates labour, Marx's creator of all value, as the antithesis of life itself. 'There is no use being alive if one must work'; this from a card-carrying member of the French Communist Party.[45] The party rescinded his membership in 1933.

The relationship between Surrealists and Communists had been rocky from the start. Shared hatred of the bourgeoisie was a shaky platform on which to sustain and build an enduring relationship. Needling the bourgeoisie and provoking scandals as ends in themselves was a one-way street. Revolutions were serious business, not a plaything for 'frolicsome terrorists'.[46]

It is inconceivable, however, that Ehrenburg had never heard of Breton, and no less inconceivable that he just stood there as Breton administered slap after slap. The Paris-based correspondent for *Izvestia* had lived in France off and on since 1925. The *gifles*, however, were real enough, as was Ehrenburg's threat. Mikhail Koltsov, a Soviet delegate at the Congress, reported the incident to Moscow and proposed that Surrealists be barred from speaking at the Congress on the grounds that 'those who settle their differences of opinions with the fist are fascists and should be avoided'.[47]

Done.

'I have to say,' Breton stated in a radio interview with André Parinaud conducted decades later, that this finally toppled the hope that for years, despite everything, we'd been reconciling Surrealist activities with practical revolutionary action.'[48]

— *2* —

Salvador Dalí spent the evening of 18 June at the movies. The film he went to see was *Frankenstein*, starring Boris Karloff.[49]

René Crevel spent the evening pursuing Breton's reinstatement. Until his recent conversion to Communism, the thirty-four-year-old author and Congress delegate had been a staunch Breton acolyte. Though no longer a Surrealist, the ousting of his one-time guru hit him hard, undercutting his efforts to work out a truce between the two warring isms on which he had pinned his hopes, with the Congress serving as a bridge on which Surrealists and Communists could meet each other halfway. In the few remaining days until then, Crevel pleaded and pleaded with the organizers to reinstate the banned delegate.

Rebuffed again and again, Crevel would call on the Dalís, Salvador and Gala, and pour out his heart, 'sobbing like a child'. Dalí told Crevel not to bother; the Congress wasn't worth it. Instead, ratcheting the argument up to the level of logical absurdity, a patented 'Dalí-esque tactic', he urged Crevel to introduce 'a motion declaring Hitler's looks and plump back endowed with a irresistible poetic lyricism'. This approach, reassured the Spanish Surrealist, would in no way undermine engaging the Führer politically.

But Crevel persisted, impervious to Dalí's advice.

The Frankenstein film put Dalí in mind of Crevel: same build, same 'protuberant face of a retarded baby'. The morning after, worried, Dalí called René at home.

A voice at the other end of the telephone urged him to rush over at once. Fire engines and a crowd met Dalí's eye as his taxi approached Crevel's building. Dalí recalled entering a room filled with firemen and René sucking on oxygen for dear life. A piece of cardboard attached to Crevel's left wrist spelled out his name in capital letters: CREVEL. Late returning home from another bout of fruitless entreaties, Crevel had pinned a note to the lapel of his jacket, stuck his head into the oven, and turned on the gas. *Je suis dégoûté de tout* — I have had enough.

Dalí wasn't all that surprised by Crevel's — attempted? — suicide, and once more drew a connection with the Frankenstein creation; Frankenstein, he remarked, 'illustrated down to the finest detail Crevel's necrophiliac obsession with death'. And in the Frankenstein film's treatment of death and rebirth, Dalí purported to see signs of the novelist's eventual resurrection. As the founding father of 'phoenixology', Dalí derived 'crever' (to perish) from Crevel and 'renaître' (to be reborn) from 'René'. Crevel would rise again.

Crevel had a long history grappling with the idea of suicide. In his 1925 novel *La Mort difficile* a jilted lover takes his life swallowing a handful of pills on a desolate park bench. That same year Breton circulated a questionnaire entitled 'Is Suicide the Solution?' Crevel responded with an emphatic 'yes'. 'Human accomplishment is nothing but a bunch of empty promises, hot air.'[50] In 1925 as well, Crevel wrote an article in which he furnished at least seven different reasons — a surfeit of intelligence being one — why suicide was no big deal. At the time, Crevel viewed the obsession with suicide as a preventive measure, like a shot against rabies.[51]

There is very little in Dalí's preface to *La Mort difficile* about Crevel's pre-Congress past: the illness (tuberculosis); the on-and-off drug habit; struggles with homosexuality; his fear of going crazy, and the tortured relationship with his mother, 'the station-master of his unhappiness'. He was fourteen when she made him look at his hopelessly paranoid father dangling from a rope.

No wonder Breton spoke of 'latent causes [that] had been brewing for some time'.[52]

In the final analysis, however, Dalí put the blame for Crevel's demise squarely on the 'Great International Congress'.

> To begin with, they eliminate all artists who betray even a smidgen of originality, and principally all those who possess or entertain the slightest subversive and thus truly revolutionary idea. Congresses are strange monsters where, in essence, glib types, physiologically conditioned, run the show behind the scenes.

Dalí wrote the preface to *La Mort difficile* in 1954, and his memory of some of the events is warped, as in his famous timepieces. But there is no mistaking his contempt for the Paris Congress.

Ezra Pound as well weighed in on Crevel's suicide. In a foreword to Crevel's *Putting My Foot in It*, Pound recalled meeting the author at Nancy Cunard's Hours Press in Normandy around 1930 and being much impressed with this 'perfectly real, authentically young man', who seemed 'perfectly healthy', though no fascist; who spoke 'perfectly good English, not frenchman's pigeon'; who peeled off his jersey to reveal a 'five-inch cicatrice on the back of his Belvedere torso'. *Putting My Foot in It*, Pound wrote, was as 'authentic and convincing' as its creator in spite of a lack of 'constructive components'. To Pound, Crevel was a 'gust of fresh air', a 'born writer', 'genius,' 'eternal youth, plunged into the tail end of a ten-tailed epoch. [...] The abundance, the sense, general and inclusive, of the utterly blithering frumpery, post-war, of Paris, of the conglomerate of countries that hadn't the sphincter strength for revolution' — for fascism, that is. 'Crevel revolted but knew nothing else'. Crevel killed himself, Pound noted, 'before the new hope had reached France'. And Pound, too, held the Congress to account.

Not Congressista, but having authors assembled, and considering the probably (understatement that …) the in short faked nature of that Congress the utter hoakum wherein any man present would have been at least momentarily drowned, one couldn't help wondering whether rather than face that swamp of hoakum (*toc, fumperpey*, masquerading as conviction, the final disgust), as the only possible gesture of absolute dissociation of himself from any such hokus-pokus Crevel hadn't chosen EXIT.[53]

In its obituary to the fallen comrade, France's Communist daily *L'Humanité* extolled the 'far-sighted writer' as a working class hero who had saved his last breath for the proletarian cause. 'It is only now that I have started to live,' Crevel told the workers of Bourges shortly before his death. 'In the workers' movement', the paper observed, 'Crevel had found the reasons for hope of which his illness deprived him.'[54]

Nothing Crevel did surprised Klaus Mann. The latter remembered his friend as somewhat of a wild man, prone to 'vehement judgments' and sudden 'intellectual somersaults'. How, for example, Crevel could have fallen for the 'rampant paradoxes' of Surrealism and their 'pugnacious oracle' with 'a big head', André Breton, was beyond Mann's comprehension. And so was the 'sudden somersault' that landed Crevel in the Communist camp. He must have cut an odd figure addressing the working men of Bourges — even without the loud clothes made out of coarse material he was wont to wear in defiance of his mother's perennial black and bourgeois finery. He lisped a little, too, Mann noted.[55]

— 3 —

*L'Humanité* was tickled pink. The organ of the French Communist Party thrilled at the prospect of the antifascist writers' Congress about to unfold under the sign of the Popular Front, the Soviet initiative promoting cooperation with non-Communists. Formally adopted in August 1935 at the 7th Congress of the Comintern, this was the new dawn Western Communists, fellow travellers, and Soviet sympathizers had been waiting for. No more consigning Social Democrats to Dante's Ninth Circle of Hell. No more casting the democracies as fascist regimes in waiting. No more unconditional subordination to the general Party line.

[T]he 'Marseillaise' was no longer derisively booed but sung with exaggerated enthusiasm directly before or after the 'Internationale.' Some time later the Communists stopped lampooning the national army as both hateful and ludicrous; in fact, on orders of Stalin they became the staunchest and even the most chauvinistic patriots of France, unresolved champions of democracy as it was practiced in the most progressive capitalistic countries.[56]

So when Hitler dismissed international working class solidarity as a myth, the French Communist Party countered with a giant demonstration calculated to make the Führer eat his words. On 20 June, *L'Humanité* invited all workers, regardless of political affiliation and trade union membership, to a day-long love-in with sports, music and other entertainments, capped by fireworks at 'the magnificent park of Montreuil'. A similar event was in the works for 14 July, Bastille Day.

Making common cause with individuals, parties and organizations prepared to stand with the Kremlin was a clever move on Stalin's part. With Hitler's victory and the rise of fascism — to say nothing about major setbacks in the twenties and thirties in Germany, Austria and China — even the most rabid Soviet enthusiast had to concede that world revolution was not about to come barrelling down the Eurasian plain. Stalin knew this as well as anyone. He was under a lot of pressure. A consummate master at dealing from a weak hand, the Soviet ruler kept busy scraping up allies wherever he could find them. In the fall of 1934 the world's first workers' state took its seat in the League of Nations. The following year gave birth to a mutual assistance treaty with France designed to keep an openly rearming Germany at bay. Currying favour with French writers and intellectuals was part of this outreach.

— 4 —

Victor Hugo imagined that the 'H' in Notre Dame's twin towers stood for his initial. The author of Les Misérables also believed in magic; his closet contained packets of hair swept up by his barber as well as nail clippings — to ward off danger.[57] Upon his death, along with the hair and nail clippings, Hugo left 'a lifetime annuity' of twenty sous per day to revolutionaries like himself who had put their lives on the line for the republic in 1830 and 'were still in this world'.[58] In Les Misérables, Valjean is arrested and sentenced to five years of penal servitude for a 40-sous theft of bread.

The curtain-raiser to the Congress was a 'magnifique hommage' to the nineteenth-century writer on the fiftieth anniversary of his death. The 20 June event, held at Paris's capacious Théâtre National du Trocadéro, featured Jean-Richard Bloch, novelist, poet, and essayist; a speech choir; an actor playing Hugo and a theatre troupe miming the death of Gavroche, the boy hero of Les Misérables. The Hugo anniversary was a good fit with the writers' Congress and a number of participants showed up for the occasion, among them Heinrich Mann, André Malraux, André Gide, Henri Barbusse, Martin Andersen Nexø, E. M. Forster and Paul Nizan.[59]

The Soviet Union had Maxim Gorky, the French Victor Hugo. By and by, the 'unparalleled genius' of French letters who 'raised a storm at the bottom of the inkwell',[60] found his way to everyman. France's Communists appreciated the iconic writer's concern for the common man: 'the grand bourgeois', friend of the left, a force of nature who transformed a beggar into a hero, as Marx had the ordinary labourer. Hugo had a sense of where history was going and 'spoke the words that needed to be spoken', opening up a universe where peace reigned and man could experience 'the honour of being a man'. For all that, Hugo failed to grasp that none of this could come to pass as long as the bourgeoisie held the whip hand. Thus Paul Nizan in L'Humanité.[61]

A year's travel in the Soviet Union had persuaded the thirty-year-old Nizan that Hugo's legacy was being revived there, in word and deed, by its writers and 'in the acts of Stalin' himself; that in the new Russia, humanism and humanitarianism were passing from the realm of fable to the realm of fact.

Hugo brought out the crowd. It had been a scorcher of a day. In the course of the evening, as though letting off steam, thousands of throats intermittently raised the 'immense cry' 'Free Thälmann!', Germany's Communist party leader imprisoned since 1933. Five years later (almost to the day) Ernst Thälmann's gaoler took a three-hour victory lap around the city of his dreams. At the all but deserted Trocadéro the conquering Führer posed for a snapshot with the Seine and Eiffel Tower in the background. Thälmann died in Buchenwald in 1944.

— 5 —

Another French writer and Congress delegate who took the measure of the Soviet Union was that evening's keynote speaker Jean-Richard Bloch. In the course of a prolonged stay, Bloch talked to workers, assessed the educational system, inspected factories and farms and made the literary rounds, including the 1934 Soviet Congress of Writers. 'Something is going on there', he wrote upon his return to France in January of 1935,

> of which we in capitalist countries have no idea. For those who have made the revolution literature is no longer what it is for us, the individual fruit of a temperament that tries to express itself in accordance with his genius, talent and environment, and which grows grows like a solitary flower in a field [...] [Over there] it is a matter of one hundred million individuals who have been told: You are worthy of culture, and we will put this culture at your disposal. We will do everything to make this happen. The bearer of this culture, in accordance with Stalin's expression, is the engineer of the soul.[62]

In Moscow, Bloch and his wife Marguerite were feted like royalty. A black Lincoln was standing by for them at Moscow's airport. The Lincoln dropped them off at the Hotel Metropol, across from Revolution Square. A 'hotel for foreigners in all its glory', marvelled Bloch, a 'real nabob's quarters: a drawing room, a piano, a bathroom'. He could have left his wallet at home. Travel on the cheap educed an aphorism worthy of La Rochefoucauld. 'One is never treated so well as when one is paying nothing.'[63]

A Dutch reporter who stayed at the Metropol in 1932 described the hotel in somewhat different terms. Philip Mechanicus informed readers back home that the Soviet Union, having discovered tourism, had remodelled the Art Nouveau hotel to simulate the 'natural habitat' of visitors from abroad so as to cash in on their 'deep pockets'. The hotel had three classes: Russians, who paid for their stay with roubles; Europeans who paid with roubles, and Europeans who paid with dollars. For the dollar-paying Europeans there was 'a real bar', tended by barmaids in short skirts, rouged cheeks and painted lips; not unlike the women that might take your order in the better West European lunchrooms, observed the correspondent for *Het Algemeen Handelsblad*. It was said that the girls picked for this 'disgraceful' job were from the 'old bourgeoisie', and also that they were 'easy'. Diehard Communists considered the Metropol a 'blight' on Moscow's hotel scene.[64]

On the road, the Blochs travelled in equally grand style. Their host, Mikhail Koltsov — 'a fantastic chap' — had outdone himself. Thanks to the exertions of the Chairman of the Writers' Organizing Committee, the Blochs had the run of a private railway carriage that included 'a library, study, kitchen, cook and two attendants'. No wonder Bloch returned to France bubbling over with warm feelings toward his former hosts and the conviction that Stalin held the key to fighting fascism.

'Bursts of applause shook the hall' when 'the great writer' mounted the stage. Bloch read some of Victor Hugo's previously unpublished writings, as well as a letter from the Soviet archives indicating that the French author had interceded with the government on behalf of a Russian revolutionary whose extradition had been requested by the tsar; concluding, he read from a Hugo letter defending universal suffrage.

That evening at the Trocadéro, reported *L'Humanité*, Hugo's spirit lived among the masses.

> It is the people's tribute to the generous poet of the people, the homage of the working masses on whom rests the future of thought and the cultural heritage the degenerated bourgeoisie is no longer capable of nourishing.

In Moscow, Bloch sparred with Radek on the question of artistic freedom and individualism, warning Radek not to 'confuse individualism with the individual'. And this: 'Comrade Radek, if you persist in condemnation, if you go on showing mistrust, I personally warn you that this will only push broad masses in the West towards Fascism.'[65] Radek:

> Comrades, what Bloch said is true. We must distinguish individualism, 'unsocia-bility', inability to go with the community, from respect for personality. The young revolution, which is an army, has to live in barracks at a certain stage in its advance — and it cannot be otherwise, for armies live in barracks. The revolution, which is an army of labour, cannot busy itself with personality, devote much time to personality, at all stages of its march, but after its victory the revolution is a soil on which personality can bloom in all its richness. We — the army of Communism — do not consist of mere ciphers. Communist society will be a million times richer in great personalities than any other type of society could be. It is enough to look at our country as it is even today. Where else in the world have we seen shepherds growing up into philosophers, brigade commanders, university professors in the space of fifteen or sixteen years?[66]

On the road from Moscow to Paris, however, Bloch had a change of heart. He now saw the need to reverse direction. Two days after his appearance at the Trocadéro, he brought his message to the Congress itself. 'For whom do you write?' he asked with his first breath. That question was no longer being asked in the Soviet Union, Bloch declared, the interests of writer and public felicitously converging on the same page. Thus it had been in France in the nineteenth century, starting with Hugo. The incredible success of *Les Misérables* created a visceral relationship between the writer and the masses. This fruitful synergy had been lost in France. Although in Moscow, Bloch went on, he had been at pains to defend the freedom of the artist, arguing that the writer who writes for 5000 readers was entitled to as much consideration and respect as one writing for 100,000, or a million, back in France he had come to the conclusion that the Western artist's presumption of absolute autonomy and obsession with technique was responsible for the split between the masses and the writer. This fixation on technique had to be broken if writers and the masses were to be reunited. How this was to be achieved Bloch did not say, other than hold out a vague hope that this relationship might yet be recouped. The time was not propitious. 'Our society', he declared, 'is dying, steeped in pessimism, reeking of the end of things.' Yet the effort on behalf of a Popular Front Bloch construed as a significant and hopeful sign.

## Notes to Chapter 1

1. Karl Radek, 'Contemporary World Literature and the Tasks of Proletarian Art,' <www.marxists.org/archive/Radek> [accessed 12 January 2012]
2. Julian Green, *Diary 1928–1957*, trans. by Anne Green (New York: Caroll & Graff, 1985), pp. 62–63.
3. George Orwell, *An Age Like This 1920–1940. The Collected Essays, Journalism and Letters*, ed. by Sonia Orwell and Ian Angus, 4 vols (Boston: Nonpareil Books, 2000), I, pp. 336, 337.
4. Julien Benda, *The Betrayal of the Intellectuals*, trans. by Richard Aldington (Boston: Beacon Press, 1955), p. 21.
5. Benda, p. 33.
6. Wyndham Lewis, *Rude Assignment: An Intellectual Autobiography* (Santa Barbara, CA: Black Sparrow Press, 1984), p. 35.
7. Lewis, p. 75.
8. Joseph Roth, *Right and Left,* trans. by Michael Hofmann (Woodstock and New York: Overlook Press, 1992), pp. 106–07.
9. Stephen Spender, *World Within World: The Autobiography of Stephen Spender* (New York: St. Martin's Press, 1994), p. 189.
10. Spender, 'Poetry and Revolution', in *The 30's and After: Poetry, Politics, People, 1930's–1970's* (New York: Random House, 1978), p. 32.
11. *The God that Failed*, ed. by Richard Grossman (New York: Bantam Matrix, 1965), p. 208.
12. Spender, *World Within World*, p. 190. Though no longer a card-carrying comrade, Spender's attitude toward Communism remained ambivalent. See Thomas von Vegesack, *De Intellectuelen: Een geschiedenis van het literaire engagement 1898–1968*, trans. by Petra Broomans and Wiveca Jongeneel (Amsterdam: Meulenhoff, 1989), pp. 181–82.
13. Cited in Walter Benjamin, *Reflections: Essays, Aphorism, Autobiographical Writings*, ed. by Peter Demetz (New York: Harcourt Brace Jovanovich, 1978), p. 218.
14. W. H. Auden, 'September 1, 1939'.
15. Leopold Schwarzschild, 'Autobiographical Notes', Leopold Schwarzschild Collection; AR 7043 / MF 571; box 1; folder 1; Leo Baeck Institute, New York.
16. Ludwig Marcuse, *Mein 20. Jahrhundert. Auf dem Weg zu einer Autobiographie* (Munich: List, 1960), p. 204. Schwarzschild returned to Germany in 1949 and died the following year.
17. Leopold Schwarzschild, *Die Lunte am Pulverfass. Aus dem 'Neuen Tagebuch' 1933–1940*, ed. by Valerie Schwarzschild (Hamburg: Christian Wegner, 1965), pp. 104, 109–10, 119, 122, 136.
18. Michael Gold, 'Notes from Kharkov', *The New Masses*, March 1931, 4–6 (p. 4).
19. Max Eastman, *Artists in Uniform: A Study of Literature and Bureaucratism* (London: Allen & Unwin, 1934), pp. 8–9. Eastman furnishes much of the background material to this congress, including the sevenstep.
20. 'Letter to Anatoly Lunacharsky', 6 May 1922, in *Lénine, Sur l'art et la littérature*, selected and presented by Jean-Michel Palmier, 3 vols (Paris: Union Générale d'Éditions, 1975), III (1975), p. 278.
21. Vyacheslav Polonsky, 'Lenin's views of Art and Culture', in Eastman, *Artists in Uniform*, pp. 217–52 (p. 222).
22. Eastman, p. 251.
23. Ezra Pound, cited in Daniel Aaron, *Writers on the Left* (New York, Avon Books, 1961) p. 134.
24. Cited in Frank Westerman, *Ingenieurs van de ziel* (Amsterdam: Atlas, 2002), p. 40.
25. Ceremonial Opening of the Soviet Writers' Congress (1934) <https://www.youtube.com/watch?v=HZUelR9jZik> [accessed 12 December 2014]

26. Westerman, p. 36.
27. Ilya Ehrenburg, *Memoirs: 1921–1941*, trans. by Tatania Shebunina and Yvonne Kapp (New York: Grosset & Dunlap, 1963), p. 270.
28. Soviet Writers' Congress 1934, Marxist Internet Archive, <https://www.marxists.org/subject/art/lit_crit/sovietwriterCongress/index.htm> [accessed 1 June 2012] Speeches cited are from this archive. This is the online version of the paperback, *Soviet Writers' Congress, 1934: The Debate on Socialist Realism and Modernism* (London: Lawrence & Wishart, 1977).
29. Eddy du Perron, *In deze grootse tijd* (The Hague: Stols, 1946), pp. 14–15.
30. Cited in Du Perron, *Grootse tijd*, pp. 15–16.
31. Yury Olesha, *Envy*, trans. by T. S. Berczynski (New York: Ardis Publishers, 2004).
32. John Scott, *Behind the Urals: An American Worker in Russia's City of Steel* (Bloomington: Indiana University Press, 1973), p. 69. Originally published in 1942.
33. Scott, pp. 70–79, 114.
34. *Belomor: An Account of the Construction of the New Canal Between the White Sea and the Baltic Sea*, ed. by Maxim Gorky (principal editor) and others, trans. by Amabel Williams-Ellis (London: John Lane, 1935).
35. The best account is Frank Westerman's *Ingenieurs van de ziel*. Also available in English: *Engineers of the Soul* (New York: Overlook Press, 2011).
36. Danilo Kiš, *A Tomb for Boris Davidovich*, trans. by Duška Mikić–Mitchell (New York: Penguin Books: 1980), pp. 133–34.
37. Eastman, citing Sergei Tretyakov, p. 5.
38. *Belomor,* p. 343.
39. Trans. by Anthony Wixley and Robert S. Carr (London: Lawrence and Wishart, n.d.).
40. The play enjoyed a long and successful run. A number of participants at the Paris Congress (H.-R. Lenormand and Lion Feuchtwanger, to name two) saw the play in the course of extended visits to the Soviet Union and recorded their impressions.
41. Shana Lutker, 'Some fistfights of the Surrealists', *Material*, 3 (2012), 53–58 (p. 56). There are a number of versions of what took place that day on Boulevard du Montparnasse. The gist, as related here, stands, however.
42. Samuel Putnam, *Paris Was Our Mistress: Memoirs of a Lost & Found Generation* (Carbondale: Southern Illinois University Press, 1947), p. 166.
43. André Breton, *Manifestoes of Surrealism*, trans. by Richard Seaver and Helen R. Land (Ann Arbor: University of Michigan Press, 1969), p. 125.
44. Putnam, p. 164.
45. André Breton, *Nadja,* trans. by Richard Howard (New York: Grove Press, 1960), pp. 143, p. 60.
46. Klaus Mann, *The Turning Point: Thirty–Five Years in This Century* (New York: Fischer, 1942), p. 183.
47. Cited in Sandra Teroni and Wolfgang Klein, *Pour la défense de la culture. Les textes du Congrès international des écrivains, Paris, juin 1935.* (Dijon: Éditions Universitaires de Dijon, 2005), p. 63.
48. *Conversations: The Autobiography of Surrealism*, with André Parinaud and others, trans. by Mark Polizzotti (New York: Marlowe & Co., 1993), p. 139.
49. Salvador Dalí, preface to *La Mort difficile* (Paris: Pauvert, 1979), pp. 7–12.
50. 'Le Suicide est-il une solution?', in *La Révolution Surréaliste*, 1, 15 January 1925, pp. 8–15 (p. 8) <http://gallica.bnf.fr/ark:/12148/bpt6k58450811/f1.item.r=Crevel> [accessed 14 February 2016]
51. René Crevel, 'Mais si la mort n'était qu'un mot', *Le Disque Vert*, 1 (1925), <http://www.psychanalyse–paris.com/908–Mais-si-la-mort-n-etait-qu-un.html> [accessed 29 April 2012]
52. *Conversations,* p. 139.
53. René Crevel, *Putting My Foot in It,* trans. by Thomas Buckley (Normal, IL: Dalkey Archive Press, 1992), pp. vii–xiv (viii, ix, ix).
54. 'L'écrivain révolutionaire René Crevel est mort', *L'Humanité,* 21 June 1935, p. 2.
55. K. Mann, *Turning Point,* pp. 182–83.
56. Manès Sperber, *Until My Eyes Are Closed with Shards* (New York: Holmes & Meier, 1994), p. 55.
57. Green, *Diary,* 13 April 1938, p. 79.
58. Walter Benjamin, *The Arcades Project*, trans. by Howard Eiland and Kevin McLaughlin (Cambridge, MA, and London: Bellknap Press of Harvard University Press, 1999), p. 749.

59. 'Travailleurs et écrivains ont rendu à Victor Hugo un magnifique hommage', *L'Humanité*, 21 June 1935, p. 1.
60. Hugo's own words. Cited in Benjamin, *Arcades Project*, p. 746.
61. Paul Nizan, 'Hugo et nous', *L'Humanité*, 2 June 1935, p. 4.
62. Jean-Richard Bloch, 'Parmi les leçons d'un congrès', *Europe,* 37, (1935), 98–108 (pp. 99–100) <http://gallica.bnf.fr/ark:/12148/bpt6k6282358r/f119.item.zoom> [accessed 15 November 2015]
63. Cited in Ludmilla Stern, *Western Intellectuals and the Soviet Union, 1920–40. From Red Square to the Left Bank* (London and New York: Routledge, 2007), pp. 18–19, 22–23.
64. Philip Mechanicus, *Van sikkel en hamer* (Amsterdam: Blitz, 1932), p. 16.
65. Ehrenburg, *Memoirs*, pp. 273–74, 286.
66. Radek, 'Contemporary World Literature'.

CHAPTER 2

❖

# The Congress, 21–23 June

## I. André Gide

*My reticences are the most passionate thing about me.*

— 1 —

André Gide's lips barely moved when he spoke. Oscar Wilde quipped that they were 'taut as those of someone who has never told a lie'.[1] Of an evening, in Algeria, toward the end of the nineteenth century, Gide fell for a 'marvellous' flute-playing adolescent with the 'slender body of a child'. Wilde led his companion, whose acquaintance he had made a few days earlier, to a place where he might enjoy the boy. Two years later, Gide once more hooked up with Mohamed. Mohamed conducted the author of *L'Immoraliste* to a shabby hotel. Made to sign in, Gide put down: César Bloch.[2]

Gide considered Shakespeare messy because the Bard's characters kept on living after the curtain falls. He preferred Racine, preferred 'that exact limitation, that non-protruding from the frame, that sharpness of outline'. To Gide, Racine was 'the summit of art'.[3]

To Maurice Sachs, Gide came across as a 'headmaster of an Upper School' who loved order and classification and wielded his pen like 'the needle of a compass'. Sachs, briefly Gide's secretary, compared Gide's writing to that of a log kept by the captain of a beautiful ship who imperturbably keeps watch on the bridge decade after decade, who shows us where our duties lie, who steers clear of the reefs and has the training ship well in hand'.[4]

Mention Gide and strong nouns materialize as in cartoon speech-bubbles: honesty; probity; integrity; non-conformity; order. For Gide moral problems carried all before it. There were those who, like Klaus Mann, found his predilection for dark-skinned North African boys 'objectionable', yet worshipped the ground he walked on. 'To thine own self be true' was the message Gide sounded in his books and embodied in his persona.

By 1935 Gide, by his own admission, had become a type. He wasn't happy about that. Types tend to morph into caricatures. He shunned the limelight, avoided crowds. Gide addressing workers of Paris's 'red suburbs' was a 'curious spectacle' indeed.[5] He reluctantly assumed the co-chairmanship at the Paris writers' Congress. Not one to stick his neck out, he would not sign a petition he himself had not helped

FIG. 3. Writers' Congress for the Defence of Culture.
Opening of the Congress, 21 June 1935 (Photo Gisèle Freund/Art Resource)

write. When Louis Aragon got into trouble with the law for a poem calling for the assassination of Léon Blum, the future socialist premier, Gide refused to sign a petition on his behalf initiated by André Breton.[6] When an association of antifascist writers tried to recruit him, he respectfully declined: 'No dear comrades'.[7] He also waved off an appeal from Italian historian Gaetano Salvemini to speak up for Lauro de Bosis. De Bosis, Italian poet and essayist, had learned to fly solely to be able to drop anti-Mussolini pamphlets from the air. A squadron of planes went after him and he was never seen or heard from again. Gide acknowledged having read De Bosis's anti-fascist literature and having been deeply moved. '[B]ut what can I do?...' he lamented in his *Journal*,

> I must explain myself to Salvemini: despite my admiration for the young hero's deed, I lack something: belief in liberty. It is most difficult for me to bring my own thought to light. The notion of liberty, as it is taught us, seems to me singularly false and pernicious. And if I approve the Soviet constraint, I must likewise approve the Fascist discipline. I am more and more inclined to believe that the idea of liberty is but a snare. [...] The 'Render unto Caesar the things which are Caesar's, and unto God the things that are God's' of the Gospel seems to me more than ever a teaching full of wisdom. On God's side, freedom, that of the mind; on Caesar's side, submission, that of acts. The single concern with the happiness of the greatest number, on the one hand; on the other, the single concern with truth. (524)

— 2 —

In 1931, the same year he refused Salvemini's request, Gide discovered Communism. 'By mood and temperament, I could not be less revolutionary', Gide acknowledged in 1933, approaching age 65. 'I personally have every reason to be pleased with the state of things.' (563) The decision for Communism ran 'contre sa chair' — against his temperament — but so was the fascist contention that civilization was based on a lie, and civilization was worth defending, and the Soviet Union offered a clear-cut alternative. 'Never', he wrote in his journal in May 1931, 'have I bent over the future with a more passionate curiosity. My whole heart applauds that gigantic and yet entirely human undertaking.'

Not Marx, least of all Marx, but the Gospel paved the way, Gide explained. He had come to see that the relationship between art and life was more complicated than was dreamt of in his philosophy; that the moral questions he formerly considered the life-blood of literature could not be divorced from social questions. 'Today I let myself be convinced that man himself cannot be changed unless social conditions first urge and help him to do so.' (502) 'I never had much of a taste for portraying the victors and the glorious of the world', affirmed the scion of an upper bourgeois Protestant family in his autobiography, 'but rather more those whose true glory was concealed.'[8]

The Soviets could not have been more delighted. Gide, long-time fulcrum of European intellectual life, was a big catch: the biggest — and he did not disappoint. 'On that high road of history where each country, each nation must sooner or later set forth, the Soviet Union has taken the lead in a glorious manner', he declared in his message to the First Soviet Writers' Congress (17 August 1934).

> Today she is giving us a model of that New Society of which we dreamed, but for which we dared not hope. In the domain of the spirit as well, it is important that the Soviet Union set the example. [...] Her task is to inaugurate, in literature and in art, a *Communist individualism* (if I dare to couple these two words customarily opposed, in my opinion quite erroneously). Doubtless a period of intemperate affirmation was necessary; but the U.S.S.R. has already passed that stage, and nothing convinces me of this more than the most recent articles and speeches of Stalin. Communism will be able to implant itself only by taking account of the particularity of each individual. A society in which each resembles the other is scarcely desirable. I would even say that it is impossible; and such a literature more impossible still. Each artist is by necessity an individualist, however strong may be his Communist convictions and his attachment to the Party.[9]

In Moscow, Radek was not slow in milking Gide's 'conversion'.

> The great French writer, André Gide, who had previously been fluctuating between a real conception of the world and the ivory tower of the recluse, an aesthete who held that in the modern world Prometheus, descending from his rock, could only win the world's ear by jesting — André Gide, confronted with capitalist reality, which was revealed to him in all its starkness in the French colonies, and confronted on the other hand with the heroic struggle which the Soviet proletariat is waging for the new order of society, declared, to the

amazement of the capitalist world, that he sided with the USSR and would be glad to lay down his life for it.

Gide's affair with Communism, like most affairs, lasted five years, and, again as in most affairs, the suitor could not bring himself to tie the knot by taking out Party membership.

— 3 —

At a banquet of French writers held at the time of the Congress, a Persian or Afghan delegate got up to present Gide with a multi-coloured robe: he had to put it on, and kept it on throughout dinner 'as a kind of comic opera Fellah', for fear of insulting the donor.[10] 'A constant need of reconciliation torments me', Gide confided in his journal: 'it is a failing of my mind; it is perhaps a good quality of my heart'. (620) Thus he was disappointed that so many delegates who should have had a chance to speak at the Congress never got to do so. 'But what can be done when faced with the eloquence of certain orators who go on at length? ... to call for, it so happens, to insist upon, everyone's right to speak. The oratorical excess of a few reduces the others to silence.' Thus he felt sorry for that woman who waited in vain for her turn to speak; she had come a long way.

> It is most likely she that I see at a distance [...], wearing a saffron-coloured peplum, seated alone. At once I approach her and, putting into my voice all the sympathy I can: 'It is fortunate, comrade, that Greece is represented here.' Then she, turning her beautiful face toward me and in an undertone: 'I am India.' So that the unfortunate representative of Greece will not even have the consolation of my remark. (584–85)

Gide's 'need for reconciliation' was much in evidence in the opening address to the Congress, 21 June. In it, he hailed the literary contributions from different countries, national in form and international in scope, as the common property of all. In next day's principal discourse, Gide essentially reiterated the literary credo staked out in his message to the Moscow writers' Congress: profoundly internationalist; profoundly French; profoundly individualist, 'though in full agreement with the Communist outlook [...]

> I have always contended that the individual can best serve the community by being most effectively himself. Today we may add to this, as a corollary, the assertion, that individuals and their peculiarities can best flourish in a Communist society; or that, as Malraux writes in a recent preface that has already become famous, communism 'restores to the individual all the creative potentialities of his nature'.[11]

Literature was no different, Gide insisted, for in literature the general triumphs in the particular; it is where all that is human reaches its ultimate realization. His overriding concern was to defend the autonomy of literature and the cause of freedom. However bourgeois his background, he had spent his life at war 'with the conventions, habits, the lies of my environment'. The present-day task of literature was to oppose itself to the culture of the past, the detestable capitalist regime of our 'sad West'.

Yet by the time the Paris Congress rolled around, Gide's embrace of Communism was starting to show serious signs of buyer's remorse. Those seeds of doubt planted in his message to the Moscow Congress the year before had started to germinate, foreshadowing a parting of the ways. In Paris, he criticized the Soviet's approach to literature on several counts. Although the Soviet Union had provided humanity with a 'spectacle without precedent', Gide acknowledged, a state in which reader and writer communed as in no other country, Soviet literature had not yet reached the point of giving the new man a face and a body. It had been brought to his attention that at the Moscow Congress workers had implored writers to produce works that reflected their lives. Gide thought this was the wrong approach; literature was not a mirror, not mere imitation: it informs, proposes, and creates. 'Culture works toward the emancipation of the mind and not to its enslavement.' Today all our sympathy goes out to oppressed and suffering humanity, Gide went on, leading up to his punchline:

> But I cannot admit that man ceases to be of interest to us when he ceases to experience hunger, suffering and oppression. I refuse to admit that he only merits our sympathy when miserable. [...] Nevertheless, I am greatly pleased that efforts are going forward toward creating the social conditions in which joy is accessible to all and joy itself contributes to men's growth.

— 4 —

In 1935, all Gide knew about the Soviet Union was second-hand, based on hearsay and reports by fellow intellectuals. That was about to change. A trip to the workers' state was in the offing. Not that Gide was all that eager to take a look. He feared being used and, perhaps even more so, what he might find there. For one couldn't just visit Russia: one had to take a stand, for or against. It would take a good deal of arm-twisting to get him to change his mind. Ehrenburg and Malraux twisted, and so did Jef Last, Gide's *ami hollandais*.[12] The thirty-eight-year-old Dutch Communist pulled out all the stops, for by this time, less than a year after the Paris Congress, Gide was on the verge of breaking with Communism. Last knew the Soviet Union well. This would be his fourth visit. There would be none of the celebrity hoopla, the Dutchman promised, to interfere with Gide's ability to get an unobstructed view. He spoke the language; enjoyed an insider's grasp of Soviet red tape; knew Moscow better than Paris and even had a bank account there (there could not have been much in it). The fear of being used and fooled was groundless. Gide would be safe under his wing. 'Ah, dear André', Last gushed, 'I will show you things there that will make your heart jump for joy.' Gide would experience such 'happiness, joy and beauty as to make you feel younger than ever and return home having glimpsed the future of humanity'. If only it were possible to go unrecognized.[13]

After much humming and hawing, Gide caved. At the time, noted a fellow Gide devotee Klaus Mann, Gide was a sucker for 'the popular wit and the almost savage vitality of the husky rebel from Amsterdam'.[14] Last was ecstatic. He could not have been happier, he informed Gide, 'had he been invited to descend with him into Dante's Inferno'. For starters, Last mapped out more innocuous pursuits: Leningrad's children's theatre, the Bolshoi, and the Parks of Culture (recreation centres for the people). They would have the time of their lives, the Dutchman promised.

Around the time of his departure for the Soviet Union, Gide received an 'open letter' from Victor Serge,[15] the writer-revolutionary banished to the Russian outback in 1933 for allegedly conspiring with Trotskyists. Serge, who wrote in French and had lived in France for years, enjoyed a devoted following among France's intelligentsia. Concerted efforts on the part of a dedicated group of supporters riding the wave of United and Popular Front politics led to Serge's release, at Stalin's behest, in 1936, several months prior to Gide's visit. Serge's letter began as follows:

> You once presided in Paris at an international writer's Congress gathered for the defense of culture, where the question of the freedom of thought in the USSR was brought up only insofar as it concerns me and, it seems, against the will of the majority of those at the Congress. I have learned that at that time you attempted several steps to save some of my manuscripts that were being held by the censor in Moscow. They are still there. [...] I thank you for all that you have done for me, as well as the impartiality you have shown towards the friends who defend me and who have been refused the right to speak.

Having read his *Journal* in secret, Serge expressed amazement that Gide, the embodiment of 'that great Western intelligentsia', seemed to know nothing 'of the tragedy of a revolution ravaged from within by reaction'.

> What is the condition of thought? A dry doctrine, emptied of all its content, strictly imposed in all domains. [...] What is the condition of the writer, i.e., that of the man whose profession is speaking for all those others who have no voice? [...] A literary mandarinate admirably organized, royally renumerated, *bien-pensant*, as could be expected. [...] We are confronting fascism, but how can we block its path with so many concentration camps behind us?

'I beg of you', Serge pleaded, 'not to close your eyes [...] and see the reality of a revolution wounded in its living world.'

— 5 —

Gide and Last, joined by four other writers (Louis Guilloux, Eugène Dabit, Jacques Schiffrin, and Pierre Herbart), took off for the Soviet Union in mid-June, planning to stay ten weeks. Maxim Gorky happened to die within days of Gide's arrival. The funeral took place on 19 June in Red Square. Gide was invited to speak, sharing the platform with Stalin and Molotov. His speech was broadcast over loudspeakers throughout the city and his photograph addressing the crowd appeared in all the papers. The fate of culture, Gide declared, was bound up with the fate of the Soviet Union.

> When the October Revolution stirred up the deep masses of the Russian people, it was said in the West, oft repeated and universally believed, that this tidal wave would swamp all art. As soon as literature ceased being the privilege of one class would it not — it was asked — then constitute a danger? It was to answer that accusation that writers from all counties grouped themselves together with the firm conviction of accomplishing an urgent duty. It is true that culture was menaced — but the peril did not come from the revolutionary and liberating forces; it came, on the contrary, from the parties which were

trying to subjugate these forces and to break them. It is War which most threatens culture, war toward which national forces inspired by hate and envy drive us. It is the great international and revolutionary forces on which the duty is laid to protect culture and to make it illustrious. Its fate is bound up, in my mind, with the fate of the Soviet Union and it shall be defended.[16]

Gide's travelling companion Eugène Dabit had been scheduled to speak at the last session of the Paris Congress but had voluntarily ceded his place so others might. Dabit's remarks, published afterward, extolled the bracing influence of proletarian literature on existing literature, erasing the distinction between manual and intellectual labor, because in the end art is 'nothing other than life'. Our eyes, he proclaimed, are fixed on the future, on 'a goal beyond our time, beyond our toil, beyond our person'.[17]

There is a photograph of Dabit, Gide, and Last being chauffeured in a luxury car with the top down. It was hot. Last sits to Gide's right, robust and tanned. Gide does not look well. His stomach was bothering him. He looks wan and frail, uncomfortable and out of sorts; a handkerchief sits on his baldpate like a limp pancake.[18]

As the tour wore on, Dabit became increasingly distressed. At the umpteenth hotel stop he and Last got into a heated argument in the course of which Dabit confessed that he would give up every one of his leftist beliefs for a single hour in the arms of the woman he loved.

Despite Last's repeated assurances, Gide's party shuttled from place to place as on a magic red carpet; every sighting set off a flurry of activities on the ground. The party's reception in Sebastopol, the port city on the Black Sea, was typical. Gide:

> Of course, there is a band on the dock and a full committee to receive us. On the sidewalks all the school children are lined up with their teachers in cheerful rows. All the children hurl roses toward our cars. The paved road behind us is covered with roses, as in a parade. Our car itself is filling up with roses that rise higher and higher. When we finally arrive at our hotel, we find the bathtubs filled with roses that eventually cover everything but our upper bodies.[19]

Someone in the party surmised, half-jokingly, that the flowers and banners that welcomed them wherever they happened to alight were the same flowers and banners that had preceded their arrival at the previous stop, being hauled from place to place in the lead car.

Banquets succeeded one another in dizzying succession; champagne flowed like water from the tap; caviar piled on as though it were fast food at the local drive-through. There were visits to the former palaces of the aristocracy and czars. Well before the end of the tour, increasingly fed up, Gide exploded in front of his travel mates: 'I am not His Majesty Amman Ula, am I?'

Bolshevo, a town populated by ex-criminals, was a mandatory stop for important mucketymucks from abroad. A resident was trotted out to relate the story of his 'rebirth'. Last listened as in a trance. Back in the hotel, Gide set the 'husky rebel' straight:

> But dear boy [...] don't you understand that it was all Salvation Army stuff? That poor sap earns a rather pretty sum from his confession, which he has repeated so often at all kinds of occasions that he knows it by heart. [...] The only time

I found him at all sympathetic was when it became very obvious how much
pleasure he still derived from the memory of his misdeeds.[20]

In a post-war publication, Gide claimed that it was not until later that he
discovered that 'only informers [...] were granted the privilege of living in this
model settlement'. 'When I visited it, it seemed to me one of the noblest and most
successful experiments in the Soviet Union and a great achievement.' He also said
that he went to the Soviet Union full of hope. 'I had arrived there a convinced and
enthusiastic follower in order to admire a new world, and they offered me, to tempt
me and win me, all the prerogatives which I abhorred in the old world.'[21]

Dabit's preparedness to sacrifice his political principles for an hour entwined in
the arms of his beloved quickly became moot: he died in Sebastopol, succumbing
to scarlet fever.

— 6 —

'A tremendous, dreadful confusion', Gide wrote in his journal within days after his
return to France. (599) It did not take him long to sort it all out. The result was
*Return from the USSR* (November 1936). Dedicated to the memory of Eugène Dabit,
it lifted the curtain on a veritable shop of horrors, not quite Dante's Inferno, but
sobering enough.[22] It was, Gide said, 'because of [his] admiration for the Soviet
Union and the wonders it has already performed' that he was going to criticize
it. Reticent by nature, he started slowly, scattering bits of praise before going on
the attack. Thus he liked what he saw in the children's pioneer camp he visited:
'handsome, well fed, well-cared for'. And 'the parks of culture' where people could
relax after a day's work were 'unquestionable successes'. From there it was pretty
much downhill. In the special car provided by the ever-solicitous Mikhail Koltsov,
'at the time a kind of unofficial Minister of Propaganda in the Soviet Union',[23] they
travelled from Moscow to Ordzhonikize in 'unlooked for comfort'. The Pullman
boasted private sleeping berths and a sitting room where meals were served. They
managed, with some difficulty, to make contact with Komsomols (youth division
of the Communist Party) in the next compartment. Gide had brought with him
some 'little toys' to relax his 'grey cells', Last recalled. The youths were at a loss to
know what he meant. 'For a true Komsomol', Gide commented, 'is always bent on
service and judges everything from the point of view of utility.'[24]

The much-vaunted new man found it 'perfectly natural', Gide went on, to stand
in line for the shoddiest of goods and foods — 'they seem to enjoy waiting' — and
thought he lived better than workers in the West. (Last, on the other hand, was
impressed by the progress made in the foodstuffs available since his last visit in 1934.)
The goods in the shop windows were 'horrifying'. Stakhanovites, shock workers,
left him cold. Soviet workers were lazy. Unequal salaries, had been reintroduced,
of necessity, and the gap was widening. 'Bourgeois tendencies' were on the rise and
a 'petty-bourgeois' spirit hovered.

The Soviet citizen's ignorance about the West was astounding. 'What they want
from us is not information but praise'.[25] Stalin was everywhere. Gide was not able

to send a telegram to Stalin and write 'you' without penning a superlative such as 'You master of the people'.

Gide was shocked by the degree of conformism. 'Everyone is like everyone else.' The model kolkhoz (collective farm) he visited was a model of 'complete depersonalization'. Every dwelling featured the same 'ugly furniture, the same portrait of Stalin, and absolutely nothing else'. Freedom of expression was non-existent. People waited to see what *Pravda*, the official organ of the Communist Party, had to say before venturing an opinion. The line was 'sacrosanct'. 'And I doubt', Gide concluded, 'whether in any other country in the world, even Hitler's Germany, thought be less free, more bowed down, more fearful (terrorized), more vassalized.'[26]

The fallout from this little book was considerable. Ehrenburg, Jef Last, and others had tried to persuade him to hold off on publishing, arguing that publication at this time would severely undermine Soviet enormous efforts on behalf of Spain.[27] Moscow was incensed. Such a 'wicked old man', Ehrenburg lashed out. In mid-December, *L'Humanité* reprinted an article from *Pravda* that struck back at the 'turncoat' with a species of venom invariably reserved for spurned lovers everywhere and at all times. The article, 'Laughter and Tears of André Gide',[28] contrasted the tears he shed and the words he spoke in the course of his visit with the views articulated in *Return from the USSR*. 'The well-known French writer André Gide', the article began, 'laughed a lot, cried a lot, during his stay in our country this summer', an aged author wallowing in sentimentality. *Pravda* next produced the telegram Gide sent from the Soviet border on his way back to France:

> At the end of our unforgettable journey across the great land of victorious socialism, I dispatch from this frontier a final and cordial greeting to the magnificent friends whom I leave with sadness, in telling them, and thus to the entire Soviet Union, Goodbye!

*Pravda* had a field day pointing out the contradictions and using Gide's own words against him — from *Return*'s opening pages praising Soviet youth to the sky, only to slander them a few pages along as a bunch of mindless parrots; from the surprise he expressed on discovering that more people knew about his books in the Soviet Union than in France, to his contention that art and literature were strangers to the masses and that 'beauty is considered a bourgeois value'. *Return* accused Soviet writers of cowardice and lack of talent; but at Gorky's funeral, *Pravda* noted, its author proclaimed that being a revolutionary writer no longer placed one in opposition. 'On the contrary, it responds to the wishes of a great number of people and, what is most admirable, of its leaders.' *Pravda*'s readers learned that Gide had made similar noises at the bedside of the terminally ill Nikolai Ostrovsky, with tears in his eyes, even as he planted a kiss on the forehead of the venerated author of *How the Steel was Tempered*. In Georgia, Gide dispatched a telegram expressing his delight and enthusiasm. There was simply no end to the lies of this 'worthy son of the French petty bourgeoisie'.

As for the allegation that there was no freedom of expression in the Soviet Union, *Pravda* went on, the old man's biggest lie merely demonstrated an utter inability to grasp the true nature of the workers' state. Gide simply did not understand that there could be no criticism where there was nothing to criticize and everyone was in agreement. Shamefully, Gide's idea of freedom of expression amounted to giving free rein to Trotskyists and other counter-revolutionaries, thus helping spread the lies of 'the enemies of the working class'. Wasn't Gide aware that the entire nation was just then involved in discussing the new constitution, and that the law outlawing abortion, 'law for the protection of the family', was being fully debated in the press? Gide, *Pravda* summed up, came in the guise of a friend and 'lied in order to hide his true face, like the counterfeiters in one of his novels'.[29] *Return* was a book of 'incomprehensible hatred'.

Gide took it all in stride. He had sobered up. He had come to realize that Communism required a commitment that transcended his own person. Revolution was nothing like dabbing your lips with a little white napkin after a two-hour lunch with Malraux at a pricey restaurant on the Place des Victoires. It was as though a huge load had been lifted from his shoulders. 'The discipline I imposed on myself for three years has not been without advantage; but today I find greater advantage in liberating myself from it than in continuing to adhere to it.' At last he was able to reveal that he had spent hours agonizing over *Das Kapital* and never understood a word of it. 'And each time I came away aching all over, my intelligence bruised as by instruments of torture.' (618–19)

## II. André Malraux

> What interests me in any man is the human condition; in a great man, the form and the essence of his greatness [...] certain characteristics which express not so much an individual personality as a particular relationship with the world.[30]

— 1 —

On 5 September 1936, André Gide dined with André and Clara Malraux. Gide had just come back from the Soviet Union and there was a lot on his mind. Should or shouldn't he? Should he tell or keep those taut lips of his shut? More was at stake than trashing a syndicated image of a country in sync with human aspirations. One false step from Gide was enough to put the antifascist struggle on the back foot, at home and abroad, at a most critical time. Gide may have wanted to solicit Malraux's input. He may well have asked for it in private prior to setting out for the restaurant. But Gide's journal is altogether silent on the subject. Dinner was excellent, and so was the 'conversation' if one-sided.

> And for two hours I am in awe before his dazzling and staggering flow of words. [...] André Malraux's great strength lies in caring very little whether he winds, or tires, or 'drops by the wayside' whoever is listening and who has hardly any other anxiety [...] but to seem to be following, rather than to follow really. [...] I come away rather crushed than exalted. (600)

Gide was not alone in remarking Malraux's torrential verbal downpour, no doubt much of it brilliant. On a roll, Malraux was like a runaway train. It was part of his Gestalt, like the nervous tic.

If reticence was Gide's 'passion', Malraux's was adventure. At twenty-two he took off for Indochina. In time-honoured colonial fashion, his travel plans included a good deal of pilfering. The stolen loot, temple statuary, was earmarked for the villas of wealthy collectors. The enterprise got him in trouble with the law and a suspended sentence. This set the stage for a small-bore career teetering on the edge of respectability. Thus he helped organize a party of adventurers in search of the legendary capital of the Queen of Sheba in the Yemenite kingdom — and subsequently tried to pass off photographs of a few skeletal buildings taken from a souped-up aeroplane and published in a French magazine as the genuine article.[31] 1936 found him fighting in the Spanish Civil War on the Republican side. Malraux enjoyed dressing up in a uniform and being called 'colonel'.[32] Although he knew very little about flying, he took charge of a brigade of airmen. His courage was never in doubt, unlike his orders, which often came out muddled. 'The leadership of the entire air corps', wrote Jef Last to his wife in the autumn of 1936, 'for lack of skilled airmen, lies in the hands of André Malraux, an amateur in this area, whose enormous dedication is offset only by his lack of technical knowledge, albeit imperfectly.'[33]

It is no accident that Malraux 'resurrected' the term *farfelu*, 'a noun designating a particular kind of crazy quixotic adventurer'.[34]

There is a photograph of nine-year-old André dressed as a musketeer awkwardly gazing into the camera. With the passing years, the awkward gaze gave way to the intense look captured in dozens of photographs. 'Every young bourgeois wants very much to be a d'Artagnan', Malraux was to remark as an adult.[35] There was a lot to be said for the Dumas creation: good looks; courage; adventurer; fighter; loyal servant. Like d'Artagnan, Malraux always seemed to be rushing off somewhere. When he wasn't off to China, Persia, or Tibet, he could be found in Greenland observing 'how the midnight sun reflects off polar bears'.[36]

— 2 —

In 1934, Malraux told Paul Valéry, another wielder of words sans merci, that what interested him 'a great deal' was 'how to reduce to a minimum the theatrical side of one's nature'.[37] It was a thought Malraux repeated the following year at the Mutualité. '*To be a man is for everyone to reduce play-acting to a minimum*', he declared on the evening of 22 June. The eleven theses he laid out paralleled the ideas articulated in the preface to the novel *Le Temps du mépris* (*Days of Wrath*), which came out around the time of the Congress.

> The history of artistic sensibility in France for the past fifty years might be called the death-agony of the brotherhood of man. Its real enemy is an unformulated individualism which existed sporadically throughout the nineteenth century and which sprang less from the will to create a man whole than from a fanatical desire to be different. [...] It was not only in Stendhal's time that the concrete conditions of social life imposed hypocrisy on the pure individualist whenever he wished to act.[38]

In his speech at the Congress, Malraux opposed such 'unformulated individualism' with the 'will to humanism'. 'The humanism we want to create and which finds its oldest expression in the long line of thought from Voltaire to Marx' (thesis VIII), he asserted, 'requires above all that we take stock of the real human being. [...] A communion with the people is possible now [...] in its will to revolution.'

The Soviet new man was the much-decorated model worker at the Magnitogorsk steel plant who refused to take a break from the building of a new world for fear they would finish the job without him.[39] To the American writer and Congress delegate Waldo Frank, Malraux's characters in *The Human Condition* and *Days of Wrath* represented a new type of Western man, an image forged in 'the flames of disaster and of struggle', superseding the 'hysterical atomic man'. The conduct of this new type of person, Frank remarked in the foreword to the *Days of Wrath* was 'premised, not upon isolation, but upon solidarity'. Frank perceived Malraux as a 'revolutionary artist [...] because every profound artist must be a revolutionary in a revolutionary period'. André Malraux, Frank concluded,

> has an honorable place among the too scant number of creative writers scattered throughout the world, who, by their translation of cosmic and social forms into forms of personal experience, are doing the artist's share in the creating of the new world order.[40]

(For Frank, as for Malraux, building socialism was first and foremost a human and cultural task, only then political and economic. The New World could not come into being, Frank told the Congress in the evening of 23 June, unless all of its parts were working together in unison. 'That, in the social body in waiting', he concluded, 'is the role of the writer.')

At the Congress, Malraux was Mr Solidarity himself. He played ball with the Soviets and ran a tight ship. He overturned the tables of the Trotskyists and kept the nether echelons of the writing guild from storming the microphone. He does not appear to have spoken up for Breton. Yet he was no Soviet stooge. On the final day of the Congress, he cautioned the Soviets not to let the literary giants beneath whose portraits they had conducted the Moscow affair to fall between the cracks and become museum pieces, but to look to them for inspiration.

— *3* —

> At last, the plane takes off for Hong Kong. The Pacific. Islands. Over there, there is the island called Balé-Kambang, which Eddy du Perron gave me when I dedicated 'La Condition humaine' to him. He died when the Germans entered Holland. He thought all politics meaningless, and history too, I believe. He was my best friend. [...] He did not believe in politics, but he believed in justice.[41]

Malraux wasn't so much an actor as someone who was constantly working on his persona. So judged Eddy du Perron, Malraux's best friend. Du Perron's island accrued to Malraux in the same manner as the filched statues: colonial theft.

André Gide had Jef Last. Malraux had Eddy du Perron. He, too, was Dutch, despite his French-sounding name. Born into the colonial caste, Du Perron grew up in what was then the Dutch East Indies. In 1921, the Du Perrons moved into a 'château' in Belgium. (In Belgium, 'castle' was a flexible concept: any really big house would do.) Upon the death of his mother in 1933, the son was left with a pittance — ruined by an inheritance, quipped Malraux. Up until then, Eddy had lived the life of an intellectual grandee, with a monthly stipend that covered his basic needs and self-published early writings. The collapse of the family fortune forced him to start earning his own keep, putting to the test his definition of an intellectual as 'someone who cannot earn a living except by the pen'. Fluent in French, in Paris Du Perron found work as a correspondent with a Dutch newspaper.

Eddy du Perron's contribution to world literature is *Het land van herkomst (Country of Origin)*, a free-wheeling autobiography that at times reads like a novel and at other times as narrative nonfiction. The book combines flashbacks of his upbringing in Indonesia fleshed out with chapters set in Europe. One chapter deals exclusively with Malraux, although his name pops up regularly throughout this unconventional account of a life.

The chapter on Héverlé (Du Perron's *nom de guerre* for Malraux) opens with a Du Perron visit. Clara had just given birth (we are in March 1933) but all Malraux could talk about was *La Condition humaine*, then being serialized in *La Nouvelle Revue Française*. The conversation bore on sexual freedom. Du Perron championed complete fidelity, Malraux the opposite. Du Perron then pointed to a scene in *La Condition humaine* that struck him as false. This is the scene in which May's husband, Kyo, forbids his wife to join him as he goes toward almost certain death; May's punishment for revealing she had recently slept with a comrade. Reminded that they had agreed to give each other unconditional freedom, Kyo shot back: but you must have known not to believe me. Du Perron thought it was cruel to have sprung this on Kyo, the timing could not have been worse. Malraux defended May's action as a necessary corrective to the bourgeois possessive instinct expressed through jealousy. André and Clara had a similar arrangement. Clara: 'You're not cheating if you tell each other everything.'[42] But that did not work out, either; they separated in 1938.

'The confessions of Héverlé', observed Du Perron, 'take place on an impersonal terrain, a sort of plateau where everything is carried on culture-historical and philosophical winds.'[43]

Differences regarding fidelity and the bourgeois possessive instinct spilled over into the political arena. Malraux professed to be an intellectual who walked the people's side of the street. Du Perron, self-proclaimed 'abject intellectual and 'filthy little swine of a bourgeois' (Malraux chimed in with 'intellectual masochist') preferred to take it all in from the sidelines.

> M.   So, you don't want to be the victim of a collectivity. I mean, in the name of what? Of individualism? Then you become easily duped by that as well. There is no reason to suppose that over a thousand years the belief in the 'I' should be any less ridiculous as the belief in fire worship for us. For the Buddhist it is already like that.
>
> DP.  Somewhere the 'I' will always remain, isn't that so? It is grounded in a sensibility embedded in the individual. [...] *His* fate, *his* sensibility, what is he to make of that if he denies the 'I'?
>
> M.   What nonsense! The manner of feeling is itself determined by the nature of

the culture. Your 'I' can't stop being part of a series of specifics dependent on country, race, education, the specific moment in time in which it exists. [...] And don't you worry; no civilization, whatever the form, can destroy intelligence.

DP. At this particular moment in history people who don't get involved in politics don't seem to exist.

M.  It is impossible at this stage of civilization to shrug off politics as mere politics.[44]

There was no escape. The revolution, from the right or the left, or war, would catch up with you no matter where, Malraux contended. Du Perron was not persuaded. 'A failed revolutionary', he told Malraux in 1934, 'is executed by his enemies and a victorious one by his friends.'[45]

That same year riots precipitated by the Stavisky scandal kept France on edge for several weeks. During those tense February days, both Malraux and Du Perron participated in a massive antifascist demonstration in support of the Republic. That is to say, Malraux marched while Du Perron sat, monitoring the showdown from the safety of an outdoor café.

— 4 —

Three months after the demonstrations and crackdowns occasioned by the Stavisky scandal, Malraux and Clara took off for a two-month visit to the Soviet Union. The end of their expedition coincided with the Moscow Writers' Congress. Invited to speak, Malraux started out as though reading from cue cards furnished by his Soviet hosts.

It will be said of you, 'In spite of every obstacle, through civil war and famine, for the first time in thousands of years they put their trust in *men*!'[46]

To the Bourgeoisie, who spoke of the *individual*, Communism will reply: *man*.

I believe in Soviet humanism to come, a humanism that is similar to but not identical with that of Greece, Rome, and the Renaissance period.[47]

The state of literature was another matter. To Malraux, Soviet writing was hopelessly one-dimensional and conformist, bereft of attributes found among the living, and advised the bullish Communist state not to get too carried away by its own propaganda.

America has demonstrated that while a literature can express a powerful civilization, that does not itself mean that it is a powerful literature, and the photograph of a great epoch is not tantamount to great literature. You, who are like one another and yet as unlike as seeds, are inaugurating a culture from which new Shakespeares will emerge. May the Shakespeares not be stifled by a pile of beautiful photographs.[48]

Writers might be 'engineers of the soul', but engineers did more than follow a blueprint. The 'highest function of the engineer', Malraux reminded his Soviet counterparts, 'is to invent'. He next drew a sharp line between the things that belonged to Marx and the things that did not. 'Marxism is the consciousness of the social; culture is the consciousness of the psychological'.

The denial of the psychological in art leads to the most absurd individualism. Because every person endeavours to think about his life, whether he likes it or not; the denial of the psychological in reality means that he who will have thought the most about his life, instead of transmitting it to others, will keep it to himself.[49]

'Art', Malraux proclaimed, 'is not a submission, it is a conquest'.

If, 'in a perfect socialist-transport system', no one could ever be run over by a streetcar, where did that leave the writer? Malraux presumably asked on another occasion.[50] Ten months later, in Paris, Mikhail Koltsov supplied a partial answer. 'Once you have sown wheat in the Arctic Circle', Koltsov pointed out, 'then nothing is impossible.' In a classless society with no one to exploit there was still plenty of room for satirists like himself. An administrator who betrays socialism was a fit target for the satirist's 'anger and venom', as were the enemies of the Soviet Union abroad. Today the Soviet reader laughs at a millionaire who cannot buy anything in the Soviet Union except the basics. 'In the books and songs a new satire is born, insolent and joyous, which defends culture, combats the shame, dirt and the slavery of the past.'

At Moscow's closing banquet attended by Russia's top brass (though not Stalin) Radek ('most certainly drunk') stumbled up to 'comrade Malraux' and wanted to know why he had asked Komsomol members what they thought about death. This, Radek pointed out, was an 'unfruitful attitude in a century in which the individual has at last been given the chance to fulfil himself in community with others'. To Radek, the French writer was just another a petty bourgeois.[51]

— 5 —

'A thousand differences play beneath our shared purpose', Malraux asserted in his concluding speech at the Paris Congress. But all in all, he thought the conference had served its purpose, and gave it a qualified thumbs-up.

That was the public posture. But the reality, Malraux well knew, was quite different. The Russian delegation especially proved a major disappointment. Excepting last-minute additions Isaak Babel and Boris Pasternak — Babel told stories and Pasternak recited a poem — the Russian delegation was a flop. Couldn't they have sent more sophisticated speakers?, Du Perron asked Malraux after the Congress. 'The first Christians also were a pain in the ass', Malraux replied, 'but they were the way of the world.' Du Perron further asked Malraux why he had bothered to participate in a charade like the Congress in the first place. 'That's the wrong way of looking at it', came the response, 'even if you are aware that you are surrounded by idiots. Quitting means ceding the place to idiots. Staying is the only thing to do, if you want to prevent the idiots from setting the tone.'[52]

As for French writers, Malraux was disappointed in their overall contribution to the fight against fascism. 'Writers have often carried weight in French politics', Malraux told General de Gaulle in an interview at the tail end of World War II.

They played an important role in the Dreyfus case. They thought they could play a similar role at the time of the Popular Front, but instead of influencing events they were made use of. [...] But in spite of all their talk about action [...] what have these intellectuals done since 1936? Drawn up petitions.[53]

## III. Ilya Ehrenburg

*We have turned all work into a creative act.*[54]

— 1 —

Most days Ilya Ehrenburg could be found at the Café du Dôme in Paris smoking a pipe or cigarette, writing, reading, conversing. The Café du Dôme, a hangout popular with the avant-garde and assorted people-watchers, was a good spot for a pipe-smoking man of letters wearing 'good English tweeds' with a 'pathological hatred of the foxtrot' from which to observe the collapse of the West. Or was it Julio Jurenito, the protagonist of Ehrenburg's *The Extraordinary Adventures of Julio Jurenito & His Disciples*, sitting there relishing the end of everything? 'Was there anything worth saving, Ilya?', Louis Aragon, whose company Ehrenburg enjoyed, might well have asked.[55] When it came to books, Ehrenburg's answer was never in doubt: Stendhal's *Le Rouge et le Noir*, for this was a work he could never put down for very long. Stendhal depicted 'characters, passions, and destinies' and 'never forgot social problems, party struggles, and politics', Ehrenburg wrote in an essay devoted to his literary idol. Stendhal's style was straightforward, his approach modern. He hated the bourgeoisie and the church. 'He said that all human misfortunes stem from falsehood. For him, the writer was a servant of the truth.'[56]

Ehrenburg loved Paris and France. The Russian-born author found joy in things the native-born Frenchmen might well take for granted. In a long essay devoted to French culture, Ehrenburg counted the ways: industrious artists and writers (Flaubert, Balzac); clarity of expression; painting (to love France is to love her painting); the ability to joke even under the direst of circumstances; cognac (he could talk for hours about the method of preparation). Ehrenburg's billet-doux ends on a lyrical note. The essence of France he found in the Loire, the river he loved the best.

> Many of the writers and artists who are dear to me grew up on her banks. [...] Tourists usually visit the Loire to admire the Renaissance chateaux. [...] Yet it is something else that draws me to the Loire. It is her flow, now rapid, now gentle; the little islands that come and go; the old trees standing like sentries on her banks; the hills with their vineyards blue with spray, the emerald pastures with their spotted cows, the little towns with their twisting streets, the belfries from which the Gallic cocks first tried their voices. The Loire is not navigable. She is beautiful, yet the people of Touraine and Anjou, who adore her, regard her with certain apprehension: she is capable of rising suddenly, flooding islands, villages, and towns. On such days she looks like a sea. Then suddenly she retreats again below the shore, lazily reflecting a tower here, an alder there. She is made of the same stuff as France, her history and her future.[57]

Olga Carlisle interviewed Ehrenburg *en pantoufles* for *The Paris Review* in his Moscow apartment in 1961.

> I looked around Ehrenburg's study — a room even more French than the other rooms, with rare leather-bound editions and white French editions of the *Nouvelle Revue Française* mixed with the hardbound Russian volumes all

around the walls (Ehrenburg owns an edition of Ronsard published in 1579). There were two paintings of Paris hanging near the desk, a small Marquet representing the quays of the Seine, and a street scene by Robert Falk — painted in soft, nostalgic colors. Ehrenburg told me that almost all the works he owned were presents from the artists, and that he had more paintings in his country house.[58]

— 2 —

Shunted to a small room in Moscow's Hotel National for the duration of the First All-Union Soviet Writers' Congress, Ehrenburg complained bitterly. One morning he was refused tea because 'the restaurant served only those who paid with foreign currency'. Denied hot water and sugar on similar grounds, he sped off to see the manager.

> Potted plants were set out all along the staircase. Floor-waiters in bright green tunics and chambermaids in rustling aprons and smart caps stood in rows; at a word of command they bowed [...] the restaurant [was] selling salt-shakers with carved cockerels [...] the orchestra was rehearsing *Down Mother Volga*. The manager explained that I must immediately vacate my room: in an hour's time a large group of American tourists was due to arrive from Leningrad.

Infuriated, Ehrenburg wrote an article critical of Soviet bowing and scraping before the foreigner and slammed Intourist, the state-run tourist office catering to foreign visitors, as 'a bad fairy tale'.

> I knew the capitalist world, where they were still burning cotton and books, where the unemployed slept under bridges, where Fascists organized pogroms; in short, it was not only despicable but stupid to be ashamed of our poverty before some hundred American tourists.[59]

There was some pushback on the part of Intourist, but the 'most gifted literary agent of the Kremlin in Western Europe'[60] was virtually untouchable; he even had Stalin's ear.

Ehrenburg entered the Hall of Pillars with several axes to grind. For one, he accused Soviet writers of avoiding 'difficult subjects'. 'In our novels', he said,

> workers often appear to be divorced from life. Yet workers are human beings. They struggle, they love and kiss, they read and dream, they are jealous husbands and lovers, sometimes they do silly things. Occasionally attempts are made to enliven a story about shock workers or a machine tractor station by inserting tidy little love scenes. But two or three kisses and a few rationed tears do not make dummies human. Some of our authors follow the line of least resistance. They find it safer to repeat monosyllabic declarations than to write about life as it really is. There are those who prefer skillful manoeuvering to the agony of creation. They avoid difficult subjects [...].[61]

As well, the Soviet journalist took a swipe at 'brigade literature' (presumably of the White Sea variety) and the direction of Soviet literary practices in general.

> Our country today has achieved hegemony. But in our books one often senses the arrogance and at the same time the subservience of the backwoods. [...]

Instead of serious literary criticism we have a red and a black list of authors, and what is truly fantastic is the ease with which they are transferred from one list to the other. [...] The distribution of material benefits should not depend on literary criticism. In the last analysis one cannot treat an artist's failures as crimes and his successes as a form of rehabilitation.

'At that time I was shaggy-haired and full of fight', bemusedly recalled Ehrenburg a generation or so along.[62]

— 2 —

Back in Paris, Ehrenburg met with leading French writers in the Maison de la Mutualité to report on the Soviet Congress. A great crowd was present.

Vaillant-Couturier, André Gide, Malraux, Andrée Viollis and Communist workers sat on the platform. In the audience were people who had also made their choice; they shouted rhythmically: 'Les Soviets partout!' Andrée Viollis who sat next to me whispered: 'Soviet writers must show that they're ready to work with everybody in the struggle against Fascism.'

Ehrenburg next went back to Moscow where he was to meet with Stalin to discuss the mood of Western writers. Bad timing. The assassination of Kirov was on everybody's agenda; Stalin cancelled the meeting. Ehrenburg returned to France and sounded out Gide, Bloch, Malraux, and Jean Guéhenno. There were problems.

Writers are not like workers: it is very difficult to get them to combine. André Gide proposed one thing, Heinrich Mann another, Feuchtwanger something else. The Surrealists shouted that the Communists had become high priests and that the Congress ought to be sabotaged. Writers close to the Trotskyists — Charles Plisnier, Magdeleine Paz — gave warning that they would speak and 'unmask' the Soviet Union. Barbusse feared that the Congress would be politically too broad and therefore unable to take any decisions. Roger Martin du Gard and the English writers E. M. Forster and Aldous Huxley, on the contrary, thought that the Congress would be too narrow and that only the Communists would be allowed to speak. Much patience, restraint and tact were needed to reconcile what seemed irreconcilable attitudes.

On his way by train to cover the Saar plebiscite, *Izvestia*'s Paris correspondent 'indulged in dreams'.

The Congress would force the doubters to choose the path of struggle. After all, Fascism was not as strong as it seemed: it derived its power from the general helpless state of hypnotism. Perhaps the Germans in the Saar would vote against Hitler?[63]

— 3 —

Ehrenburg's novel *The Second Day* came out in the Soviet Union in the spring of 1934. It did not pass muster with the censors and had been 'red-listed', the Soviet category for works deemed deviationist, and may well account for the author's prickliness later that year.[64]

*The Second Day*, or 'how the east was won', is set against the background of the construction of the Kuznetsk iron ore plant, built in record time with 'iron will' in 'the heart of Asia' where the 'earth was frozen three meters down'. Its protagonist, Volodya Safonov, 22, a student, can't find his footing in the new scheme of things. Aware 'that spring had predated the Revolution', he had yet to be convinced that a blast furnace was more beautiful than Venus de Milo. To a visiting journalist representing a major Paris paper who wants to know if ancient history is being taught, Volodya explains,

> 'Everything's viewed here from the perspective of diamat [dialectical materialism]. [...] The students, I gather, don't suffer in the slightest. I'm not typical, you see. I live on an island. My comrades are eternally cheerful. That's probably why I suffer.' (207)

The comrades are doers. 'Only the occasional imbecile has heard of Homer — that type of person is called a nonfeasor.' (209) Up on the Paris literary scene, Volodya shared his impressions with the journalist. 'I've read about the "malaise". It seems to be the main theme of your young writers. What's unsettling them?' he asked. 'The mechanization of life? Ossification? Cultural decline?' The Surrealists, adrift in confusion, he went on, were typical manifestations of the 'disease'.

> On the one hand, there's the cult of dreams, the assertion of a meta-reality. In philosophical terms, that's the purest idealism. On the other hand, they're gravitating towards Communism. Perhaps that's a sign of protest? I don't know if they understand what Communism is ... On earth, that is [...]. (207–08)

Volodya was acutely aware that Surrealists and incurable 'nonfeasors' like himself were destined for the dustbin of history. Here he is addressing a group of students on 'cultural construction'.

> Today I was talking to a Frenchman. He's a journalist. He told me that in France the students don't read poetry. They want to have a good time. They study just to get their diplomas. They know a lot, but they can't do a thing. In France there's a poet named Valéry. He's hard to understand. Sometimes he's as obscure as Pasternak. He's a real poet. The Frenchman told me that no one reads Valéry because he's 'deadly dull'. Valéry wrote somewhere that in order to act one must know only the minimum. I used to think the same. I thought you could build factories because you didn't know Dante. That sounds like a paradox — but it's not all that stupid. And yet I think that Valéry is wrong. He lives without air. It is impossible to know and to act. There's a kind of knowledge that dooms one to inaction. I know it well — that's dead knowledge. In order to build a factory, you must know something — that's a precise, limited knowledge. That which you're striving towards is the water of life. I'll tell you straight — you know very little. But you already know a good deal more than those French students with their diplomas and their Boul' Mich' [Boulevard Saint-Michel, street in the Latin Quarter filled with cafés, a hotspot bustling with students out to have a good time] [...] Their prime aim is to occupy a ready-made place in life, while you want to create the life you'll live. That's why knowledge per se is important to you. Can there be any doubt as to who will inherit the future? (218–19)

'Doomed to inertia', young Volodya kills himself, not for the love of a woman but the inability to project that kind of love onto a blast furnace.

— 4 —

An altogether different Ehrenburg showed up in Paris: linear, provincial, defensive: Mr. Feasor incarnate. Eddy du Perron, who attended the proceedings, compared the Soviet speakers to soldiers loath to betray the weaknesses of their own army while at war.[65] In Paris, Ehrenburg was like that pastry chef in *The Second Day* out to prove that Siberia was no backwater of civilization.

> A delegation from America came for the start-up of Blast Furnace Three. A banquet was arranged for them. Kupryasov, the chef, [...] determined to show these Americans that they certainly did not slurp cabbage soup out of bast slippers round there, [...] made an ice-cream cake in the shape of a blast furnace, with sponge-cake doused in rum flambé and with raspberry syrup streaming out of the apertures. (334)

Speaking in the evening of 22 June, Ehrenburg blasted Western views of the Soviet Union. '"Our adversaries say our society is primitive, your orchestra is composed solely of drummers, you have impoverished life".'

> They show us with the face of the crowd, or, worse, with a machine in place of a face. Everyone knows that we have built huge factories, but what is less well known is that for us these factories are not temples but instruments, and that our life has but a single goal: the growth and triumph of man.

Surrounded by love and confidence, writers in the USSR were key actors in helping build 'a beautiful new world', through the moral and spiritual advance of the working class. 'Just as young people will ask questions of a metallurgist, so they look to the writer to understand themselves, to understand their neighbour and the new humanity.' Writers themselves were works in progress, groping toward new terms with which to express new feelings. 'We can say, without embarrassment, that our books are stutter-steps, but they are the first steps of a new language of men'. Shakespeare in the kolkhoz inspired farmers, creators in their own right, of wheat and rye, to increase the harvest. Exposure to *Othello* helped them grow, even if they did not always quite get it.

(That same afternoon Fedor Panferov happened to furnish the key to help *Othello*-challenged workers understand the Bard's tragedy. In the course of explicating socialist realism, Panferov compared the reaction of two sets of audiences to a performance of *Othello*: Western and Soviet.

> Othello, impelled by his anger, kills his beloved wife, whom he suspects of having deceived him. He then kills himself. The audience furiously applauds Othello, carries him off on their shoulders like a hero. The Soviet spectator, attending the same play, concedes that the play is written by master and applauds his genius. It is brilliant, but Othello's action is absurd. First of all, his wife did not deceive him; and, even if she had, he had no right to take her life, for everyone can and should love whomever they fancy.)

'When a bourgeois doesn't understand a work of art, he blames the artist', Ehrenburg soldiered on. 'When our worker doesn't understand a painting or a poem he blames himself. [...] I have seen workers in the Moscow museums before the canvases of Matisse and Picasso, they said: "We must come back here often, then perhaps we can figure it out and feel it"'. (Picasso drew Ehrenburg's portrait; Matisse favoured him with a sketch.) To finally grasp a poem by Mayakovsky or Pasternak filled the workers with immense pleasure. The Revolution was like a stone thrown in the pond, with ever-widening circles.

'A truly disinterested art', Ehrenburg concluded his address, 'consecrated not to the savagery of the status quo but to the development of man is only possible in a new society'. The Soviet Union had made a creative act out of all work. There was no division between art and the people, as in bourgeois society. The West possessed the morality of the wolf; the bourgeois novel depicted 'man's deformation'. Bourgeois culture was moribund.

— 5 —

In her memoirs Nadezhda Mandelstam came down hard on writers and intellectuals co-opted by the regime. Ehrenburg is a partial exception, one of the few. 'He was always the odd man out among the Soviet writers, and the only one I maintained relations with all through the years. He was as helpless as everybody else, but at least he tried to do something for others.' In 1967, Osip Mandelstam's widow attended 'Shaggy's funeral. ... [T]here was a great crowd [...], and I noticed that the faces were decent and human ones. It was an antifascist crowd, and the police spies who had been sent to the funeral in force stood out very conspicuously. It was clear, in other words, that Ehrenburg had done his work well, difficult and thankless though it was.'[66]

## IV. René Crevel

The Congress did its part in memorializing the deceased author, intending to fill Crevel's original time slot with the speech he had planned to give. That speech, however, was discovered too late to be included in the programme. Instead, the Congress reprised Crevel's 1 May address to the proletariat of Bourges. To the lapsed Surrealist Louis Aragon went the honour of delivering it in the evening of 22 June.

Crevel's 1 May speech affirmed an 'indissoluble bond' between manual and intellectual workers. 'An intellectual who is conscious of himself and the world in which he lives has no other choice but to stand elbow to elbow with the exploited.' The familiar laundry list of bourgeois bad behaviour passed in review — no less real for being familiar and a laundry list: dumping wheat in the ocean, setting fire to coffee, burning books, exploiting workers, plundering their overseas colonies. Crevel called for a united front against fascism and war, the achievement of worldwide socialism, the abolition of frontiers, and the free exchange of goods and ideas. Irreconcilable contradictions compelled states to become fascist, build prisons and concentration camps. Nothing, however, Crevel stressed, could break the bond between workers and intellectuals, adducing, as a case in point, the example of Spanish intellectuals who started a newspaper and a workers' university within their prison walls in support of striking miners in the Asturias. Crevel ended with an appeal to intellectuals everywhere 'to unite with the proletarians of all countries'.

When Aragon had stopped speaking, the entire hall rose as one, paying final tribute to the late author and fallen comrade.

Crevel's 1 May speech only feebly resembled the speech he had meant to give. 'The Writer, the Individual, Society' likewise proclaimed the indestructible bond between writer and worker, albeit in a higher key. In it, Crevel pictured the latter-day 'Botticelli of the pen or brush' abandoning the sandy beaches of *The Birth of Venus* for the muscular epics taking root in the soil of the Soviet Union. Crevel's highlight reel of Western civilization featured dozens of greats from Aristotle and Heraclitus to Rousseau and Rimbaud; from Bacon, Locke, Diderot, Wilde, and Proust to Hegel, Feuerbach, Heidegger, and, naturally, Marx and Engels. Not a few of the great thinkers, Crevel noted, boasted Communist bloodlines.

In his novel *Der Vulkan* Klaus Mann created Marcel Poiret, a character modelled on his late friend. How weary, stale, flat, and unprofitable seem to him all the uses of the world. Fists pressed against his temples, Marcel explodes:

> I'm so fed up with words! It is as though I have to swig dirty water and to spit it out again. The great ideas have been deflated, worn out — and nothing new in sight to which we can hold onto, pull ourselves up on! Everything has already been said, exhausted. The nineteenth century was enormously garrulous, through and through rhetorical, in love with the word, trusting in it as though it were a fetish. It has all been drained away now. The crisis of the twentieth century, which has left traces in my life like a disease, is the crisis of big words. Democracy is finished because it clings to words that have been emptied of their meaning. Fascism, the new barbarism, will easily triumph: it beheads corpses. We must embrace a new innocence. Words won't get us there, only deeds. The big words stick to us like dirt. [...] Only one fluid can wash these off: blood. Will it be our blood? Then we have to spill it. Better to make it flow than have it clog up our veins like a soft mush. We shall kill and suffer, no longer speak and write. Enough of talk! Enough of writing! Enough of thinking! Perhaps other generations will again derive joy and benefit from words and thought. Not us — no longer us! We will no longer pose arguments with which to confront the fury of the reactionaries, but a new rage, a new obsession. We have to become dumb and blind and be prepared to die. Only thus can we atone for the guilt of our fathers.[67]

In the end, Marcel goes off to fight in the Spanish civil war on the Republican side, spilling blood and dying a hero's death. It was a generous gesture on the part of Mann to bestow a dignified exit on a friend who 'chided and cursed like a young god annoyed by human viciousness and intoxicated by earthly wines'.[68]

## V. Menno ter Braak (1)

— 1 —

Menno ter Braak had to be told that indoor cats require litter boxes[69] yet sufficiently worldly to recognize fascism's unparalleled threat to democracy's fragile infrastructure from the very first. Ter Braak was twenty years old when Mussolini took power in Italy; thirty-one when Hitler assumed the chancellorship. Thus he

Fig. 4. Menno ter Braak
(Photo Emiel van Moerkerken/Fotoarchief Bruno van Moerkerken)

spent his entire adult existence (he died in 1940) living in the shadow of fascism and devoted a goodly portion of it deconstructing and condemning it.

Menno ter Braak grew up in a middle class household in a small town on the Dutch-German border. His mother was related to Johan Huizinga, the Dutch historian who made his name chronicling the death throes of the Middle Ages. Menno, too, went in for history. Enrolled at the University of Amsterdam, he left his mark on the student publication *Propria Cures* (it still exists), contributing articles on film, literature, and politics. In his very first contribution, 'The Appreciation of Form', the facility of expression and the brilliant phrasing — *language is to literature as dogma is to religion* — there is already present, in embryo, that uniquely *Braakian* touch that would make him Holland's foremost cultural critic in the years ahead.

Upon completion of his doctorate on the Holy Roman Emperor Otto III, Ter Braak taught history in secondary schools while keeping a finger in the literary pie. Free-lancing and collaborating on literary magazines, he built a reputation as a perceptive and hard-to-please reviewer — 'Demolition Menno' (in Dutch: 'Menno Ter Afbraak'). Nietzsche was God and Ter Braak his apostle, a gadfly tasked with exposing, or unmasking, to use the term he himself preferred, modes of thinking that did not live up to the self-styled pedant's literary standards. Staunchly anti-fascist, a friend who said anything nice about National Socialism was a former friend.

For Ter Braak, the conventional analysis of National Socialism as the revolt of the petty bourgeoisie squeezed between big business (department stores) and organized labour was only the tip of the iceberg. Its real lifeblood was hatred. National Socialism, 'the emancipation of rancour' and 'pure resentment', was unthinkable without hate. The person consumed by rancour nurses 'the idea of revenge as an artist "l'art pour l'art".' National Socialism was a movement of losers — *ratés* — filled with malice toward their betters, with Jew-hatred, 'the easiest and most giving of hatreds', leading the charge; its half-civilized followers subsisted on phrases. Ter Braak summed up: in the National Socialist trinity, hate is primary, hatred of Jews secondary, the 'scientific' argument tertiary.

> The 'right of everyone' appears to inhere in the unlimited right of everyone to hate everyone else; to loathe and imprison any individual in a concentration camp who doesn't accept the egalitarianism of the rubber truncheon as the highest ideal and the 'leader' as the highest symbol of hysterical resentment.[70]

National Socialism's vaunted *Volksgemeinschaft* as a community of equals and a true democracy was neither, for it lacked the underpinnings that in a truly democratic environment keep lies, propaganda and resentment ('one to the most essential attributes of our culture') in check. While fascism and Marxism, the Christian ideal of equality minus the afterlife, converged in a number of ways, Marxism at least rested on a body of knowledge absent in its 'rancorous reaction'. It came down to knowledge versus humbug, clear-headedness versus mysticism and mystification.[71] Not that Ter Braak had a great deal of faith in the liberal-democratic system, but as long as it left people alone to have their say he saw no reason to complain. That's where he drew the line: freedom of thought; beyond it gaped the abyss.

— 2 —

'The conscience of [Dutch] letters'[72] was the very model of the respectable burgher, not the type to disturb the peace after eleven o'clock at night. Or take his cause to the streets. But one's life, which is the life of the mind, was worth fighting for. 'We damn well cannot allow ourselves to be told what to think by a bunch of despicable club-wielding louts'.[73] A founding member of Holland's Committee of Vigilance against Fascism, Ter Braak helped take the fight to the enemy. Composed of Dutch intellectuals, 'regardless of political conviction', the committee meant to defend the domain of the spirit against the depredations of National Socialism. Intellectuals made up the committee's core constituency. Their job was 'to unmask the lies and to translate the drumbeat of bombastic phrases into ordinary language'. For all that, Ter Braak had no illusions about the ability of intellectuals to influence events, in spite or because of the 'monstrous overestimation of their powers'.

Ter Braak published two novels, neither memorable. *Hampton Court* (1931) drew the observation that it was written for the 'unhappy few because one has to be terribly unhappy, or bored to death, and on top of that tormented by an irrepressible determination to derive pleasure from reading a story like *Hampton Court*'.[74] Fiction was not this critic's forte.

Ter Braak was one of two Dutch delegates scheduled to speak at the writers' Congress; the other was Jef Last. Unlike Last, however, he was not all that keen on going, reckoning there was little point in attending a Congress that would hold few surprises. 'I think the result will disappoint', he wrote to Eddy du Perron in Paris, 'but the experience seems to me rather worth the trouble.'[75] Ter Braak was to speak on Saturday 22 June. Earlier in the day he sent a postcard to his wife, Ant, in The Hague. 'The Congress', he wrote, 'is a kind of gigantic mass demonstration for something that's unclear to any of us. Much terrified to have to mutter on tonight, in French, into a microphone, in front of an enormous hall.'[76]

— 3 —

It is a truism that writers reveal themselves with every word they put on paper, and no one knew this better than Ter Braak, who regarded the writer's character — personality — as 'the first and last criterion in the judgment of the artist'.[77] ('My I is a form of polemics, like my writing.'[78]) The reports Ter Braak submitted to *Het Vaderland*, the sophisticated liberal newspaper in The Hague he served as cultural critic, reveal as much about the correspondent as it does about the Congress and its participants. Of the two, the first covered Friday evening's opening session and the two Saturday sessions, afternoon and evening.

The bulk of Ter Braak's article discussed the difference between Communist and non-Communist authors and the concomitant contributions by Congress's two chairmen, as evidenced by the subheading, 'Gide and Malraux Dominate'. Ter Braak admired both immensely and went to some lengths to rationalize their subservience to Soviet-dictated house rules. 'As things stand', he wrote,

> one can assume that with the important speeches on Saturday evening by André Gide and André Malraux, individualists 'converted' to Communism, the

dividing line between 'bourgeois' and 'Communist' has already been clearly drawn. Indeed, the power of a new faith — rooted in a mystical identification of the individual with his fellows — expressed by these two grand and pure individuals was fascinating to behold, so much so that even their opponents repeatedly burst into applause. Nevertheless, here we once more encounter the irrational element that is not amenable to logical reasoning at congresses. Gide and Malraux have found in Communism — permanently or temporarily? that is the question that must have engaged a great many in the course of listening to their speeches! — a certainty that has not abrogated their former individualism but rather has made it serviceable. No one familiar with their work will doubt that only the purest motives are in play, a need to seek human dignity in a new conception of the world whose errors one takes into the bargain.

Ter Braak conceded that Gide's opening address played into the hands of the Communists and left non-Communists apprehensive about the direction the Congress was taking.

The writers opposed to dictatorship, but equally to dictatorship as manifested in the Soviet Union (about whose suppression of the opposition and of freedom of thought the Congress until now has been silent in just about every language spoken there), will look upon the organization of congresses of this nature with due scepticism. They have been invited to a writers' Congress and most likely assumed (like this writer) something in the manner of an opportunity for writers to engage each other in a discussion that might well lead to a positive outcome from an organizational standpoint. That, however, is not what the 'stewards' of this Congress had in mind. In reality, in the colossal hall of the Palais de la Mutualité capable of swallowing entire masses, it is the *spectators* who play the leading role.

Returning to Gide and Malraux, he absolved both of bad faith despite carrying a torch for the Soviets.

As mentioned earlier, the integrity of the two individuals who dominate the Congress, Gide and Malraux, are beyond reproach, and whose Communism, even to those who reject it, is looked up to as an attempt to combine a critical individualistic standpoint with a mystical collective conviction. As Gide, in his deep, melodious voice commences speaking it is clear from the very outset that we are dealing here with a first-rate personality, a righteous and astute thinker. The same holds for Malraux, the author of *La Condition humaine*. This zealous advocate of human dignity has coupled that zealotry in a most unique manner — with a powerful Nietzschean inflection! — to the idea of Communism. He speaks almost entirely off the cuff, and excellently, with all the 'histrionics' of the people's tribune yet without the hokum that tends to accompany such histrionics. For 'the party' (of which, as far as I know, he is not yet a member) he is not nearly disciplined enough, and it remains to be seen whether he will ever become so, if he will ever be able to put up with party discipline when compelled to subordinate his personal integrity to political slogans. For both Gide and Malraux it is the mystique that conquers the dogma. And because they, though mystics, remain keen intellectuals, the fervour with which they present their convictions betrays not the slightest hint of the commonplace or implausibility. They espouse a kind of modern *credo quia absurdum*, rooted in a powerful feeling for human brotherhood and a rather understandable aversion for the old ideologies on which they long ago have turned their backs.

Ter Braak was less charitable toward the 'official spokesmen' of Communism, and least of all to Ilya Ehrenburg, an author he detested both as a person and a writer: a literary quack.

> His fame is due in no small measure to the Western European bourgeois, which he mocks nonstop with the voice of a superbly trained auctioneer. Ilya Ehrenburg is Communism's missionary for Paris and surroundings. He knows the tricks of Western thought and how to ridicule it in an incomparably cheap manner (like someone who has bought a brand new suit and now looks down on people wearing old ones). Therein lies a substantial reason for his enormous success with the public of the Mutualité. It goes without saying that the worthy Ehrenburg is always right, and it is this very rightness that turns him into a caricature of Malraux and Gide. While speaking, Ehrenburg repeatedly turned in triumph to Gide seated behind him on the podium as though to underscore the point: 'It is the former bourgeois Gide, presently on our side, whose authority ratifies all these astute platitudes'.

As for Communist delegates in general ('almost without exception robust fellows with an astonishing lack of humour and understanding of European intellectual life'), Ter Braak dismissed their contributions as insufferably jejune:

> [...] [T]here is nothing Western Europeans might find attractive [...] in the naïvely optimistic, arrogant speeches, at times bordering on the comical, of typical 'new' Russian writers like Messrs Luppol, Koltsov or Panferov endlessly extolling the blessings of the Soviet regime in the most superfluous terms and brazenly uttering the most insipid banalities. Having listened ad nauseam to this endless primitive and muscular chatter, one would surely be inclined to agree with Spengler that Bolshevism no longer exists in the Soviet Union. What does exist is a smug ideology erected on platitudes by European writers that may well be suitable for internal consumption but as cultural 'export article' lacks every value except of that of cheap propaganda.

The way the Congress was set up placed 'bourgeois' authors at a distinct disadvantage.

> To be sure, surveying the writer-delegates, the 'bourgeois' author especially, discerning a courteous but also very partial crowd, can have few illusions regarding the 'objectivity' of these surroundings, to which the photographers with their irritating flashbulbs add their bit. Here speeches turn into demonstrations, subtleties are lost in the microphone through which one has to make oneself comprehensible (so as not to be incomprehensible!), inadvertently turning one's voice into a trumpet. Is this a *writers'* Congress? More so, it is a spectacle of more or less known 'stars', among which the Communists (on account of their greater skill playing to the crowd) as a rule have the public's approval. [...]

> From everything I have said with regard to the 'direction' of the Congress it follows that the 'bourgeois' elements, by no means inadequately represented, are required to operate in an unfavourable atmosphere. Because the discussion almost invariably gives way to demonstration, there is but little room for criticism that rises above crude commonplaces, and where they do rise to the surface, they are not given their due. Take the speech by Julien Benda, also known to us as the author of *La Trahison des clercs*, who presented a somewhat

historicizing but very good argument differentiating between Western and Russian world views, a difference, according to him, 'not of degree, but of essence'. But Benda does not play to the house, like those right-thinking Russians; his arguments are too personal to have an impact, and so he was easily outmanoeuvred [...].

(On opening night Julien Benda, a Ter Braak favourite, had thrown down the gauntlet. Did the civilisation Communism strove to create, he asked, represent the fulfilment and advancement of Western values or a break with them? 'Does Lenin signify a break with Montaigne or complement him?' Jean Guéhenno and Paul Nizan responded for the Communists. Humanism, an ailing Gorky weighed in from afar, was 'incomprehensible to wolves and wild boars on two legs', exalting the proletariat as the only class capable of grasping its universal meaning for all of humanity.)

As things stood, there was little to look forward to, concluded Ter Braak.

> The tendentious manner in which the Congress has been organized seems to me to preclude any practical result ('for the defence of culture'), inasmuch as discussion of the real meaning of the word is precluded. There may very well be some benefit to having writers from all corners of the world, irrespective of their politics, discuss the character and the dangers that currently threaten culture. Yet there can be no real unified action on behalf of this 'cultural heritage' as long as there is no agreement among those at risk on how to go about it. [...] Undoubtedly, the most important outcome of this Congress (we can safely predict at the halfway mark) is to increase scepticism among the 'bourgeois' authors (that is to say non-Communist) vis-à-vis the cultural aims of the Soviets.

— 3 —

Speaking after Ehrenburg — 'in itself a curious sensation' — Ter Braak attempted to give a definition of the idea of 'freedom from an individualistic standpoint'. En passant, he blasted the Dutch delegation at the international P.E.N. gathering, held in Barcelona the previous month, for being the only one to have voted against Klaus Mann's resolution on behalf of Ludwig Renn and Carl von Ossietzky, 'a shameful repudiation of our tradition'.[79]

Ter Braak's 'Discours sur la Liberté' fully justified the speaker's reputation as a dyed-in-the-wool liberal. His opposition to fascism, he said, was rooted in individualism. Individualism was of a piece with freedom. Freedom, however, was but a word, subject to changing interpretations, depending on circumstances and past history. Even the Nazis had 'a certain idea of freedom', Ter Braak asserted, not unlike the concept of 'libertas' advanced by St Augustine in the Middle Ages. Augustine's 'libertas', however, had about as much in common with the liberty propagated by the French Revolution as peace did with 'pax', which in the medieval world amounted to waging 'permanent war against the devil and his cohorts'. The time had come, Ter Braak asserted, to revert to the nineteenth-century idea of freedom, capable of withstanding dictatorships on both left and right.

> I am convinced that intellectuals today have the duty to defend certain ideas of the nineteenth century, the same ones they were fervently attacking only years

ago. There is no other choice, because their freedom, that is to say their human dignity, can only manifest itself in opposition, and not only in bourgeois society.[80]

The postcard Ter Braak dashed off to his wife admitting stage fright was not mere play-acting. Eddy du Perron, who was present, registered the audience's reaction:

> Ter Braak [...], reading [...] an article conceived for a Congress without loudspeakers, witnessed the writers' table behind him emptying, excepting the chairs Heinrich Mann and Jean-Richard Bloch, who were obliged to remain, as half the audience facing him streamed to the bar amid the sustained applause of folding chairs.[81]

# VI. Bertolt Brecht

— *1* —

The overalls Brecht wore on occasion were made to measure and cut from the finest cloth. So claimed Ludwig Marcuse, the philosopher and theatre critic Brecht sued for a matter unrelated to the overalls.[82] To Brecht translator and admirer Sergei Tretyakov, Brecht was nothing like your typical German. The typical German would not be caught dead appearing in public without a stiff collar, tie, and 'trilby with a broad brim'. Brecht wore a torn cap and a leather tie that kept his rumpled shirt from appearing even more rumpled. The tie wound up in Sergei's wardrobe, a gift. Brecht's hooked nose reminded Tretyakov of Voltaire or Ramses.[83] The Austrian film maker Berthold Viertel thought Brecht resembled Schiller, adding that his face was 'as German as Hitler's was un-German'.[84]

In the summer of 1943 Christopher Isherwood visited Brecht and his wife, the actress Helene Weigel, at their Santa Monica home. Brecht appeared to Isherwood as though garbed in a judge's robe.

> My position as a member of a religious sect was about to be judged according to Marxist law. My judges were polite, but beneath their politeness was contempt. To them 'religion' meant ecclesiastical politics — politics of the capitalist front. But even if I had convinced them that Prabhavananda [Isherwood's guru] had nothing to do with vested interests of this sort, they would have remained hostile to him. Brecht said — I am not quoting his exact words — that a saint needs thousands of sinners to make his career possible; meaning that any attempt to lead a spiritual life is mere self-indulgent individualism. I sat silent, almost sorry that I couldn't defend Prabhavananda and myself with an equally silly dogmatism.[85]

Brecht knew the feeling. 'I often think of a tribunal before which I am being questioned', he confessed to Walter Benjamin the year after he found himself in exile in Denmark.

> 'What was that? Do you really mean that seriously?'
> 'I would then have to admit: Not quite seriously. After all, I think too much about artistic matters, about what would go well on the stage, to be quite

serious; but when I have answered this important question in the negative, I will add a still more important affirmation: that my conduct is *legitimate*.'[86]

In 1947, thirteen years after this exchange, Brecht faced the House Un-American Activities Committee, a tribunal of US Congressmen out to prove the German author was a Communist. Brecht had rehearsed his part with six lawyers. The *Los Angeles Times* of October 31 reported that Brecht denied he was a Communist.

> Brecht, who spoke with a heavy accent and puffed at a long cigar with easy poise, explained that he was answering the $64 question because he was a guest in this country. [...] The committee quizzed Brecht on poems which its investigators termed 'revolutionary'. The poet said he wrote them to stir his fellow Germans against Hitler. He protested that the translations read were inaccurate and of one translation he said, 'That is bad.'

Wisely, Brecht flew back to Europe the day after the hearing.

— 2 —

At twenty-one, on the heels of German defeat in World War I, Brecht took a seat on the Soviet Workers' and Soldiers' Revolutionary Council of Augsburg. A political greenhorn. 'Years after i had made my name as a writer i still knew nothing of politics and had not set eyes on a book by or about marx.' Absent an ABC of politics, Brecht lacked the underpinnings of a full-blown *Weltanschauung*. A projected play set in the American heartland cleared the underbrush. The Chicago 'market in wheat was one huge swamp', impervious to human cerebration. Stymied, Brecht hired Marxist guru Karl Korsch. Korsch fed his pupil dialectics, history's forklift, 'and for the first time, my own scattered practical experiences came to life'.[87] There wasn't all that much to digest, really. Once you grasped the concept of productive, i.e. property relations and all that entailed, you were home free. Brecht appears to have caught on quickly.

Brecht was no mean teacher himself. His plays were conceived as *Lehrstücke*, teaching tools. Epic theatre created a classroom setting by removing the barrier, 'the abyss', between the actors and the audience. Poems, prose, and lectures rounded out Brecht's multifaceted lesson plan.

Brecht's irresistible rise coincided with the equally irresistible rise of fascism.

Shortly after Hitler took office, Brecht met with a number of anti-Nazi writers. Hitler was in power. What now? Brecht said he was prepared to stand his ground: launch appeals, give speeches, issue proclamations, put on plays — provided he was given four or five armed bodyguards from the fighting units of the reliable left prepared to use their guns. 'A bodyguard'? Heinrich Mann asked in disbelief. 'To protect, or to watch us? To protect, or take us into protective custody? To protect, or to betray us?' Brecht had no answer.[88] Within days, Brecht found himself in exile in Denmark.

In the spring of 1935, Brecht visited the Soviet Union — 'refreshing in every respect' — and befriended the omnipresent Mikhail Koltsov. Koltsov was part of the Soviet hospitality industry, charged with making Western writers feel good about Russia's new deal. Upon his return to Denmark, Brecht provided the Soviet delegate to the Paris writers' Congress with a blueprint for dealing with the non-Communists. 'In Paris', he urged,

> I think you should try to involve people in work: a writer is most interested in writing. (He'd have no objection to the end of the world if he could be sure his book about it would still manage to appear.) For instance, under the motto: 'Against systematic intellectual befuddlement by etc.' you could bring out a *New Encyclopaedia* of the best authors, a series of publications in which they could attack the slogans of fascism and militarism, each in a two-to-ten page article, in other words, ten to fifteen writers would comment simultaneously on every stultifying thesis put forward by the fascists. Such an encyclopaedia would be a rallying point and would soon attract specific groups of readers.[89]

— 3 —

At the time, Brecht himself was busily assembling materials for an 'encyclopedia' of his own. Brecht's encyclopedia was a projected novel about bourgeois intellectuals, a Gibbonesque register of crimes and follies of the smart set that had helped smooth Hitler's path to power. He would not be attending the Congress merely to give a speech but to collect materials for his projected 'Tui' novel.[90] 'Tui' was a bastardization of the German word for 'intellectual': *Intellektuell*. In Brecht's hands, *Intellektuell* became Tellekt-Uell-In: Tui for short. Monitoring the reaction of bourgeois intellectuals challenged to enter the fray against fascism was expected to yield fresh material and broaden the scope of his investigation. The Congress would serve to flesh out the typology of the bourgeois intellectual crippled by a blind spot that had helped bring down the Weimar Republic. It was precisely this blind spot Brecht sought to address at the Congress.

'A Necessary Observation on the Fight Against Barbarism', delivered in the afternoon of 23 June, was built around a single theme cast in the form of two appeals: 'Comrades, let's think *about the roots of evil!*'; and: 'Comrades, let's talk about the property relations!'. Intellectuals, Brecht said, were wrong to assume that the brutality of fascism was unnecessary to secure the prevailing system of productive relations. The two were joined at the hip. Fascist cruelty was part and parcel of the economic system and grew out of property relations. In other words, fascism was no outgrowth of barbarism. Nor was it a product of a faulty education. Fascism, too, believed that education had fallen short, underplaying the physical courage indispensable in war. And fascism, too, had ideals. Culture and barbarism were not separate issues.

> Many among us writers have not yet understood, have not yet discovered the root of the barbarism they fear. This is a huge hindrance in the struggle. They always run the danger of considering the cruelties of fascism as *unnecessary*. They stick with property relations because they believe that the cruelties of fascism are not necessary to defend them. But these cruelties *are* necessary to the preservation of existing property relations. This is where fascists don't lie; this is where they tell the truth.

And fascism had no problem with savagery, Brecht pointed out; indeed, it revelled in it.

Like every good teacher, Brecht illustrated with a concrete example. In Denmark, a decent country that had given him a home away from home, thousands of cattle were being slaughtered every week; they had become too costly to keep alive. The too-costly-to-feed mentality was built into the capitalist system and applied to workers no less than to cows. But salvation was at hand, for a 'great doctrine' was sweeping the globe. 'This doctrine, simple like all great doctrines, has taken hold of the masses that have most to suffer from existing property relations and the barbaric methods by which they are defended. [...] In one-sixth of the earth's surface', Brecht pointed out, 'there was no destruction of food or culture'.

Incapable of grasping the underlying economic mechanisms that pulled its switches, bourgeois intellectuals were unfit to lead the charge against fascism; as long as they were left alone to go on writing, they did not care enough to put up a fight.

A self-confessed upper-class intellectual, Brecht proved, to himself at least, that a bourgeois intellectual *could* change his spots.

— 4 —

Brecht worked on the *Tui* novel off and on for a decade and a half without ever completing it; it would always remain a 'fragment': *Der Tui-Roman. Fragment.* Brecht was no Erasmus. The unfinished satire is a one-liner, lacking the wine-stoked feathery touch of the Dutchman's *Praise of Folly.* But then, fascism presented a far greater threat to civilization than the sale of indulgences. These were ugly times indeed.

Who are the Tuis? Tuis are citizens of the middle kingdom of Chima. They are intellectuals in the epoch of capitalism.

* A Tui believes that 'consciousness determines being'
* A Tui is a bourgeois intellectual who abuses his intellect
* A Tui has a mind for hire; Tuis assisted the Kaiser in keeping civilian morale up during the war
* A Tui helped draft the peace agreements and the constitution, ushering in the 'The Golden Age of the Tuis'
* A Tui is a defender of the status quo; Tuis are master bootlickers
* A Tui mind tends to run ahead of the facts, 'like a scampering dog'
* Tuis can't see the forest for the trees. A system in which political freedom coexists with economic slavery beggars their understanding, whence their confusion
* A Tui isn't smart enough to understand that cruelty is an integral part of fascism
* A Tui is a writer/intellectual who failed, or refused, to play by the Marxist rules
* Tuis unwittingly helped dig Chima's grave, and thus their own
* Tuis are delusional

Preoccupied with defending the status quo, a new movement rises under their very noses: the Fe-esch. The Fe-esch, National Socialists, are led by a triumvirate of depraved Tuis: 'the army spy' Hu-ih (Hitler), the author of a book composed of 53,000 solecisms; Gogher Gogh (Goebbels), and Angerlan (Goering). The Fe-esch embody the rebellion of the lower, most inept Tuis against the higher. Fe-esch ideals triumph, the people die.

The more enlightened Tuis find themselves in deep trouble. Some are jailed, others run for their lives. Where had they gone wrong? They had protected the property, profits and privileges of their rulers and bolstered them in every other way. A sizable contingent fled 'head over heels' to warmer climes, where they gnawed on the bitter root of exile, a reference to the émigré community in southern California that included Brecht himself. There they wandered amid palm trees, endlessly complaining, gorging on steaks, muttering threat after threat. In time, their opinions came to resemble the shabbiness of their coats. Their hopes likewise took a beating. Yet, incapable of grasping the source of their misery, they stubbornly retained their faith in *Geist über alles*. 'When they heard that literature was being strangled, they joyfully exclaimed! That will destroy them!'. ('The Third Reich doesn't seem to be collapsing for want of decent literature', wryly observed Brecht in a letter to Alfred Döblin midway through 1935.[91])

Brecht was quite pleased with the information he had picked up at the Congress. 'As for me', he informed Karl Korsch, 'I've been at the Writers' Congress where I collected quite a lot of material for my *Tui* novel. It's depressing how few ideas come to one.'[92] And to George Grosz, he wrote (around July):

> We have just rescued culture. It took 4 (four) days, and then we decided that we would sooner sacrifice all else than let culture perish. If necessary, we'll sacrifice ten to twenty million people. Thank the Lord, enough of the persons prepared to shoulder the responsibility for this were present. We proceeded at once boldly and with caution. Our brother Henricus Mannus submitted his oration in favour of free speech to the Sûreté [French security police] before delivering it [unconfirmed rumor.] A slight incident attracted notice. Toward the end, brother Barbussius devoured brother Andreus Gideus whole on the open rostrum. The episode ended tragically, for I'm told that an onlooker committed suicide out of boredom. — Fascism was unanimously condemned. What for? Because of its *unnecessary* cruelties.[93]

The notes to the *Tui* novel contain a number of allusions to the Congress. Concerning Barbusse and Gide, we find: 'The battle of the speeches Barbusse-Gide: Gide kind, Barbusse kinder. Therefore Gide hates Barbusse and speaks like Christ. Barbusse goes to the toilet and files down his teeth with the same file he uses to file his sentences. [...] Resolution is passed on behalf of freedom of speech — as if a resolution is enough to bring it about; good will makes humanists. Lectures produce culture.'[94]

Brecht's 1935 poem 'Über den Satz 'Die Barbarei kommt von der Barbarei', den man oft hört' ('Regarding the oft-repeated phrase that barbarism stems from barbarism') took this line of reasoning to its illogical, non-dialectical conclusion. 'If barbarism comes from barbarism, then good must come from good; thieves taught to love their neighbour will stop stealing milk from the mouths of babes; 'And beauty is beautiful, even if it is up to the neck in dung.'

Europe's dung kept on rising. At the Second International Congress of Writers for the Defence of Culture, held in Valencia in 1937, Brecht kept pace with the latest developments. Guernica, he said there, had opened the eyes of many. Upping the ante, Brecht no longer thought it was a question of defending culture with weapons of the spirit but of fighting fire with fire.[95]

— 5 —

Ludwig Marcuse distinguished three Brechtian incarnations. The first two were charming and caring; the third 'arrogant, vicious, and scornful'.[96] Brecht the know-it-all, Isherwood's hanging judge, showed up at the Congress. He was vicious toward bourgeois intellectuals of the misguided variety, lavished his charm on the members of the Soviet delegation and fellow travellers, and, presumably, reserved the caring for the Mutualité's janitors.

## VII. Klaus Mann

*To tell the story of an intellectual in the period from 1920 to 1940 — a character who spent the best time of his life in a social and spiritual vacuum; striving for true community but never finding it; disconnected, restless, wandering; haunted by those solemn abstractions in which nobody else believes: civilization, progress, liberty.* Klaus Mann, 11 August 1941.[97]

— 1 —

'Intellectuals have no sex appeal, that's the trouble with them.'[98] Did Klaus Mann arrive at this conclusion at the International Congress of Writers for the Defence of Culture? It is impossible to say. There is no indication, however, that Thomas Mann's eldest son came to Paris solely to test out his hypothesis, as Brecht had for a projected novel impugning spineless intellectuals. If Mann is to be believed, the Paris writers' Congress had to be the most sexless assemblage of men and women — overwhelmingly men — ever. But if by 'their problem' he meant to correlate the lack of sex appeal with its outcome, Mann's perspective opens up intriguing possibilities. Salvador Dalí, as noted, thought that a focus on Hitler's looks and plump back would yield the kind of results the organizers of the Congress had in mind. Even so, Mann's contention defies common sense: over a hundred delegates from eighteen countries (counting only those who spoke) and not a single one worthy of a second look?

Granted, sex appeal, like beauty, is in the eye of the beholder. A consensus is clearly lacking. The second part of Mann's proposition, however, is a slippery slope. Take E. M. Forster. The author of *A Passage to India* did not know how men and women were 'joined' until he was thirty and then waited another seven years before he had his first sexual experience. Was it the lack of sex appeal or the case of a moralist lurking behind those light-blue eyes? Or was it because he 'never ceased to be baby-like'?[99] Forster was fifty-six years old when he attended the Congress and as fearful for the future as he had been of his mother finding out that her son was gay. If fascism triumphs, he informed the audience from the stage of the Maison de la Mutualité, we might as well give up on civilisation as we know it.

> They [his colleagues of the British delegation] may perhaps say that if there is another war writers of the individualistic and liberalizing type, like Mr

Aldous Huxley and myself, will be swept away. I am sure that we will be swept away, and I think that there may be another war. This being so, my job [...] is an interim job. We just have to go on tinkering with our old tools until the crash comes. [...] After it — if there is an after — the task of civilisation will be carried on by people whose spiritual development has been different from my own.

Maxim Gorky represented the other extreme. Stripped naked in front of a mirror, casting an approving look at his own reflection and grinning from ear to ear, the Russian author indexed his life in terms of the number of books he had written and the women he had slept with. 'Sixty-three years old [...] Women [...] about 2000. Works [...] about thirty. Not bad. Not bad.'[100] By 1935, Russia's pen-wielding Lothario was too ill to attend the Paris Congress and died the following year. A gigantic headshot of the celebrated Soviet writer formed the backdrop to one of the sessions.

If anyone deserved to be called 'sexy', it was André Malraux. Congress's co-chairman was a dynamic presence. His looks and bearing invariably drew movie star comparisons. While one noted his 'exceptionally pretty hands' and 'beautiful face',[101] another toasted his 'romantic forehead'.[102] A character in a Mavis Gallant story described the young Malraux as 'dark and tormented, the windblown lock on the worried brow, the stub of a Gauloise sending up a vagabond spiral of smoke'[103] — Malraux's iconic photograph of the dashing intellectual. To Mike Gold, the author of Man's Fate evoked the 'aviator type'.[104] Gold himself, 'dark-eyed, hand-some-featured, with wide, lush lips',[105] cut no mean figure himself.

Ilya Ehrenburg's splendid mop of unruly hair begat Lenin's 'Shaggy Ilya'. The Dutchman Jef Last was a hunk and had his way with the men, inducing a former cook in the Russian Marine to don his old uniform, precipitating a no-holds-barred tryst peppered with hosannas to the workers' state and the Great Helmsman himself.[106] The other Dutch delegate, the clean-shaven, horn-rimmed literary critic Menno ter Braak, wore the label 'pedant' with pride; a closed book sexually. The pipe-smoking, avuncular Dane Martin Andersen Nexø, the author of Pelle the Conqueror, telegraphed goodwill and homespun wisdom. Johannes Becher may have looked striking in a leather jacket and helmet posing beside his beloved motorcycle, but in ordinary street clothes the expressionist poet looked, well, ordinary. Austrian journalist Egon Kisch, 'world's funniest man',[107] hadn't earned the moniker 'racing reporter' dodging women. Henri Barbusse 'had the visionary look of a John the Baptist'.[108] Mikhail Koltsov had a sexy signature, but that was about it.

The former Nazi Bodo Uhse was a chain-smoking alcoholic, but at 31 still rather passable. To Mann, Louis Aragon had 'the laughter of a bloodthirsty child and the elegant verve of a bullfighter who is out to seduce a rich American heiress'.[109] Isaak Babel was impish, but no prize. Jean-Richard Bloch had dark, expressive eyes. Lion Feuchtwanger was in excellent shape. His fitness trainer of a wife held back a soft-boiled egg for breakfast until her husband had completed the requisite number of deep knee bends.[110] Gide impressed Mann with 'the noble shape of [his] physiognomy' and 'coquetry'[111] — but sexy? No. On the other hand, Mann found much to ponder in the 'limpid depths' of René Crevel's eyes: 'huge, shiny stars widely opened', emitting 'flashes of golden and bluish-green sparks'.[112]

Brecht had 'a beautiful, hard face', reminiscent of medieval German woodcuts.[113] Prune-faced Alfred Kerr had the worst taste in ties.[114] Ludwig Marcuse had 'the head of a lion,'[115] majestic but hardly titillating. In contrast, Boris Pasternak, 'delicate and pensive',[116] was too sexy for words. A photograph taken at the Moscow writers' Congress (which Mann also attended) depicted the poet sitting in rapt attention, chin on fist. Musil had the demeanour of a man without qualities. There is no telling whether Mann considered himself an exception to the rule.

Women were poorly represented at the Congress. Amabel Williams-Ellis (née Strachey) was no Cleopatra. Anna Seghers could be considered sexy in a strait-laced kind of way. Magdeleine Paz was not unattractive, but close-cropped hair and dowdy dress created a schoolmarmish effect. Then again, women weren't Mann's cup of tea. Nor was the Paris writers' Congress a beauty contest.

— 2 —

Klaus Heinrich Thomas Mann completed his first autobiography, *Kind dieser Zeit*, 'on the threshold of life'. He was 25. At 26, his father already had one literary classic under his belt: *Buddenbrooks*. Mann's eldest son chose to follow in his father's footsteps, as though by force of primogeniture. There were pluses and minuses. Not quite eighteen, Klaus was appointed second theatre critic at a Berlin newspaper. The downside was less attractive, stretching the son's ability to cope. At the end of *Kind dieser Zeit* Mann writes that he had not yet found the reader prepared to think of him as his own man. 'They judge me *as the son*.'[117] And again, four years on:

> Resentment and respect, protest and gratitude are insolubly intermingled. Fame and authority of the father become a stimulus, a thorn, an obsession to the striving son. Inevitably he will try to imitate the paternal model and at the same time underline his own originality.[118]

The gilded literary cage didn't seem to faze him. To friends and acquaintances Klaus came across as cheerful and witty; 'he didn't waste his life shivering enviously in that huge paternal shadow', recalled Christopher Isherwood.[119]

Klaus Mann's literary output is considerable. It has been said that much of it was written in haste; father concurred. The son lacked the father's 9–5 *Sitzfleisch*. Assuredly Klaus was more engaged with the world. One novel, *Mephisto*, appears to have stood the test of time. Every writer should be so lucky.

In his late teens, down and out in Berlin and burdened with debt, Klaus's thoughts ran to suicide — and not for the first time. In his (unpaid) hotel room young Klaus made the necessary preparations. It is impossible to think of down-and-out Klaus in the same vein as George Orwell down and out in London and Paris, however. Money problems had to be the least of it. There was a history of drug abuse. The actual end came in 1949, in Cannes, overdosing on sleeping pills.

Mann was of that generation born before the Great War but not old enough to have served in it. The 'world of yesterday' had gone up in smoke. What was to replace it? The answer arrived soon enough. For now, Mann embarked on the life of a young European, as distinct from German, intellectual. Mann and his coevals identified as European *and* intellectual, in protest against German nationalism and in defiance of 'the fashionable idolatry of "blood and soil"'. 'Playful and open-minded, we floated between the classes and nations, even between the literary camps and tendencies.'[120]

Politically, Mann related in *Kind dieser Zeit*, he could never be other than on the left. In this he resembled his uncle Heinrich, whom he looked up to like an older brother. In World War I, Thomas Mann had supported the German war effort Heinrich unequivocally opposed. The political distance between Klaus and his father narrowed appreciably in the course of the Nazi era.

Within a year of publication of *Kind dieser Zeit,* Klaus found himself living in exile, a hobbling condition that stayed with him like a pebble in a shoe for the remainder of his life. Mann's émigré novel *Der Vulkan* (1939) taught there was no getting around the times, nor the shadow of one's émigré self. 'Exile is hard' summed up one of its characters.

— 3 —

Ineluctably caught up in the fate of Europe in the thirties, Mann kept track of the moment. His first stop was Amsterdam, a city that filled him with wonder and gratitude — 'beautiful and incomparable', he wrote in an essay extolling its myriad charms. The essay appeared in *Die Sammlung*, an émigré journal edited by Klaus and underwritten by Querido, a Dutch publishing house based in Amsterdam committed to bringing out exiled German authors.[121] The journal's cover prominently displayed the names of its literary patron saints: André Gide, Aldous Huxley, and Heinrich Mann; the Mann brand had its charms. 'This journal', Klaus submitted in the preamble to the first issue, 'wants to serve literature [...] that high endeavour that does not just belong to one people but to people everywhere.' Inside were contributions by Jakob Wassermann, Joseph Roth, Heinrich Mann, and other well-known authors.

Mann's journal was in trouble from the start. Although *Die Sammlung* was conceived as a literary journal, it could not but have a pronounced political profile, for such were the times. The first issue came out in the autumn of 1933 and raised hackles.[122] Thomas Mann, René Schickele, Alfred Döblin, Stefan Zweig, and Robert Musil, among others, repudiated Mann's publication on political grounds, and at the behest of their German publishers informed the proper Nazi authorities, cash flow trumping odium.

With the Nazis putting the clamps on émigré publishing and sales inside and outside Germany, the political dust-up quickly dropped from sight. Not so the journal's financial woes. *Die Sammlung* was on permanent life support, the glittering array of contributors notwithstanding (contributions rarely lived up to the writers' reputation, however). It paid so little, if it paid at all, as to border on the grotesque. One example suffices. In May 1935 Walter Benjamin submitted a twelve-page review of Brecht's *Threepenny Novel*, and was offered 150 French francs (then roughly $10). Benjamin had asked for 250 and refused to let Mann have it for less, upon which the commissioned work was returned to him even though it had already been typeset. 'I would obviously have swallowed Mann's impertinence had I foreseen the result', Benjamin informed Bertolt Brecht. 'I showed myself not clever enough for this world and did so at a point at which cleverness would have meant a lot to me.' (Benjamin was not the only author 'not clever enough for this world' and willing to swallow his pride for a pittance.)[123] When, in September 1935, *Die Sammlung* folded for lack of cash, it had 400 subscribers worldwide.[124]

— 4 —

The year before the journal's demise Mann was in Moscow attending the Soviet Writers' Congress. Mann's impressions, 'Notes in Moscow', appeared in *Die Sammlung* in October 1934.[125] The general impression was that of a country striving toward a new El Dorado, churning out a new species as though it were a cheap two-pound sausage worthy of exhibiting in a major European city, as in Yury Olesha's novel *Envy*. The Soviet Union, Mann asserted, was a democracy of a peculiar sort, in the sense that the dictatorship drew its power from the people vigorously engaged in public life: 'real, passionate, vital'. From film making to theatre, from the collectivization of agriculture to aviation, the work of building socialism filled hearts and minds to overflowing. The Soviet capital had the force to concentrate all of one's thoughts on the future. Foreigners were told they were making a journey in a time machine, previewing, as though it were a movie trailer, 'the land of the future, the foundation of a new world'. In their drive to catch up with the capitalist states, the Soviet people were obsessed with setting and breaking records. 'The record-setting achievement of a female parachutist held everyone in thrall, but so did a new play or novel.' The subway under construction was on everyone's lips. Mann detected little difference between the Muscovite at play and the Muscovite at work: both were pursued with boundless energy and enthusiasm; 'the tennis court and water slide are as much part of their lives as the factory and the collective farm'. People laughed a lot. Such *joie de vivre* was nothing if not infectious.

It was as though Mann had landed in the middle of Dziga Vertov's *The Man With the Movie Camera*. In the evening, back in his room, Mann felt exhilarated, as though returning from an adventure.

In the Soviet Union literature was 'not merely a decorative arabesque on the fringes of society', Mann observed, 'but an active part of public life'. Everyone was reading, from the Red Army recruit to the telephone receptionist; publishers battled paper shortages to keep up with the demand. There existed a vital connection between 'literary producers and their consumers, writers and public, literature and the people'. Workers, sailors, soldiers, and Young Pioneers not only paid homage to the assembled writers, but also exhorted them to pay attention to their specific needs: sailors demanded sailors' songs, female kolkhoz workers an epic celebrating the heroic contributions of women. The classics, both Russian and Western, were popular. Muscovites queued not just for groceries, cinemas and buses, but also at newspaper stalls. There was a strong demand for foreign authors like Céline, John Dos Passos, Lion Feuchtwanger, and Heinrich Mann, to name a few. In the course of one of his walks, Mann came across a shabbily dressed woman on a park bench reading Proust. The French writers who attended the Congress were warmly greeted. The press reported the proceedings at great length.

As noted earlier, Maxim Gorky was the man of the moment. The Soviet people worshipped 'the undisputed pope of Socialistic letters' like a god. 'Whenever Gorky rose, the vast audience seemed awe-struck — petrified with attention'. Every time he opened his mouth to speak, he had to fend off the photographers like 'pesky flies'. A predominantly proletarian audience listened as in a trance. The cult of personality reached such dizzying heights that Gorky himself found it necessary to protest against it.

Of an evening Mann and other visiting authors were invited to the Russian author's splendid dacha on the outskirts of Moscow. Seated at a long table they ate the caviar and drank the vodka and peppered Gorky, 'enthroned amidst them like a somewhat irritable oracle', with questions. Just as the grandmaster of Russian literature was being asked for his opinion of Céline and Dos Passos, a triumvirate of high government officials (Molotov, Kaganovich, and Voroshilov) barged in 'as though it were a factory delegation' and sat down fraternally among the guests. Concerning Céline and Dos Passos, Gorky was afraid the fine print of socialist realism still eluded these western writers. Louis Aragon raised 'the dangerous theme' of the status of individualism. 'How would you, Maxim Gorky', Aragon asked, 'respond to the liberal objection that Communism suppresses the personality and its free development?' Communism, Gorky retorted, opposed individualism as such yet was the only form of state that guaranteed the free development of the individual.

But all that glittered was not gold. The spectacle of 'dangerously pounding soldiers' being greeted with cheers did not sit well with Mann. The ubiquitous presence of the military and the military spirit made the German exile feel queasy. Granted, there had to be a Red Army and it had to be strong, but the need for a loud, demonstrative military presence at a literary gathering eluded the recent refugee from Nazi Germany. Alarmed, he found himself unable to applaud.

And there were other criticisms. Mann panned Gorky's opening speech as lacking in substance: rigid, formulaic, choking on Marxist dogma. He thought even less of Radek's: 'crude and formulaic', and not without errors. In the ensuing debate, Radek dismissed *Ulysses* as 'merely individualistic, without social content'. Mann was not pleased, and even less with Radek's gloss on Proust. What could an author capable of differentiating between seven smells at one and the same time possibly have to say to socialist realism, Radek wondered. 'In the homes of the Soviet worker there was only one smell — that of cabbage.'

Mann was unconvinced that Radek's 'vulgar irony' passed for truth in the Soviet Union. Change, Mann concluded, was in the air. Already more was being demanded from writers than mere reportage and a politically correct attitude. Stalin's 'engineers of the soul' were a thing of the past: Soviet critics were starting to demand beauty. 'With beauty enters mystery, the irrational.' Mann was persuaded that the high-flown optimism in the literary sphere was a symptom of growing pains destined to disappear as the threat from abroad receded and the phase of 'heroic construction' came to an end. The new literature would no longer blame capitalism for man's incurable ills and dismiss love's slings and arrows as a distraction from the class struggle. That generation would no longer be satisfied with a Song of Songs on collectivization of agriculture. A Soviet *Werther* was just around the bend, the visitor from the West predicted.

To the Soviets the preoccupation with metaphysical questions seemed comical, if not downright counterrevolutionary; death was perceived as the natural conclusion to a life spent working for the common good. But no political system, Mann reflected, could remedy every existential ill. Enduring human tragedies like loneliness, mourning, and the awareness of life's transience — these could not simply be chalked up to the 'the decadent lifestyle of a late bourgeois generation'.

Finally, the German émigré asked the question of questions: what, in the final analysis, *was* the function of literature at a time humanity faced, if not extinction, a dire threat to cultural values held dear by both Communism and the bourgeois West? Was literature an effective tool to combat barbarism and to preserve a writer's freedom?

Eight years later, Mann revisited the Moscow Congress in *Der Wendepunkt*. Mann's 'second' autobiography sheds new light on the happenings in Moscow. While the earlier account gives the impression that he was free to come and go as he pleased, Mann now confessed that he 'saw as much or as little as our guides were supposed to show us'.

In 1934 Moscow was building up to a united front, and Mann, though not a Communist, fellow traveller, or even a Marxist, was doing his part, labouring under a self-imposed constraint to cut the most important ally in the struggle against fascism some slack. Much had happened in the intervening years. The bloom was off the Soviet rose. The show trials had come and gone, as had the Popular Front and the Nazi-Soviet Non-Aggression Pact. In 1942, looking back, Mann ratcheted up his criticism a notch or two. Gorky took another beating. At the Congress, Gorky 'whispered patriarchal platitudes in a piping, pitiful voice', a pathetic foil for the 'brilliant rhetoric of the Frenchmen Louis Aragon and André Malraux', as well as his Russian counterparts Ilya Ehrenburg, Boris Pasternak, Alexei Tolstoi, Bukharin, and, yes, even that 'red-bearded schemer' Karl Radek. The get-together at Gorky's 'royal estate' had been bumped up to coincide with the termination of the Congress. The great Gorky, the man of the people, lived in 'regal splendour. The women received us decked out in Paris fashions; the food arrived in Oriental profusion.' 'If I had said such things at Moscow's writers' Congress', Mann acknowledged in 1942,

> it would have led to an extremely painful scandal. But it is not in my nature to assume the role of provoker and to undermine the harmony of such a festive gathering. What would have been the sense of that? The true believers who led the Congress and had invited me to take part knew very well that I didn't belong to their church. Yet they wanted me there, and I don't regret having accepted the invitation.[126]

Mann was 28 years old when he attended the Moscow Congress. It is easy to see why the Russians were pleased to have him. The editor of an important literary journal moved in rarefied intellectual circles. 'Mann' was a marquee name.

Mann's *Der Wendepunkt* opens with a chapter entitled 'The Myths of Childhood'.

In it, the author relates the pains his parents took to cover up some 'ugly' family business. Looking back, Mann reflected — with the Russian experience in mind?

> No, it probably didn't occur to me at bottom to doubt the 'orchestration of the young' in which the family drama was presented to us [the suicide of an aunt and/or suicide/murder of a ne'er-do-well uncle in Argentina], which certainly does not mean that I actually *believed* this veiled version. 'Believing' presupposes a positive impulse, a conscious and deliberate act; 'not doubting' is a negative, passive act. Perhaps one shies away from finding out the truth solely from inertia or out of courtesy; or, perhaps, simply because one senses *that it would do no good to know the whole truth* (emphasis in the original). [...]
>
> No one will find the truth without first looking for it. The search as such is almost like a discovery. If you look hard enough, you'll always find it. To every probing question there at last comes an answer. Often to one's chagrin.[127]

— 5 —

'Bad omen for the Congress', Klaus Mann recorded in his diary on 21 June, alluding to René Crevel's suicide. At the conclusion of the first day, Mann wrote:

> The start of the Congress was not good. No connection between the various speeches, no connection between speakers and public. Kisch had the nerve to speak three quarters of an hour, in German, barely on the level of a union meeting. Musil, too, very weak. Innumerable acquaintances. They talk a lot about René, various opinions regarding the cause. Oh well, I know them; Éluard sees deepest and comes closest. Agonizing heat. Overwhelming desire to leave.[128]

Mann's heart just wasn't in it. But with the Popular Front about to become official, he put on a brave public face. His observations on the Paris Congress appeared two months after the event in *Die Sammlung*, excerpted below.[129]

> This important Congress, attended by some of Europe's most prominent intellectuals, had a dual task: on the one hand, a demonstration of all antifascist intellectuals against the fascist enemy; on the other, a wide-ranging discussion regarding the moral and intellectual foundations on which intellectuals can come together and from there carry on the struggle along a broad united front.
>
> The writers assembled in Paris consider fascism the most dangerous enemy of culture, its survival and progress. On this, they are agreed; this is the point of it all. Which is why the permanent organization established upon the conclusion of the Congress stated: 'This bureau, made up of writers with differing philosophical, literary and political beliefs, is prepared, within its own specific terrain, that of culture, to combat war, fascism and every threat to culture in general.' This resolution was signed, among others, by André Gide, Maxim Gorky, Aldous Huxley, Heinrich Mann, Selma Lagerlöf, Romain Rolland.
>
> There can be no doubt that this Congress brilliantly fulfilled its function as a procession of *the* great antifascist names. As for me, the emotional high point of the antifascist demonstration was the spontaneous homage paid to Heinrich Mann: everyone rose in his honour when he accepted the chairmanship. Up until then, the audience had risen only once: in honour of someone who was no longer in our midst, René Cevel.

The second significant component of the Congress, the discussion, was more difficult. A German representative, Rudolf Leonhard, provided a summary in his discourse about the difference between the 'traditional literature' and a 'new collectivism without traditions'. Leonhard, a staunch Communist, assured writers that writers had nothing to fear from collectivism. Such reassurances failed to convince those 'reared on the norms of Western culture and enamoured of its culture', noted Mann. It was left to Mann's hero, André Gide, to provide a possible way out of the impasse, proposing a formula designed to kill two birds with one stone: 'He who is the most individualist can most effectively serve the whole.'

Gide's first appearance was an event in itself, recalled Mann four years later.

> It became very quiet in the hall when André Gide mounted the podium. He spoke without rhetorical flourish, but the effect was enormous. Everyone felt that the threat to peace, personal freedom and Western culture must be very great indeed when this man, the greatest of living French writers, sacrificed his precious isolation to address the mass with pleas and solemn appeals [...] to shout out to his fellows: take heed, comrades! Something horrendous, something beyond repair, will befall us lest we pull ourselves together and set aside our differences in behalf of our struggle for a dignified future. Fervent applause gratefully acknowledged André Gide's appeal.

Gide's crafty formula and alarums failed to turn the tide. In the end, the gulf separating traditional and collectivist approaches to literature, Mann acknowledged, was unbridgeable. To the Soviets and their supporters the term 'individualist' sent shivers up their spine, while 'liberals' failed to bite on reassurances that 'we writers, we individualists, have nothing to fear'.

All in all, Mann had his doubts whether a large Congress replete with loudspeakers and an impatient, impressionable crowd was the ideal format in which to discuss, let alone overcome, complex philosophical differences. At the least, Mann resolved, the Congress had provided a forum in which to raise and hash out such differences. This in itself Mann perceived as a hopeful sign. 'Paris furnished the best proof', Mann wrapped up his report,

> that existing problems between antifascist writers need not result in destroying the united front. All are agreed on the rejection of barbarism. On other points there are differences of opinion. These are being discussed on an ongoing basis. Such a discussion is the most beautiful demonstration of the good will to keep on working together.

As in 'Notes from Moscow,' Mann revisited the Paris Congress long after the dust had settled, inserting some new, if insignificant, touches.[130] The Danish writer Nexø's head received an honourable mention: 'beautiful and benign, at once paternal and childlike'. Huxley seemed to have traded in the cynicism of *Point Counterpoint* (1930) for a more upbeat model in *Eyeless in Gaza* (1935). André Malraux's speaking ability was terrifying, like his writing. Ehrenburg increasingly assumed the role of liaison between the most recent French literature and the literature of his own country. Aragon was following in the footsteps of Balzac and Zola. The on-stage discussions spilled over into the corridors. There was Ludwig Marcuse, the lion-headed author of books on Loyola and Wagner, and Anna

Seghers, the people's tribune, talking things over with Erwin Piscator, the director of *Revolt of the Fishermen*, a film based on Seghers's award-winning novel. Menno ter Braak was no longer the talented but swollen-headed, pretentious and thin-skinned character from a pipsqueak country, an earlier characterization,[131] but 'a confirmed liberal and brave defender of great European values'.

— 6 —

Mann spoke in the afternoon of 23 June. 'The Struggle for Youth' addressed the fascist appeal to adolescents. That 'cynical seducer' National Socialism exploited the credulity of the young even as it led them to the slaughter in a new war. All of Europe's youth was at risk, not just Germany's. 'Why are we losing so many of our young people?' Mann asked. Harking back to 'Notes on Moscow', Mann ventured that socialism had been defined too narrowly. For all its greatness, Marxism failed to address a number of existential questions and could not satisfy every need. Mann contended that one could espouse Marxist economic theory without marrying the materialist philosophy. Too often the implementation of Marxism had lapsed into dogma; too often what was missing was 'a certain degree of tolerance, of liberty of conscience.' Youth deserved better.

The year before in Moscow, Jean-Richard Bloch postulated that the revolution in France would have to funnel some of the enduring legacies of the French into the 'powerful current of Communist thought', specifically its emphasis on the individual and liberty. Failure to do so would throw the western masses into the arms of fascism, Bloch warned. Bloch's speech affected Klaus like 'a pebble thrown into the pond', opening up broad and important perspectives.

In Paris, Mann shared one of those perspectives with the largely proletarian audience. In place of an all too rigid materialist worldview Mann championed socialist humanism. Touted as the complete antithesis of fascism, Mann's 'socialism' incorporated serviceable aspects of Christianity and Antiquity and was open to all opposed to racism, imperialism and the 'poison of nationalism'. 'Socialist humanism will honour its mentors and its great men [...] but it will not stoop to a blind cult of personality.' Writers and intellectuals were expected to do their bit and make their voices heard. 'We fail if we don't succeed in reaching the youth.'

Editing a highbrow literary journal and commitment to a united front imposed constraints. Not so the diary. 'Paris was hard to take', Mann wrote there.

> The Congress, too, appeared to me, on the whole, as having failed — or was it because of my poor showing? A few strong impressions: the speeches by Gide and Malraux; the ovation for Heinrich when he took over the presidency; the ovation for René. Dissatisfied with my own speech, although outwardly it went tolerably well.[132]

Mann was exhausted, the heat overwhelming. With apologies, in writing, to uncle Heinrich and Gide, he quit Paris before the Congress closed up shop. 24 June found him in Switzerland, shopping, meeting with authors, visiting friends and parents.

## VIII. Ludwig Marcuse

The person who has lived through this century and hasn't become a sceptic is beyond help.[133]

— 1 —

Every time Ludwig Marcuse sat down to write he was reminded that nothing was simple. *Es ist immer komplizierter* — It is always more complicated — was the creed that governed his writing life. The inspirational motto, Ludwig's philosopher's stone, had been mounted on the wall facing his desk like a commandment from on high.

This piece of wisdom still lay well into the future when the seventeen-year-old embarked on a study of philosophy in Berlin. 'A young student whom I knew well', Marcuse reminisced twenty-one years later,

> entered the university in the autumn of 1913. There he lost his bearings completely, like the best among his pals, because he believed wholeheartedly in the principles enunciated by the great German idealists of the eighteenth century: that the university existed to provide him with a universal education. As a Jew, he was a loyal protector of the German tradition and he began studying philosophy. School had taught him that the world had begun with the Greeks; about Jews he of course knew nothing. [...] But not a single professor in any seminar was able to point the way to the end-goal of German idealism, to the freely formed personality. Why not?[134]

Ludwig Marcuse — philosopher-journalist-literary critic — had a bone to pick with the heirs of Kant, Lessing, Humboldt and Hegel, latter-day purveyors of German idealism who continued to pay lip service to Kant even as they supported the war effort and from there graduated to pledge their mortar boards to Hitler. As one such philosopher quoted by Marcuse put it: 'Hitler is not less than the idea; he is more than the idea, because he is a reality.'

German idealism, argued Marcuse, had been demolished by some of its finest flowers: Marx, Engels and Nietzsche. 'But if Marx', demolition's principal architect, 'has undermined the moral philosophy of German idealism', Marcuse wrapped up his case against the faux idealist philosophers in the summer of 1934, 'he did so for the love of an all-pervasive sense of justice.' For all its ferocity, the Third Reich's onslaught on German idealism by way of Karl Marx was destined to fail, predicted Marcuse, drive it underground, but not kill it. At the time, Marcuse was living abroad, having settled in Sanary-sur-Mer on the French Riviera, well out of reach, for the time being at least, of Hitler's philosophical cohorts.[135]

In 1935, at the Paris Congress, the German exile struck a similar optimistic note, albeit tacked on as a rider to an otherwise bleak assessment. Marcuse's contribution, 'Le cas de l'humanisme', fell under *autres discours*, a category reserved for participants who for one reason or another (suicide, illness, previous engagements, yielding one's slot) were unable to address the Congress live. 'The Case of Humanism' dwelt on the rise and fall of humanism and, as with German idealism, its enduring relevance.[136] In it, Marcuse contended that the humanist tradition that had taken shape between the fifteenth and eighteenth centuries and had gone to seed in the nineteenth was far from exhausted, seeing the trouble the Nazis were taking to will it out of existence.

In step with Congress's agenda, Marcuse urged all sides to pour their energies into combating fascism instead of arguing ad nauseam about the relative merits, say, of collectivism versus individualism, when, in the nature of things, 'the fruits of this planet' belonged to all and accrued to those prepared to exercise what he called 'the will to achieve *humanitas*'.

— 2 —

Europe's literary establishment, similar to literary establishments elsewhere, was a network of more or less thin-skinned individuals prone to infighting, jealousies, friendships, enmities, and literary vendettas. Literary critics in particular evoked dislike and, not infrequently, great hatred. The very sighting of German theatre critic Alfred Kerr on opening night, 'arms crossed and frock coat buttoned up to his neck', had been known to strike fear into the hearts of directors and actors alike.[137] Menno ter Braak was another critic with a knack for making enemies. Klaus Mann was one, Marcuse another.[138] For the likes of these, meeting their critic face-to-face at the Congress was bound to be somewhat unsettling.

Toward the end of 1934, Ter Braak published an article critical of German émigré authors like Marcuse. Rather than producing new work prompted by their recent fall from grace and embracing 'their European task', Ter Braak charged, they by and large trod well-worn paths, churning out historical novels and fruitlessly engaging 'the false mysticism of Blubo idolators Blubo' (Blubo, short for *Blut und Boden*, Blood and Soil). Moral outrage ventilated in such books as Heinrich Mann's *Der Hass* and Ernst Toller's *Eine Jugend in Deutschland,* both published shortly after Hitler came to power, though understandable, was a dead end, he averred, and advised them to move on. A final rebuke bore on the lack of self-criticism: émigré authors avoided panning one another in print.[139]

Marcuse was an exile, and a highly incensed one.

The philosopher's reply appeared the following week in *Das Neue Tage-Buch*, the émigré journal published in Paris that carried the Dutchman's lament.[140] For one, Marcuse denied that there was such a thing as 'émigré literature', i.e. literature that could no longer appear in Germany, arguing that the common denominator cited by Ter Braak simply did not exist. Marcuse further pointed out that Heinrich Mann's *Der Hass*, a book of essays and documents delving into the origins of Nazi hatred, articulated a world view that harked back to Wilhelmine Germany.[141] Besides, two years was scarcely a sufficient block of time to warrant the assessment hazarded by Dutchman.

Three months after the Paris Congress and nine months after his original article and Marcuse's response, Ter Braak found that nothing had changed: 'And now the illustrious authors of the emigration', he wrote,

> flee into the past, that is, into topics that enable them to make allusions to, and comparisons with, the present situation, yet on the whole detracts from

the seriousness of that situation. Heinrich Mann visits Henry IV, Ludwig Marcuse Ignatius de Loyola, Gina Kaus Catherine the Great, Alfred Neumann Napoleon III, etc.; the list is by no means exhausted.[142]

Marcuse had a hard time letting go. 'Since he expected Thomas Mann and Alfred Döblin to achieve superhuman powers upon crossing the border', Marcuse remarked in his memoirs twenty-five years later, 'he was disappointed to find that they were the same people they were before.'[143] Ter Braak had been dead for twenty years.

— 3 —

To judge by these same memoirs, Marcuse was a lively presence at the Congress despite forfeiting, for whatever reason, a place at the speakers' table. 'I did not then believe', he began his recollection of the Congress,

> that one could defend culture, yet talked myself into believing that one could intimidate beasts of prey through a parade of world famous men armed with pens, brushes and similar dinky weapons. In the meantime even the most naïve have come to realize that this is not possible. A fighter plane and Paul Valéry are values of a different order with an immutable relationship to power: the bomber can indeed kill Valéry but not the other way around.
>
> [...]
>
> There were long speeches, some stating the obvious, others reproachful; often interesting, more often excruciatingly boring. There were protests, both raucous and prudent. A resolution was crafted as cautiously as though it was a complicated trade treaty, for the interests of many participants had to be taken into account.

Like Ter Braak and Klaus Mann, Marcuse made no secret of his admiration for André Gide — nor of his dislike of Robert Musil.

> At the speakers' table sat two men who absorbed my attention so completely that I barely heard what was being said. One was André Gide, whom I encountered for the first time. As he did not move a muscle, it was impossible to know whether he was present or somewhere else. His face was in constant motion, a play of facial expressions that was impossible to read. His lips never moved, the nose did not twitch, the eyes did not light up or flash or do anything eyes are capable of doing. And yet his eyes were like a bustling bazaar. I found myself caught up in all that activity and found it difficult to pull myself away from it. At the time I was still unfamiliar with his writings. After reading his journals I had a better grasp of this restless activity, reflecting that perhaps people with more to hide than those with a humdrum inner life have to find ways to express themselves that far exceed the familiar knitting of eyebrows and the protrusion of chins.
>
> When I was able to take my eyes off Gide, they reluctantly wandered over to Musil. In 1930 I was one of the first who had proclaimed his *Man Without Qualities* 'A Masterpiece', a designation I had never used before or since. From then on we had an amicable relationship. During the last three years I had often heard that his behaviour had become erratic; in the highly rarefied atmosphere of the Congress his speech was downright reserved; 'unpolitical', as he put it: 'I have kept my distance from politics for my enter life because I did not sense a

talent for it.' He did not talk about 'hygiene', either, he informed the Congress, suggesting that these topics were unworthy of sharing with others. [...] Why on earth had this most gifted individual shown up to say such foolish things? [...] Should I greet him?

(In the course of a long speech delivered on opening night, Musil quoted what he designated as Nietzsche's 'terrible but altogether premonitory' remark that 'the victory of a moral ideal is obtained by the same immoral means as all other victories: through violence, lies, defamation, injustice.' Musil took issue with authoritarian regimes generally, on account of 'the simple fact that we are used to parliamentary democracy' [...] which 'leaves culture with a large margin of freedom.' Equating fascism and Communism was not *de bon ton* at this Congress.)

How different from Heinrich Mann! Thomas Mann's older brother, at sixty-four an enduring symbol of 'the other Germany' dating back to the previous century, commanded Marcuse's 'unflagging admiration'.

> There he was: a well-groomed patrician of around 60, quite like a French senator, with a still impressive moustache and modest goatee — reserved, unaffected [...] a dedicated liberal who even in a time of demagogues remained convinced that one could win the masses over by employing the language of reason.

Fleshing out Mann's portrait, Marcuse went on to cite from letters the aging exile wrote to him in Sanary from his home in Nice, 160 kilometres up the coast. One such, dispatched around the time of the Popular Front, explained why he was supporting the Soviet Union: 'the enemy of my enemy are my friends'. The good times, like the bad, he reflected in another letter, are short-lived. And in yet a third letter he wanted Marcuse to know that his faith in reason was by no means absolute: 'everything that concerns reason remains questionable, the best only possess half of it'.[144]

— 4 —

In November 1936, Marcuse boarded a train in Paris en route to the Soviet Union. Stopping over in Vienna, he briefly hooked up with Joseph Roth. Roth wished him well: 'Fahre mit Gott in die Hölle', he said — 'God go with you to hell'. 'I did not understand him. I was a monotheist and knew only one devil: the homegrown one.'[145] Roth, Habsburg loyalist unto death, hated Communism with a passion.

At the Russian border there was the by now proverbial warm welcome by a writers' delegation and the equally proverbial Pullman sleeper set aside for 'honoured guests'. Along with his wife, Sacha, Marcuse brought a 1000-page manuscript on Richard Wagner, whom he disliked intensely. A manuscript that size in a foreign language, German, was bound to raise eyebrows. It took some time for the customs officials, assisted by a posse of translators, to sort it all out. 'I may never have had such devoted readers', quipped Marcuse years later. Exiled German author Willi Bredel appeared on the scene to vouch for Marcuse, and the train pulled out at last. Bredel was the author of *Die Prüfung*, one of the first eyewitness accounts of life in a Nazi concentration camp. In the Soviet Union he helped edit, with Bertolt Brecht and Lion Feuchtwanger, the Moscow-based German literary journal *Das Wort*, an offspring of the Paris writers' Congress and Front politics; the first issue appeared in July 1936.

Marcuse entered the Soviet Union at a sensitive time. The first show trials had come and gone and the sequel was just around the bend. The latter were orchestrated between 23 and 30 January 1937. A request by Marcuse to attend one of those trials was turned down. Johannes Becher, another German expatriate, heaped praise on Stalin for having cleaned house. 'And for all this we have to thank comrade Stalin', jubilated the German expressionist poet with a thing for leather. Every important Russian writer, reported Marcuse, heartily applauded the poet's unequivocal endorsement. 'Whoever has lived through this century and has not become a sceptic is beyond help', observed the onetime student of German idealism with the benefit of hindsight.

Like many distinguished foreigners, the Marcuses were lodged in Moscow's Hotel Metropol. The hotel was chock-a-block with a colourful cross-section of people from just about every Soviet republic. A restless type, Marcuse asked for two rooms, one for himself and one for Sacha. This was refused, Marcuse recalled, on the ground that he lacked 'class consciousness'. It was pointed out that in the Soviet Union even the highest-ranking general in the East had to sleep in the same room as his spouse. Marcuse's memoirs tell of another *faux pas*: a steadfast refusal to visit an automobile plant. Before long, Marcuse writes, he was dismissed as a 'typical product of the decadent West'.

Assuredly, the usual perks lavished on 'honoured guests' made up for the relatively minor inconvenience of state-mandated doubling up. Spoiled Western intellectuals with dubious leftist credentials might carp all they liked, but however bleary-eyed for lack of sleep they ate the caviar, drank the vodka, and indulged the car and chauffeur on round-the-clock standby. Lemons, however, the self-described 'bred-in-the-bone sceptic' noted, were unavailable in the proletarian state. Sunday evening meals were prodigious feasts attended by many a Soviet dignitary and privileged writer, the kind of gourmandizing gatherings where the absence of lemons might easily have gone unnoticed.

Like Gide, Marcuse found that to most Russians Western Europe was the heart of darkness. Russians had a hard time processing information that did not square with their ideas of the West; the fact, for example, that Paris and London had subways that went back well before the Russian revolution. Be that as it may, in no other country was Hegel's *Aesthetik* being serialized with a huge print run; and where else did bar girls study geometry and physics 'while sweeping the floor', as in the Hotel Metropol? It was enough to drive a philosopher crazy.

Sacha returned to France without Ludwig, who stayed on to sample life in the USSR for some time yet. Sacha's homeward journey did not get off to a good start: forced to share the sleeper with the 'arch-communist' Pierre Vaillant-Couturier, she complained vehemently. As at the Metropol, the one-size-fits-all rule also applied to trains. Russia did not believe in separating the sexes on sleepers.

Gide, too, was omnipresent, a part of every conversation. Marcuse had packed a copy of *Return from the USSR* but found no takers among Russia's writers. *Pravda*, the Party newspaper, had laid down the line: Gide was a 'representative of high capitalism'; after all, what did Gide know about hunger? Gide's ghost popped up even in so harmless a transaction as a request for aspirins. 'Down here Gide's friend [Eugène Dabit] died', Marcuse's interpreter explained, apologizing for the delay in obtaining the aspirins. 'If something like that were to happen to another European writer, they'd accuse us of being murderers.'

Altogether Marcuse spent six months in the Soviet Union. In the second week of May, he travelled to the south of Russia. 'I saw much and learned little.' He took few notes. He ran into beggars, visited schools, inspected bacteriological institutes and paid his respects at the monuments to the casualties in the civil war. Among his strongest memories was that of a celebrated woman flier. Although Marcuse does not mention her by name, this had to be Valentina Grizodubova, the future recipient of the 'Hero of the Soviet Union' award, the top distinction in the land. Valentina's picture was everywhere, Marcuse recalled, including his own suitcase. On his way back to France, inspectors at the border beamed with delight and duly waved him on.

The trip home was far from pleasant. Ensconced in a first-class compartment, he crossed the Romanian border penniless and arrived in Paris famished. Back in Sanary, Marcuse was able to relax and reflect. Situating his Soviet experience in broader context, he arrived at three important conclusions. First, that 'the great Karl Marx' had made a cardinal error when he singled out the capitalist order as the last stage in the exploitation of labour. Second, that the philosophy of the industrial state was carrying all before it, the 'replacement of everything that once was *Bildung* with whatever is practical and useful'. Third, and evidently most importantly, that things are always more complicated.

— 5 —

Marcuse's memoirs came out in 1960, 'Gespräch mit meinen Freunden' in 1937.[146] The latter registered the philosopher's impressions five months into the visit, long enough to have formed opinions he was prepared to share with others. First the bird's eye view:

> What have I seen? Old czarist castles and monasteries, very informative museums of a vanished world; fantastic workers' clubs; courtyards that go back in time [...]; tall buildings, trolley buses, Soviet cars; a few grannies crossing themselves before crossing the street, and many young people who surely have no idea how to make the sign of the cross; very few loafers and many workers; 30 terribly serious plays, 25 loftiest of films, not a single cabaret (they don't have those here); [...] more things of the momentous and heroic sort than light-hearted [...]. May 1 is not yet so gaily celebrated as the Fourteenth of July — and far more focused.

The worm's eye view turned out to be rather more complicated. 'Conversation with My Friends', an imaginary discussion with émigré intellectuals set in a small bar behind Paris's Odéon Theatre, addressed 'God-go-with-you' friends. Marcuse's article addressed 'God-go-with you' friends like Joseph Roth and the painter who had taken him to a fancy Czech restaurant the evening before his departure and, laying a hand on his shoulder, urged him to eat his fill; and, finally, the sceptics among readers of the *Die Neue Weltbühne* and the world at large.

Marcuse seems to have got along just fine without God, neither starving nor tripping over Russia's famished. And spoken his mind. To his regret, he had not been able to attend the trials. No matter; our knowledge, he averred, was hardly limited to the things we observe with our own eyes. He had read the transcripts. And he was satisfied. 'One would have to believe in bewitchment to think that endless speeches brimming with logic, acumen, witticisms, and self-assurance' had no other purpose than 'to prove a deathly lie'. 'You are disappointed with me, my friends. I descended into the underworld and have no dark and creepy things to report.'

To be sure, Marcuse continued, there were more people than goods in stores; our kind of freedom was non-existent, and the silent were, well, silent. Great authors produce little from fear they were out of step with the reader. They had been dealt a rough hand. Admittedly, the Soviet Union was not made to order for everyone sitting around this table. Even so, the Soviets had given Western writers the opportunity to seek out the freedom they had lost at home. Putting things in perspective, Marcuse mentioned the great sacrifices made by 170 million ordinary citizens to make something beautiful of their country. Babies well cared for, children raised without fear, free education, doors open to all who want to better themselves. The servant sweeping his room was learning English, the lift operator German, the waiter French, the concierge geometry: 'that is the solid foundation for the ever suspect, notoriously fragile optimism'.

In the Soviet Union all is becoming. There is no today, only yesterday and tomorrow. The Soviet house is a work in progress and there's no telling what it will look like upon completion. The Union is young enough to raise expectation, old enough to urge even the most confirmed sceptics to hang fire. 'Whoever among us does not enthusiastically share in the happenings there, misses out on the greatest moral achievement of our day.' Western critics tended to jump to conclusions and pass them on as truths. 'Scepticism', Marcuse concluded, 'is a great virtue, but the danger for the brightest is to become more stupid than the stupidest from fear of being deceived'.

## IX. Menno ter Braak (2)

— *1* —

*The Problem of Individualism is Missing*[147]

Menno ter Braak had seen enough. With two days to go the correspondent for *Het Vaderland* packed his bags and took the train back to The Hague. On the train the critic from the Low Countries decompressed with a copy of Stendhal's *Rome, Naples et Florence*. Temperamentally unequipped for 'the church with loudspeakers', to wit, the Congress, Ter Braak ranked Stendhal's ruminations on the 'manners and contours of Italian society', opera, the arts, architecture, salons, and 'tales of love', above that of Julien Sorel's hard-nosed endeavour to make his mark in a world shot through with corruption and hypocrisy.

> It is a land of informality, and yet of natural grace and manners; of rational cynicism, and yet of decent respect towards the established superstitions; of an ignorant and vicious despotism, and yet (for such is the fertile nature of the Italian mind) of a despotism which itself breeds heroes out of slaves and conjures up painters, sculptors and musicians by the very restraint which it imposes upon all more direct and forceful means of expression.[148]

— 2 —

Ter Braak's second report on the Congress appeared in *Het Vaderland* on 25 June and covered the two Sunday sessions, afternoon and evening. There was no indication, Ter Braak found, that anything had changed from one day to the next; everything was already known.

> We are dealing here with interests that are of an entirely different order than one would have expected from the designation 'Congrès des Écrivains pour la Défense de la Culture'. Who's to blame? Not necessarily the organizers, who invited enough non-Communist authors, some of whom had accepted but did not put in an appearance; Thomas Mann being among the latter. [...] However, the 'bourgeois' authors in attendance dissolve into the mass. Understandably, they no longer have any illusions about the remainder of the Congress. [...] No new perspectives were opened up. [...] The Marxist writers are tiresome, although they often speak well since they can always switch, with unfailing certainty, to the dogma of their lesson plan.

Having concluded that the Congress was a lost cause, Ter Braak decided just to 'sit back and enjoy the many colourful by-products that a collection of more or less celebrated authors is bound to generate'.

> For instance, it is a pleasure to see the Danish writer Andersen-Nexö, who is here with his compatriot Karin Michaelis, incessantly sucking on enormous pipes; a typical old gent, rather stiff and martial in his appearance. And one can never get enough of Alfred Kerr, an émigré whose speech consisted almost entirely of lamentations concerning his own fate. In his appearance, Kerr combines the veneer of a nineteenth-century dandy with the dignified modesty of a clergyman: his tie may be considered one of the highlights of the Congress. If this sounds like gallows humour, so be it, in so far as one would have expected something rather different from a Congress associated with the names Gide and Malraux.

The defence of culture was doomed to failure, Ter Braak proceeded, 'as long as the Russian authors are unprepared to concede a smidgen of doubt in their own excellence'. For the Russian writer,

> the problems of Western thought don't exist; he has already dismissed it before he has even considered it. As such, I am absolutely convinced, after having listened to these people that, for all their vitality, they are so steeped in the bliss of their 'construction' mania that they have become blind to the rest of the

world. Ever since they have put world revolution on the map they go on and on about the new metro in Moscow, in a tone of voice of someone proclaiming the highest things.

For Westerners, he said, reprising his own speech, 'the heart of the matter is the problem of individualism', how to stay true to its meaning, 'free from nineteenth-century illusions and dictatorships of both left and right. That is a *problem,* but not one that exists for the Russians'.

The Dutchman continued to be puzzled by the demeanour of both Malraux and Gide, but especially Gide. 'What is Gide's Future?' Ter Braak asked in the subheading. It was no small matter when 'a thoroughly respectable and European figure' such as Gide 'was being sucked into the orbit of a journalist like Ilya Ehrenburg'. Not that Gide's fundamental 'intellectual rectitude' was on the block.

> For the time being Gide is still too much what he was to leave an impression of a pawn being pushed around; his speech was convincing and full of wisdom. But already his position as 'individualist' has become untenable. At the Congress he is the hero, and the role of hero is a bad fit for an 'immoralist' of Gide's stature. The real hero of all congresses is Ilya Ehrenburg, who seems have been made for this kind of heroism and thus absolutely determined to make the most of the occasion.

Toward the end of the article, having given notice that he was leaving, Ter Braak took one last swipe at Ehrenburg, pitting him against an author they both loved. 'I wonder', Ter Braak mused,

> what will happen once this optimism in Russia has spent itself; when an Ehrenburg will again be perceived as a clever and glib propagandist; when a metro in Moscow will no longer be treated as a piece of historical-materialist metaphysics; I believe that at such a time the collective diehards of every stripe who now appear to be so overwhelmingly in the right apropos the 'naïveté' of a Stendhal will be reduced to utter helplessness. At this Congress 'pour la défense de la culture' Stendhal, had he wanted to speak, would have been a complete anachronism. But I reread, far from the hall of the Mutualité, *Rome, Naples et Florence,* and experienced the undiminished charm of his 'naïve' wisdom, more than one hundred years ago and yet as fresh as if it were born yesterday. Stendhal wished for himself readers in 1935. Well then, he has them, this bourgeois, this individualist. But who will read Ehrenburg in 2035, when his style of reporting has been exceeded by thousands of other reporters? After this Congress I more than ever put my money on naïveté.

— 3 —

The Congress left a bitter after-taste that lasted for weeks. That the likes of Gide and Malraux had become 'the *victims* of others, of the politicians' was a bitter pill. Ter Braak went on to express his 'amazement regarding the attitude of Gide and Malraux, who, if they at all costs wanted to take a stand, should have stood with Trotsky.'[149] As for himself, he went back home 'more of an individualist then ever'. 'Moscow is not much better than Berlin', he wrote to his friend, the poet and literary critic Jan Greshoff.[150]

Jan Greshoff left Holland for Cape Town, South Africa, in 1939, and urged Ter Braak to follow suit before it was too late. 'Dear Jan', Ter Braak wrote back,

> This letter is intended as a final sign of life in the event that today or tomorrow air traffic comes to a halt and war breaks out. [...] For now I am resigned. As long as I have been a conscious living creature I have tried to fight for something that today apparently is becoming an issue in an uncivilized manner: human dignity, or whatever you want to call it. I don't fancy that that's on the side of the English, but I only know that it is no longer possible to lead a dignified life in Europe.

After speculating on the possible outcomes of a 'second Munich' — Eastern Europe down the drain, Hitler marching on Western Europe the following year, the prospect of living under German 'sphere of influence' — Ter Braak continued:

> in that case I'll try to emigrate to South Africa next year because by then there won't be anything left for me to do here. I doubt it, though; and then the question remains if we will meet again in this world. I don't have to remind you once more how much your friendship has meant to us, for tomorrow it may be too late; and if not, there is no harm in having said so.[151]

'You and I', observed Du Perron in conversation with Ter Braak not long after Hitler came to power, 'are too good to end up under the heels of any social beast, regardless of the boots. No one escapes his fate.'[152]

Anticipating a likely fate, Menno Ter Braak killed himself on the day Holland fell to Germany, 14 May 1940. That same day Eddy Du Perron succumbed to a heart attack.

In a post-war tribute to Ter Braak, Thomas Mann memorialized the acerbic critic as a 'good Dutchman and good European'. 'Surely', Mann concluded, 'it was this absolute commitment of intellectual and moral feeling, this extreme "honnêteté", to use one of Nietzsche's favourite expressions, that killed Ter Braak.'[153] The poet H. A. Gomperts likewise used the term 'honnête homme' to describe the Dutch gadfly, adding that he 'died like a Roman'.[154]

## Notes to Chapter 2

1. Maurice Sachs, *Heksensabbat, verslag van een ondraaglijk leven* (Amsterdam: Arbeiderspers, 1967), p. 168.
2. André Gide, *Si le grain ne meurt* (Paris: Gallimard, 1955), pp. 338–44.
3. André Gide, *Journals 1889–1949*, trans. by Justin O'Brien (Harmondsworth: Penguin Books, 1967) p. 567. Further references to this source are given after quotations in the text.
4. Sachs, pp. 169, 177.
5. Klaus Mann, *André Gide and the Crisis of Modern Thought* (New York: Creative Age Press, 1943), p. 249.
6. Frederick John Harris, *André Gide and Romain Rolland: Two Men Divided* (New Brunswick, NJ: Rutgers University Press, 1973), p. 117.
7. The antifascist writers organization in question was the Association des Écrivains et Artistes Révolutionnaires, founded in March 1932. Gide, *Journals*, 13 December 1932, p. 549.
8. *Si le grain*, p. 29.
9. *The André Gide Reader*, ed. by David Littlejohn (New York: Knopf, 1971), p. 808.
10. H.-R. Lenormand, *Les Confessions d'un auteur dramatique*, 2 vols (Paris: Albin Michel, 1953), II, p. 338.

11. Gide's reference is to Malraux's preface to *Days of Wrath*, trans. by Haakon M. Chevalier (New York: Random House, 1936), p. 7.

12. *L'ami hollandais. Jef Last & André Gide*, dir. by Pieter Jan Smit (The Netherlands, SNG Film, 2005).

13. *André Gide-Jef Last: Correspondance 1934–1950* (Lyon: Presses Universitaires de Lyon, 1985), pp. 26–33.

14. K. Mann, *Gide and the Crisis*, p. 258.

15. Victor Serge, 'Open Letter to André Gide' <http://www.marxist.org/archive/serge/1936/xx/letter-gide-htm> [accessed 15 June 2012]

16. *God that Failed*, 158–59.

17. Teroni and Klein, pp. 523–26.

18. See Jef Last, 'De persoonlijkheid van André Gide', in AO — Reeks Boekje 1287 (Amsterdam: Stichting IVIO, 1969), p. 13.

19. Robèrt Gillesse, *De Tijd der idealisten: Jef Last in de jaren dertig* (unpublished dissertation, Rijksuniversiteit Leiden, 1994), p. 79.

20. Gillesse, p. 79.

21. *God that Failed*, p. 166.

22. André Gide, *Return from the U.S.S.R.*, trans. by Dorothy Bussy (New York: Knopf, 1937).

23. K. Mann, *Gide and the Crisis*, pp. 260–61.

24. *Return*, p. 12.

25. *Return*, p. 31.

26. *Return*, p. 42.

27. Gide's book was also quite the topic of conversation as the Second International Congress of Writers for the Defence of Culture held in Valencia/Madrid/Paris in 1937. Vegesack, p. 181.

28. 'Ris et larmes d'André Gide,' *L'Humanité*, 18 December 1936, p. 4.

29. The allusion is to *Les Faux-Monnayeurs*.

30. André Malraux, *Anti-Memoirs*, trans. by Terence Kilmartin (New York: Holt, Rinehart and Winston, 1968), p. 8.

31. Curtis Cate, *André Malraux: A Biography* (New York: Fromm International, 1995), pp. 188–98.

32. Marleen Rensen, *Lijden aan de tijd: Franse intellectuelen in het interbellum* (Soesterberg: Aspekt, 2009), p. 115.

33. Gillesse, p. 131.

34. *Anti-Memoirs*, p. 9.

35. Eddy du Perron, *Het land van herkomst* (Amsterdam: van Oorschot, 1989), p. 287.

36. Du Perron, *Land*, p. 288.

37. *Anti-Memoirs*, p. 4.

38. *Days of Wrath*, pp. 5–6.

39. *Magnitogorsk — Forging the new man*, dir. by Jan Pieter Smit (The Netherlands: 1966).

40. *Days of Wrath*, pp. ix-xviii (xviii).

41. *Anti-Memoirs*, p. 333.

42. Cited in Du Perron, *Land*, p.126.

43. *Land*, p. 20.

44. 'Gesprek met Héverlé,' in *Land*, pp. 152–64 (pp. 153–54).

45. Eddy du Perron, *De smalle mens* (Amsterdam: Querido, 1934), p. 78.

46. Cited in Claude Tannery, *Malraux, the Absolute Agnostic, or, Metamorphosis as Universal Law* (Chicago: University of Chicago Press, 1991), p. 81.

47. David Pryce-Jones, 'André Malraux: Politicizing literature, fictionalizing politics', *The New Criterion* (March 2005) <http://www.newcriterion.com/articles.cfm/andre-malraux-politicizing-literature-fictionalizing-politics-1287> [accessed 12 June 2013]

48. Cited in Ehrenburg, *Memoirs*, p. 274.

49. Cited in Du Perron, *Grootse tijd*. pp. 16–17.

50. Arthur Koestler, 'Explorations', in *The Yogi and the Commissar and Other Essays* (London: Jonathan Cape, 1964), p. 126. Malraux is not mentioned by name.

51. Cate, pp. 207–08.

52. Cited in Du Perron, *Grootse tijd*, pp. 33, 30.

53. *Anti-Memoirs*, p. 90.

54. From Ilya Ehrenburg's speech at the Congress.

55. Putnam, pp. 93–95.

56. 'Lessons of Stendhal', in *Chekhov, Stendhal, and Other Essays* (New York: Knopf, 1963), pp. 145–85.

57. 'Some Characteristics of French Culture', in *Chekhov*, pp. 143–44.

58. Olga Carlisle, 'The Art of Fiction', in *The Paris Review* (1961) <http://www.theparisreview.org/interviews/4636/the-art-of-fiction-no-26-ilya-ehrenburg> [accessed 5 October 2012]

59. *Memoirs*, p. 265–66.

60. K. Mann, *André Gide and the Crisis*, p. 252.

61. Cited in Anatol Goldberg, *Ilya Ehrenburg, Revolutionary, Novelist, Poet, War Correspondent, Propagandist: The Extraordinary Epic of a Russian Survivor* (New York: Viking, 1984), p. 145.

62. *Memoirs*, p. 276.

63. *Memoirs*, pp. 287–90.

64. *The Second Day*, trans. by Liv Tudge (Moscow: Raduga, 1984).

65. Du Perron, *Grootse tijd*, p. 39.

66. Nadezhda Mandelstam, *Hope Abandoned*, trans. by Max Hayward (New York: Atheneum, 1974), p. 16.

67. *Der Vulkan. Roman unter Emigranten* (Amsterdam: Querido, 1939), pp. 198–99.

68. *The Turning Point*, p. 121.

69. Simon Vestdijk, *Gestalten tegenover mij. Persoonlijke herinneringen* (Amsterdam: De Bezige Bij, 1992), p. 87.

70. Menno ter Braak, 'Het national-socialisme als rancuneleer', *Verzameld Werk*, 7 vols, 2nd edn (Amsterdam: van Oorschot, 1980), III, pp. 575–94 (p. 583).

71. 'Fascistische gelijkheid', in *Verzameld Werk*, III, pp. 317- 49 (p. 333).

72. Simon Vestdijk, 'Ter Braak na de oorlog', in *Over Menno ter Braak* (Amsterdam: Oorschot, 1949), p. 22.

73. Cited in Du Perron, *Land*, p. 354.

74. Anton van Duinkerken cited in 'Menno ter Braak, Politiek en Cultuur: 3 Generaties, 3 Forums', ed. by Jan Fontijn, Frank Ligtvoet and Carel Peeters (Amsterdam: Stichting Literaire Aktiviteiten, 1982), p.11.

75. *Briefwisseling tussen Menno ter Braak en Eddy du Perron* (Amsterdam: van Oorschot, 1965), 6 June 1935, p. 213. Du Perron was part of the Dutch delegation but did not speak.

76. Ant Ter Braak-Faber <http://www.mennoterbraak.nl/tekst/braa002brie11_01/braa002brie11_01_0204.php> [accessed 9 December 2014].

77. Fontijn and others, 'Politiek en Cultuur', p. 13.

78. *Menno ter Braak*, Schrijversprentenboek 5, publication of the Nederlands Letterkundig Museum en Documentatiecentrum, The Hague (2nd edn, Amsterdam: Bezige Bij, 1980), p. 5.

79. Imprisoned by the Nazis, Renn was released the following year. Ossietzky was awarded the Nobel Peace Prize in 1935. He died in 1938, of tuberculosis, in a hospital under Gestapo surveillance.

80. 'Schrijverscongres te Parijs', *Het Vaderland*, Kunst en Letteren, 24 June 1935, p 9.

81. *Grootse tijd*, p. 33.

82. Marcuse, *Jahrhundert*, pp. 131–32.

83. Sergei Tretyakov, 'Bert Brecht', in *Brecht as They Knew Him,* ed. by Hubert Witt, trans. by John Peet (New York: International Publishers, 1974), p. 69.

84. 'Brecht, Robbed of Citizenship', in *Brecht as They Knew Him*, p. 81.

85. Christopher Isherwood, *My Guru and His Disciple* (New York: Farrar Straus & Giroux, 1980), p. 137.

86. *Reflections*, p. 204.

87. Bertolt Brecht, *Journals, 1934–1955*, ed. by John Willett and Ralph Mannheim, trans. by Hugh Rorrison (London: Routledge, 1993), 1935, pp. 4–5.

88. Hermann Kesten, *Lauter Literaten. Porträts. Erinnerungen* (Vienna: Kurt Desch, 1963), p. 394.

89. *Letters 1913–1956*, trans. by Ralph Mannheim and ed. by John Willett (New York: Routledge, 1990), p. 204.

90. *Der Tui-Roman. Fragment* (Frankfurt a.M.: Suhrkamp, 1973).
91. *Letters*, p. 205.
92. *Letters*, p. 206.
93. *Letters*, p. 208.
94. *Bertolt Brecht Werke,* Prosa 2: Roman Fragmente und Romanentwürfe, ed. by Werner Hecht and others, 30 vols (Frankfurt a.M.: Suhrkamp, 1989), XVII, pp. 154–56.
95. 'Speech at the Second International Writers' Congress for the Defense of Culture', <https://www.marxists.org/subject/art/lit_crit/works/brecht/fascism-culture.htm> [accessed 9 February 2016].
96. *Jahrhundert*, pp. 133–34.
97. *Turning Point*, p. 347.
98. *Turning Point*, p. 119. Unattributed descriptions are my own.
99. Christopher Isherwood, *Isherwood and His Kind* (Minneapolis: University of Minnesota Press, 2001), p. 106.
100. Cited in Lenormand, *Confessions*, II, p. 377.
101. Sachs, p. 284.
102. Sperber, p. 52.
103. Mavis Gallant, 'Speck's Idea', in *Paris Stories* (New York: New York Review of Books, 2002), p. 149.
104. Aaron, p. 321.
105. Aaron, citing Eastman, p. 104.
106. Gillesse, p. 229.
107. Klaus Mann, *Het keerpunt: een autobiografie,* trans. by Willem van Toorn (Amsterdam: Arbeiderspers, 1987), p. 369. This is the Dutch translation of Mann's *Der Wendepunkt*. The English translation leaves out information deemed irrelevant to English-speaking readers.
108. Cowley, p. 59.
109. *Turning Point*, p. 182.
110. Erika and Klaus Mann, *Escape to Life: Deutsche Kultur im Exil* (Munich: Spangenberg, 1991), p. 54. (Originally published by Houghton Mifflin, Boston, 1939).
111. *Gide and the Crisis*, pp. 22, 32.
112. *Turning Point*, p. 120.
113. *Escape to Life*, p. 79.
114. Menno ter Braak, 'Schrijverscongres,' *Het Vaderland*, Kunst en Letteren, 24 June 1935, p. 9
115. *Escape to Life*, p. 181.
116. *Keerpunt*, p. 368.
117. *Kind dieser Zeit* (Hamburg: Rowohlt, 1967), p. 195.
118. *Turning Point*, p. 196.
119. *Christopher*, p. 265.
120. *Turning Point*, p. 123.
121. 'Amsterdam', *Die Sammlung* (February 1934), 326–28.
122. See Klaus Hermsdorf and others, *Exil in den Niederlanden*, pp. 119–20.
123. *The Correspondence of Walter Benjamin, 1910–1940,* ed. by Gershom Scholem and Theodor W. Adorno, trans. by R. Jacobson and Evelyn M. Jacobson (Chicago and London: University of Chicago Press, 1994), p. 484.
124. Hermsdorf, p. 125.
125. 'Notizen in Moskau', 72–83.
126. *Keerpunt*, p. 371.
127. *Keerpunt*, 45.
128. Diary entry 21 June 1935 <http://monacensia-dev.visuallibrary.de/content/pageview/12190> [accessed 13 January 2014].
129. 'Die Schriftsteller in Paris', *Die Sammlung*, 12 (1935), 724–25. Mann's observations on the Paris Congress appeared in the publication's last issue, two months after the event.
130. *Escape*, pp. 179–81.
131. Léon Hanssen, *Menno ter Braak 1902–1940: Leven en werk van een polemist*, 2 vols (Amsterdam: Balans, 2001), II, pp. 250–51.

132. Diary entry 24 June 1935.
133. *Jahrhundert*, p. 122.
134. 'De Duitse strijd tegen het Duitse idealisme', in *Die Sammlung: Een bloemlezing uit het emigranten-maandblad*, ed. by Gerda Meijerink (Amsterdam: Querido, 1983), p. 148. The original article appeared in *Die Sammlung*, August 1934.
135. 'Duitse strijd', pp. 152–55.
136. We do not know why Marcuse was unable to give that speech. Teroni and Klein note that the 'talk' was revised and enlarged and cite additional variations (pp. 530–31).
137. *Jahrhundert*, p. 199.
138. Klaus Mann was unhappy with Ter Braak's reviews of his 'first' autobiography *Kind dieser Zeit* and *Flucht in den Norden*, both published before 1935.
139. 'Emigranten-Literatur', in *De artikelen over emigrantenliteratuur 1933–1940*, selected and introduced by Francis Bulhof (The Hague: Uitgeverij BZZTôH, 1988), pp. 146–50. Ter Braak's controversial article appeared 29 December 1934.
140. 'Zur Debatte über die Emigranten-Literatur', in *Artikelen over emigrantenliteratuur*, pp. 155–59.
141. 'Zur Debatte', p. 156.
142. Menno ter Braak, 'King Christina. De emigranten vluchten in de geschiedenis. Barok en hysterie', *Het Vaderland*, Kunst en Letteren, 29 September 1935.
143. *Jahrhundert*, p. 179.
144. *Jahrhundert*, pp. 202–06. Marcuse put the Congress in 1938. Facts cited by Marcuse, combined with external evidence, leave no doubt that he was referencing the 1935 gathering.
145. *Jahrhundert*, p. 218. Unless otherwise indicated, the account that follows is from these memoirs, pp. 218–39.
146. 'Gespräch mit meinen Freunden', *Die Neue Weltbühne*, 21 (1937), 655–58.
147. *Het Vaderland,* Kunst en Letteren, 25 June 1935, p. 9
148. Stendhal, *Rome, Naples and Florence,* trans. and foreword by Richard N. Coe (London: John Calder, 1959), p. xxi.
149. *Briefwisseling Menno ter Braak/Eddy du Perron, 1930–1940*, 24 June and 4 July 1935. (Amsterdam: van Oorschot, 1965), pp. 226, 233.
150. *Briefwisseling Menno ter Braak/J. Greshoff 1926–1940*, 24 August 1935 <http://www.mennoterbraak.nl/tekst/braa002brie22_01/braa002brie22_01_0156.php> [accessed 9 December 2014]. Greshoff, like Du Perron, was part of the Dutch delegation but did not speak.
151. Ter Braak to Jan Greshoff, 26 June 1935.
152. *Land*, p. 540.
153. Thomas Mann, 'In Memoriam Menno ter Braak', in *Over Menno ter Braak*, pp. 8–9.
154. *Menno ter Braak*, Schrijversprentenboek (Amsterdam: De Bezige Bij, 2nd printing, 1980), p. 36.

FIG. 5. Lion Feuchtwanger
(Photo Florence Homolka/Feuchtwanger Memorial Library)

# CHAPTER 3

❖

# The Congress, 24–25 June

## I. Lion Feuchtwanger

I have never been able to look upon world history other than as a
bitter and unceasing struggle waged by a thinking few.[1]

Eyewitnesses are the worst sources[2]

— *1* —

Lion Feuchtwanger and Ludwig Marcuse knew each other well. In the thirties they lived across the road from one another in Sanary-sur-Mer. In the nineteen-forties and fifties they made their home in southern California, Feuchtwanger in Pacific Palisades, Marcuse in Beverly Hills, an hour's drive apart. In Pacific Palisades, Feuchtwanger and his wife Marta occupied a palatial mansion, Villa Aurora, overlooking the Pacific Ocean. There were few visitors. Lion did not go out much except for some brisk early morning walks to stay in shape. He had his library, a writing table positioned with a view of the ocean, and worked from morning until well into the evening. 'I can write up to seven pages on the typewriter within one hour, and write poetry up to four pages during the same time. I lose twelve ounces during the hour of writing poetry.' He slept six hours daily and spent four-and-a half minutes exercising.[3] Now and then, breaking the routine, Lion and Marta played host to a handful of guests. Feuchtwanger read from his works, followed by home-made apple strudel topped with whipped cream.[4] And from time to time, the 'anchorite' at 520 Paseo Miramar dashed off a telegram to the Kremlin wishing Stalin nothing but the best.[5]

There had been two great influences on his writing, Feuchtwanger acknowledged in 1938 on the occasion of the complete Russian edition of his works: the imperialist war and Soviet socialist society. For the bourgeoisie, he wrote, literature was a luxury, a 'highly sophisticated pastime' without a vital function. For the Soviet citizen, on the other hand, literature was a commodity. The Soviet experience had helped free him 'from certain class prejudices into which I was born and spent the largest part of my life,' and thus helped him turn his back on 'dangerous aestheticism'. There was one more area in which the Soviet experience had conditioned his approach. Soviet nationality policy had been instructive in resolving the dilemma of dual loyalty: one could simultaneously be a citizen of a nation and a citizen of the world.[6]

— 2 —

Lion Feuchtwanger grew up in Munich, where his father, an Orthodox Jew, owned a lucrative margarine business (he would 'sell' his business on Friday and 'buy' it back on Monday). Lion studied literature and philosophy in Munich and Berlin, earning a doctorate in 1907. In World War I he spent 'seventeen days as a prisoner of war'.[7] Before switching to historical fiction, Feuchtwanger wrote and directed plays, occasionally with Bertolt Brecht.

Feuchtwanger made a name for himself in Germany and abroad, especially the latter, with two historical novels, one set in eighteenth-century Württemberg, the other in Bavaria in the early 1920s: *Jud Süss Oppenheimer*, in 1925, and *Erfolg. Drei Jahre Geschichte einer Provinz*, in 1930. The former told the story of the 'court Jew' Jud Süss, moneylender to the Duke of Württemberg, who ends up paying for his protector's profligate ways by death on the gallows. *Erfolg* exposed the sleaziness of Bavarian politics and justice and featured a Hitler proxy. In 1940, *Jud Süss Oppenheimer* found its way to the German screen. 'Based on a true story', it said in the opening credits, and a slick perversion it was. Germany's most expensive feature film to date, *Jud Süss*, produced under the auspices of Joseph Goebbels's Ministry of Public Enlightenment and Propaganda, was a far cry from such over-the-top 'documentaries' as *The Eternal Jew* with its opening scene of rats, i.e. Jews, crawling out of the sewer to spread disease among the unwashed masses.

In 1925, Feuchtwanger purchased a mansion in a leafy, upper class section of Berlin. 'I had my books around me. From my garden a peaceful little pine-grove sloped gently down to a peaceful little pond. I was content.' Eight years later Nazi thugs ransacked the author's splendid Berlin villa and destroyed his beloved library.[8] On 10 May, *Jud Süss Oppenheimer* and *Erfolg* went up in flames in a literary auto-da-fé that consumed thousands of books branded as 'unGerman'.

At the time of Hitler's advent to power, 'the Nazis' best-hated author'[9] happened to be on a lecture tour in the United States and was advised by the German ambassador in Washington not to return to his homeland. The Feuchtwangers decided to settle in France.

— 3 —

In the 1920s, German writers and artists discovered Sanary-sur-Mer. In the thirties, the fishing village on the French Riviera began filling out with Hitler's unwanted highbrows, and this is where Feuchtwanger chose to put down new roots upon his return from America. Marta, Feuchtwanger's wife since 1912, rented a cream-coloured villa overlooking the Mediterranean surrounded by flowers, succulents and fig trees, and Feuchtwanger got back to work, turning out one book after another and rebuilding the extensive library destroyed by the Nazis. And those books weren't just for show. At home in many languages, ancient and modern, Feuchtwanger was as erudite as he was industrious. In *The House of Desdemona*, unfinished at the time of his death in 1958, the learned author ranged far and wide to illuminate the evolution of historical fiction, a genre of literary he loved unabashedly.[10] This was one love that did not go unrequited, conferring a life-style most writers can only dream of. His books sold better abroad than in his native Germany. 'The success of his books in America', noted a French journalist, 'permits him to live like a lord of literature [...]'.[11]

Sanary-sur-Mer suited Feuchtwanger to a T. 'I had my books around me. Olive-groves sloped down to a deep, azure sea. I was content. I had not the remotest idea of ever moving from that house.' The Sanary idyll came to an end in the spring of 1940. In mid-May the threat of war prompted the French government to issue an order for all German nationals residing in Paris and surroundings to report for internment. The 56-year-old Feuchtwanger reckoned he was safely out of reach. When it became clear he had miscalculated, it was too late. 'Again and again', he observed in *The Devil in France*, his memoir of his internment in Les Milles in the south of France,

> I have surrounded myself with things I enjoyed owning; again and again I have set up a very ample writing table at a place from which I could look out over a beautiful landscape; again and again I have ranged a few thousand books about me. [...] In other words, without too many evasions, what held me was my fundamental laziness, my attachment to my comforts, my lack of imagination.[12]

Feuchtwanger, Ludwig Marcuse remarked in his memoirs, lived inside four walls like the 'rings of a fortress'. The first was a highly developed sense of self. 'His success confirmed the high opinion he had of himself.' Soft-spoken and composed, it was not easy to get a rise out of him. The second was the pride in belonging to the oldest *Kulturvolk* in the world, a descendant of the people who had brought reading and writing — reason, 'God's first-born child' — into the world. The third, a very thick wall, was an 'unproblematic world view.' And, lastly, wherever he happened to be — Munich, Sanary-sur-Mer, Pacific Palisades — he surrounded himself with books.[13]

For all his bookishness, Feuchtwanger engineered escapes from two internment camps and made a break for the United States via Portugal. 'As I look out of the window of my hotel in New York over Central Park', he mused in October 1940, 'with its lines of skyscrapers to right and left, as I look out over the great, throbbing city bustling with the pursuits of peace, I ask myself again and again: Can this be real? Am I really here? And if so, how?'[14]

— 3 —

Feuchtwanger arrived in Paris on 23 June. Being told that he was to give his speech in French was only the first of a series of frustrations. 'The organization leaves something to be desired', he recorded in his diary.[15] 'I am travelling with a secretary and translator. We are working frantically.' A life-long problem sleeper, anxiety about the French kept him awake. The next day, racing against the clock (he was scheduled to speak that evening), he called in a second translator as well as a third secretary. He arrived at the Congress at 8.30, exhausted and fighting stage fright. By the time he got to speak, it was close to midnight.

In his discourse he linked his resort to, and defence of, historical fiction to combating fascism. 'As for me', he asserted in 'Du sens et du non-sens du roman historique',

> ever since I began writing, I have endeavoured to write historical novels on behalf of reason, against stupidity and violence, against what Marx calls the descent into the void of history. [...] [T]he historical novel is the weapon that best suits me and I fully intend to continue to avail myself of it.

The historical novel, Feuchtwanger's forte, would seem to need no defending, least of all by Feuchtwanger, a skilled and successful practitioner whose book sales spoke volumes — 'the greatest representative of the historical novel of our time', according to Marcuse.[16] But defend it he did, and where better to strike a blow for this oft-disparaged medium than at a writers' congress? 'Rare are those', he said, 'who contest the usefulness of writing *contemporary* novels; rare, too, are those who question the usefulness of historical *research*. And then again there are untold others who refuse to give historical *novels* any credit whatsoever.'

In a nutshell, Feuchtwanger argued that historical novels were better able to convey history than history proper. The writer of historical fiction is an artist expressing his personal view of the contemporary world, transmitted in a pleasing, accessible format by means of 'distancing'. The historical novelist was no different from the authors of the Greek tragedies, the Old and New Testaments and Shakespeare's histories. They, too, expressed their views on contemporary life through works of art set in the past and their impact was still being felt centuries and millennia later. Besides, the accuracy of everyday histories was 'extremely contestable' because the facts can be arranged as historians see fit. The artist-historian made no pretence of being bound by the facts.

The speech came off just fine, he wrote in his diary, but it was 'all a waste because of the bad organization'.

The experience appeared to have soured Feuchtwanger on this and other such congresses. In *Paris Gazette,* his novel set amid the German émigré community in Paris in 1935, the main character, Sepp Trautwein, drew a parallel between do-nothing congresses and a couple of joiners quarrelling about Trotsky instead of attending to the door they were hired to fix.

> Oh, if instead of worrying over these great affairs they would only worry about the small ones first! If instead of calling congresses and discussing large political resolutions, they would only open an office for providing useful advice and reliable information about the getting of passports![17]

Socially, though, Paris was top-notch. Friendships were renewed and new acquaintances made. Feuchtwanger mentions speaking with Babel, Tolstoi, Heinrich Mann, and Leopold Schwarzschild. The Russians especially had received him warmly. 'Gorky had praised *Erfolg*.'[18]

The following day, Feuchtwanger paid a visit to the Russian embassy.

— 4 —

Feuchtwanger visited the USSR in the autumn of 1936, accompanied by the photographer and artist Eva Hermann, Ludwig and Sacha Marcuse. Feuchtwanger stayed ten weeks. Feuchtwanger, as always, recalled Marcuse, was of good cheer and unflappable, even when, at the Czech-Polish border, guards combed through his and Eva's numerous suitcases, sending shirts and skirts flying, and snapped his fountain pen in half to see if by any chance he was in possession of the Spanish crown jewels someone had recently made off with.[19]

Feuchtwanger arrived in Moscow on Tuesday 1 December. A delegation of Soviet authors and photographers were on hand to greet him and he gave many interviews. The government organ *Izvestia* wrote:

> In the course of the last years Feuchtwanger has become one of the most read authors among us. To what does he owe this success? Everything Feuchtwanger has written, whether historical novels or [...] or realistic works treating contemporary events, is permeated with a fervent love for humanity and a no less fervent hatred of barbarism.

'I am greatly moved by the warm reception that I found in the Soviet Union', he told the *Deutsche Zentral-Zeitung*, a German-language newspaper published in Moscow, 'especially by the refreshing encounter with my young Moscow readers'. As for the things he meant to accomplish in the Soviet Union, Feuchtwanger mentioned discussing film scripts (*Erfolg* and *Die Geschwister Oppenheim*); contacting the editors and translators of his plays; and consulting with his fellow editors of *Das Wort*, the émigré journal published in Moscow. 'Most of all, I will endeavour to connect with leading individuals and the masses of the Soviet Union.'[20]

Throughout his ten-week stay Feuchtwanger was feted like a king. His diary seemed to take note of each and every occasion. The crème de la crème of Soviet society was trotted out to meet and greet him: diplomats, film directors, playwrights, writers, performers, and so on. Plays, films, and operas, much of which met with his approval, filled most evenings. A visit to an automobile plant named after Stalin elicited the comment '*Grossartig*' — fantastic.

The very plush red carpet the Soviet rolled out for the esteemed author stopped short of his hotel room, however. Hotel Metropol did not do well by him. Diary entry 1 December: 'Since everything is full up because of a Soviet Congress, I am provisionally lodged in a very bad and comfortless room and can't unpack. I lunch with Eva, very bad and very expensive. I am given a fur coat. The room smells hideous. I am proud of the reception and unhappy about all this discomfort.' 'Much honour and little comfort', he said of the room he was assigned the next day. Other complaints involved taps that did not dispense water, light switches that failed to produce light, the taste in furniture, and the service.[21] There would be no end to his accommodation woes.

In the course of his visit Feuchtwanger contributed three articles to *Pravda*. 'Fascism and the German Intelligentsia' (28 January) amounted to a short course on Nazi disgust with intellectuals, succinctly conveyed in a simple, declarative sentence: 'A man of German blood can never belong to the intelligentsia.' Already in 1930, Feuchtwanger noted as well, he had predicted the extinction of intelligent life in the event of a fascist takeover.[22] 'An Aesthete in the Soviet Union' (30 December) argued that André Gide, the aesthete in question, was too constrained by aesthetics to grasp the true nature of Communism. Gide was surprised to find things did not quite mesh with his Paris-centric worldview; that Western-style freedom of the press was non-existent, for example. The new Soviet Constitution, adopted in December 1936 and ratified the following month, Feuchtwanger explained, was unlike bourgeois constitutions in that it bestowed true freedom and equality rather than their phoney equivalents. Stalin's 'glorification' did not originate in the Kremlin but was a product of a grateful citizenry indebted to the embodiment of socialism as the source of bread, meat, growth, security, and good government. 'Gide,' Feuchtwanger summed up, 'preferred to focus his attention on the absence of toilet paper.'[23] The third article appeared on 30 January, about which more later.

On 7 January, *Pravda* published a photograph on page 7 of a broadly smiling Feuchtwanger clad in a double-breasted suit and tie flanked by nine smiling members of a factory reading group. Two days later Feuchtwanger appeared with Stalin on the paper's front page.

'Exceptionally unpleasant day', Feuchtwanger recorded in his diary on 8 January. The room was cold; he had not slept much and had forgotten to take a laxative. His appointment with Stalin was at noon. The translator was not up to speed. Stalin danced around the question regarding the writer's freedom. Other topics touched on the Stalin cult, democracy, and the forthcoming trials of Karl Radek and Georgy Piatikov. Asked, on camera, to give his opinion of the First Secretary immediately after the interview, Feuchtwanger said that his first impression was that Stalin was extremely down to earth. He further credited Stalin with a sense of humour and revealed that the First Secretary had struck him as 'an ideal leader of the people' [...], 'a true representative of 170 million Soviets'.[24] The conversation lasted more than three hours. Feuchtwanger returned to his hotel room 'completely exhausted'. 'All the newspapers', he recorded in his diary on 9 January, 'report my interview with Stalin in grand fashion.'

Feuchtwanger's doings did not go unnoticed by the foreign press. A week after the interview with Stalin, Feuchtwanger spoke to representatives of several English-language papers and news sources, including *The New York Times* — in all instances, 'somewhat carelessly'.

On 23 January, Feuchtwanger sat down in a crowded courtroom and listened to the prosecution lay out its case against the 'Anti-Soviet Trotskyist Centre' spearheaded by Radek and Piatikov. The proceedings wore on from morning until well into the evening. The translator, Julia Anenkova — 'stupid Anenkova' — got on his nerves.[25] Despite a nagging cold, he sat through half a dozen sessions, including the last one. Indicted for treason, espionage and 'wrecking', the accused entered the courtroom packed with 300 spectators. In the end, Feuchtwanger acknowledged that he had been impressed with the speeches of the accused and expressed doubt about the sentencing. 'Radek's pardon throws everything in doubt, a farce.'[26] Radek was sentenced to ten years of hard labour in a penal colony.

In 'First Impressions of This Trial', which appeared in *Pravda* on 30 January, Feuchtwanger stated that he had been satisfied with the proceedings and that there could no longer be any doubt that Trotsky played a significant role at a critical moment in time as the mastermind behind the actions of the accused, indicative of a return to the right. The historical meaning of the trial, Feuchtwanger concluded, was that of creating 'a new barrier against war'.[27]

— 5 —

In the third week of February, back on the Riviera, Feuchtwanger faced a by now familiar dilemma: to tell or not to tell. His return from the Soviet Union had been marked by 'visceral attacks in the press'.[28] For in 1937 the Soviet Union was less popular among intellectuals than in 1935–36, when Gide had come out with his shattering exposé. Dismissing tell-all as 'short-sighted and without merit', Feuchtwanger opted for the riskier course, 'for no writer', he declared, 'who has seen something great should ever withhold evidence, even if the thing is unpopular and his words are distasteful to many'.

The result was a slim book titled *Moscow 1937: My Visit Described for My Friends*. 'I sympathized inevitably', Feuchtwanger wrote in the foreword, 'with the experiment of basing the construction of a gigantic state on reason alone, and I went to Moscow hoping that the experiment was succeeding [...] If a social system is to prosper, it must be built upon judgment and reason. [...] 'I have never been able', he went on,

> to look upon world history in any other way than as a bitter and unceasing struggle waged by a thinking few. I have always ranged myself on the side of reason, and it was thus inevitable that I should sympathize with the gigantic experiment which is being conducted from Moscow.[29]

For an 'honoured guest' to be visiting at 'a disturbed time it was not always easy', Feuchtwanger conceded, 'to find a suitable form for such criticism or terms which avoided at the same time indecision and tactlessness'. The 'disturbed time' referred to the second batch of show trials then unfolding.

The substance of that slim book did not in essence deviate from the *Pravda* article about Gide, and the Russians had reason to be pleased: they could stop worrying about Feuchtwanger pulling another Gide. The expanded version reached a much wider audience, however. Gide pronounced the Russian worker lazy, which only showed a lack of understanding of the foundational Marxist principle from each according to his ability, to each according to his need. Gide complained about the younger generation's lack of interest in the world at large. Not so, said Feuchtwanger; and while Gide spoke of Muscovites' 'indolence', Feuchtwanger was impressed by their 'activity and industry'. Russia's capital exuded an 'atmosphere of harmony and contentment, even of happiness'. Housing was a problem, yes, as was bureaucracy, but the 'citizens of Moscow joke about these minor inconveniences'. On the whole, economic planning was doing its job, and life was getting better by the day. Old and young were well cared for. 'How sturdily and with what calm confidence do they [the young] face life, feeling that that are organic parts of a purposeful whole.' If Gide was taken aback by the disparity of income, Feuchtwanger saw it as a necessary stage in the building of a system based on the distribution of wealth. Gide's perception of rampant conformism was true, Feuchtwanger acknowledged, but only up to a point; 'Bolshevist self-criticism' was no empty phrase, either. What else did he find? That the Five Year Plans in all likelihood had been subject to sabotage. That books were prized possessions. That authors who 'strike the note of historic optimism in all their works' enjoyed preferential treatment; that artists 'tied to the state's apron strings' risked endangering their creativity. That freedom of speech and press was 'by no means ideal.' That Moscow's thirty-eight theatres drew large, appreciative crowds.

As a Jew, Feuchtwanger was not a little impressed with the progress being made on 'solving the ancient, vexatious, and apparently insoluble Jewish question'. To Feuchtwanger, Stalin's formula for dealing with the nationality question, 'national in form, international in substance', seemed tailor-made for his beleaguered people. Jews felt 'in harmony' with the new state and quickly adapted to the new dispensation. Already, Feuchtwanger learned, Jews had bested the Don Cossacks in agriculture, and not only in agriculture: they had also 'proved to be better riders'.

*Moscow 1937* also revisited the interview with Stalin and the trial he had been cleared to attend. Feuchtwanger found Stalin, a slight figure 'lost in the vast room of the Kremlin', to be reserved, congenial, and troubled by his idolization. Stalin detailed the charges against Piatikov, Radek, Bukharin, and Rykov, and 'spoke bitterly and with feeling of the writer Radek', his one-time friend and adviser. While Feuchtwanger had had his doubts about the earlier Zinoviev trial, in Moscow's courtroom, he related in *Moscow 1937*, 'doubts melted away as naturally as salt dissolves in water', adding: 'If that was lying or prearranged, then I don't know what truth is'. Trotskyists, Feuchtwanger concluded, as he had in the 30 January article in *Pravda*, were likely to 'have come to an arrangement with the Fascists'.

Not surprisingly, in the chapter comparing Trotsky and Stalin, the former came out second best: a 'great writer' but no 'great statesman'. In Moscow, Feuchtwanger had been impressed with Stalin's humility; in Sanary, he accused Trotsky, whom he had never met, of 'unparalleled arrogance'. Trotsky was 'the rocket soon spent, Stalin the warming, lasting fire'. The glow emitted by Stalin lasted well beyond ten weeks.

Feuchtwanger had seen enough to conclude that the Soviet experiment was succeeding, that there was more 'light than shadow'. 'What I have understood is excellent', he wrote, citing Socrates, 'from which I conclude that the rest which I have not understood is also excellent'.

In the *Pravda* piece on Gide, Feuchtwanger wrote that by publishing his thoughts at a time when Spain was under attack Gide played into the hands of the opponents of socialism. *Moscow 1937* likewise was written with an eye on the European political situation, Popular Front and the Spanish Civil War. Appreciative of the attention lavished on his person, he appeared loath to turn on his generous hosts, which explains why he did not lace his account with the frustrations he encountered in the course of his sojourn.

Feuchtwanger's response to the abuses Western writers had seen and reported was that 'history cannot be made with gloves on'. The dictates of a socialist economy required 'a temporary modification of what is today called democracy'. '[W]hich do you prefer', he challenged,

> that the great mass of the people should have less meat, bread, and butter and, instead, that you should have greater freedom of writing, or that you should have less freedom of writing and the great mass of the people more bread, meat, and butter? That, for a writer of responsibility, is no easy problem.

'One does not dare', Feuchtwanger remarked toward the end of this little book,

> to defend oneself against the oncoming barbarism with the fist or even only
> with words, one does it half-heartedly, with vague gestures. [...] One breathes
> again when one comes from this oppressive atmosphere of a counterfeit
> democracy and hypocritical humanism into the invigorating atmosphere of
> the Soviet Union. [...] It does one good, after all the compromise of the West
> to see an achievement such as this, to which a man can say Yes, yes, yes, with
> all his heart; and because it seemed ungrateful to keep this 'Yes' within me, I
> wrote this book.[30]

Presumably Ludwig Marcuse was among the friends Feuchtwanger addressed in
*Moscow 1937.* Marcuse read it and concluded that the Villa Aurora occupant was the
kind of traveller who sees much but learns little.[31] 'His dogma kept him from seeing
the facts that stared him in the face'; that, Marcuse resolved, was Feuchtwanger's
'political Achilles heel'. Feuchtwanger was a rather better judge of Nazism. On
receiving the news that Hitler had taken power, the first words out of his mouth
were: 'This means war'.[32]

— *6* —

Feuchtwanger lived through some of the most turbulent times the world had ever
seen. During these same years a new medium, film, was coming into its own as a
form of art and popular entertainment. Menno ter Braak, an early champion of film
in its avant-garde form (he was a founding member, in 1927, along with Joris Ivens
and others, of the Netherlands Film League), was quick to spot a filmic element
in Feuchtwanger's novels, although not of the kind he considered particularly
engaging. The thing Ter Braak found 'insufferable' was Feuchtwanger's 'irritating'
habit of 'painting with words', swaddling his characters in double and triple
adjectives. Excessive description, contended Ter Braak, catered to readers with little
imagination. No fan of American escapist film making, the Dutchman discerned
a similar dumbing-down in Feuchtwanger's works, sacrificing the power of words
on the altar of 'staging', as though he were working on a film in which every facial
expression and physical attribute had to be scripted.[33]

By contrast, post-war German television producers eagerly embraced Feuchtwanger's alleged 'description mania', adapting a number of his novels for television
in the vein of Britain's Masterpiece theatre: *Erfolg, Die Geschwister Oppenheim,* and
*Exil.* The so-called *Wartesaal Trilogie* is available for home viewing in a boxed DVD
set containing seven disks. A blurb that appeared in the media retailer *Weltbilt*
retailed the trilogy as follows:[34]

> Lion Feuchtwanger, one of the most widely read German-language authors
> of the twentieth century, created one of the most impressive and artistic
> works of German exile literature. He made historical events comprehensible
> and recorded the horrors of fascism for posterity, so that they would never be
> forgotten.

## II. Unpopular Front

'The Congress has become rather fascinating after all, in that the
left opposition got in some powerful blows.'
Eddy du Perron to Menno ter Braak, 26 June.[35]

— *1* —

The wheels started coming off the evening of Monday 24 June. Until then, the
Soviets had things pretty well in hand. With few exceptions, speaker after speaker
paid tribute to the 'great experiment', the cradle of 'the new man', the wave of the
future, 'history's last laugh', the uncontested leader in the struggle against fascism
and in the defence of culture. After three days it indeed began to look as though
the Russians were in the clear. Breton had been effectively marginalized and every
effort to bring up Victor Serge cut off at the pass. Speakers critical of the Soviet
Union had been polite and respectful. Nevertheless, the official story of a people
united on a forced march on the road toward a wrinkle-free society was not one
destined to survive the Congress.

Throughout the Congress, the big guns had filled the prime-time evening
slots. But the writers on the periphery of the literary firmament had not come to
Paris merely to gaze in awe at the stars, and the organizers had set aside Monday
afternoon to unleash the second tier. That session, piggy-backing on the previous
evening's, centred on Nation and Culture. Five of the thirteen speakers from
countries that had become fascist (two Bulgarians, one Latvian, one Greek and
one Portuguese) lamented the resultant suppression of free thought. Two spots
went to German exiles. Writers from several Soviet Republics confirmed that their
independence under Communist rule had created the conditions in which their
respective cultures could at last spread their wings. One such, Ukrainian poet and
playwright Ivan Mikitenko, hailed the discovery of 'the soul of the Soviet people'
as the greatest discovery ever. Poland's Samuel Loeb Schneiderman contended that
Jews topped the list of proletarian writers. Stalin's dictum about writers being the
engineers of the soul was cited more than once as a springboard to creativity. The
afternoon session passed without incident.

The evening session tackled The Problem of Creativity and the Dignity of
Thought. The speeches traced a familiar trajectory: part analysis (literature and
society); part venting (horrors of fascism); part cheer-leading (blessings of Soviet
Communism); part literary debate (socialist realism v. Western literature); part
soul-searching (what to do?); and part dullness (a large part). Dullness in itself is
no crime, but dullness designed to keep uncomfortable truths under lock and key
is something else again. The session started out tamely enough. The French film
critic Léon Moussinac credited the Russian revolution with rescuing 'the great
cultural human values and preparing the culture of the future'. Nikolai Tikhonov
extolled Soviet optimism. Anna Seghers embroidered on 'L'amour de la Patrie' and
rued the absence in the German language of 'literary frescoes' with the social sweep
of a Balzac, Dickens, or Dostoevsky. The translator into English of Stalin's White

Sea epic, Amabel Williams-Ellis, disclosed that only a very small percentage of the British reading public read serious literature.

Gaetano Salvemini was next. The exiled Italian parliamentarian and liberal historian began by pointing out that it was wrong to conflate bourgeois societies that persecuted writers with those that did not, citing Heinrich Mann as an example of an author who was left quite alone in pre-Hitler Germany but had to flee for his life in 1933. E. M. Forster's plaint about the shortcomings of British liberty — 'the dictator-spirit working quietly behind the façade of constitutional forms' — struck the fugitive from Mussolini's Italy as not a little simple-minded, given that in Mussolini's Italy Forster's remark carried a prison sentence of some two dozen years. And however harassed, writers in bourgeois-democratic countries like Great Britain, France, and the United States at the very least could expect to die with their 'dignity of the spirit' intact. Criticize, but know where to draw the line, Salvemini cautioned.

Compared to the Soviets, Western writers like E. M. Forster were getting off lightly. The Soviet delegates, said Salvemini, citing Gide's speech, portrayed their country as one 'which promises intellectual freedom for all of its children' (payback for Gide's refusal to sign a petition on behalf of Lauro de Bosis?). Nonsense! exclaimed the professor. A nation that insists on muzzling an enemy that no longer poses a threat, Salvemini pressed on as if faced with a classroom of dim-witted students, demonstrated a profound lack of confidence in its ideas and intellectual capacity of its people: freedom was the 'right to heresy, non-conformity vis-à-vis the official culture'. Trotsky's *History of the Russian Revolution* was banned in the Soviet Union. 'It is in Russia that Victor Serge is a prisoner.' There was only one logical conclusion, and the liberal historian supplied it: 'In Germany there are concentration camps, in Italy penal islands, and in the Soviet Union there is Siberia.' In the context of the Congress, there was no greater heresy.

Salvemini's speech created quite a stir. 'Immediately following Salvemini's speech', wrote an eyewitness,

> the public split into Trotskyists and Stalinists, and the atmosphere became charged with politics. The adversaries insulted one another in the jargon and arguments of the two factions that divided Russian opinion. We were no longer in France, at a conference devoted to the defence of freedom of speech, but somewhere else, in Moscow, in a Communist party cell. There were remarks, shouts, near blows. Malraux, agitated and manoeuvring feverishly, declared, under threat of expulsion and in total submission to Stalinist orthodoxy, that the question of Victor Serge was closed.[36]

The Popular Front needed Stalin, ruler over a sixth of the planet's surface, more than Trotsky, a fugitive perpetually on the run with nothing to show for his troubles but the clothes on his back.

Victor Serge was no stranger to the French left (he wrote in French). For more than a decade Serge had been publishing works of both fiction and non-fiction. The novels (*Men in Prison* (1930), *Birth of our Power* (1931) and *Conquered City* (1932)) in particular had impressed the critics. A number of French writers formed a committee aimed at securing his freedom, infuriating Moscow. Among these

Henry Poulaille, a staunch defender of proletarian causes but no friend of Stalin's Russia, had been invited to speak at the Congress, provided he left Victor Serge out of it. Poulaille refused and was scratched from the speakers' list. In the evening of the 24th, Poulaille, accompanied by half a dozen comrades, entered the Mutualité determined to be heard, only to be ejected 'manu militari' in plain sight of the wooden bas relief in the lobby with its four frolicking maidens locked in sisterly embrace: *Si tous les gens du monde /Voulaient se donner la main* (If all the peoples in the world would join hands).

In the meantime the Congress resumed its formal course. Heinrich Mann proffered that the suppression of dignity of thought avenged itself on society as a whole, and flattered the writers assembled at the Mutualité as 'the defenders of an illustrious tradition'. Lion Feuchtwanger, trusting reason to prevail, put in a good word for writers of historical novels like himself, advocating parity with conventional fiction. Tristan Tzara contended that there existed no greater poetic value than that which coincided with the proletarian revolution. Jan Petersen, masked so as to hide his identity, brought the Congress up to speed with respect to the activities of the German anti-Hitler underground literary scene.

— 2 —

Malraux was wrong: *l'affaire Victor Serge* was far from closed. In less than twenty-four hours the match struck by Salvemini lit the torch Magdeleine Paz had brought along for the occasion. A photograph, taken in the afternoon of 25 June, depicts Paz standing behind a skirted table, prim and proper in a dark dress offset by a white, doily-like collar, flanked by Henri Barbusse, Paul Nizan, André Malraux, André Gide, and Bodo Uhse. Malraux again presided and read a declaration from the German delegation proclaiming the right to asylum a human right. Dispensing with the ritualistic pro-forma incantations to the world's only workers' state, Paz wasted no time getting to the point: the disparity between a Congress convened to defend 'the dignity of the word' and the plight of Victor Serge, banished to the Russian hinterland for doing exactly that.[37]

Magdeleine Paz had a long history of working on behalf of righteous causes. Pacifist, feminist, socialist, human rights advocate (including those of blacks), Paz was not cowed by the Soviet-imposed conspiracy of silence. Having made Serge's cause her own, drumming up support among the movers and shakers of France's literary establishment, she approached Romain Rolland. Today Rolland is best remembered — if remembered at all — as the author of *Jean-Christophe*, a ten-volume doorstop of a book long since mouldering on antiquarian bookshelves. Rolland's voice carried weight and his reputation as an irreproachable pacifist transcended national boundaries. Asked to join the committee to free Serge, Rolland responded that he supported their efforts on behalf of freedom of expression, but no more. 'I am convinced that as soon as he returned, he would put himself at the head of the Trotskyite opposition', and went on to say that although he considered Serge a great writer, he could not lend his name to an opposition he considered harmful, 'especially at this hour'.[38]

Rolland thought the world of Stalin, 'ascetic and thoughtful'. In the late spring of 1935 Rolland was the guest of honour at a dinner hosted by the Kremlin denizen. What, Stalin asked, could he do for this excellent friend of the Soviet Union? This was the moment, scripted as in a play, Rolland had been waiting for all evening: 'Free Serge', Rolland responded as if on cue. 'Serge, Serge', replied his host, mulling over the name as if he couldn't quite place it. 'But he is only a petty Soviet bureaucrat.' 'Petty bureaucrat, perhaps', countered Rolland, 'but without doubt a great French writer.'[39]

As this scenario was unfolding, Victor Serge had got hold of a newspaper with a photograph of the French author shaking Stalin's hand. 'Look at the face of that man', he said to his fourteen-year-old son Vlady. 'If we are going to be saved, it will be now or never.'[40]

(Serge, however, had neither been impressed with Rolland's efforts nor with the support of writers generally. 'Believe me, my dear friend', he wrote to Trotsky months after regaining his freedom, 'I have no illusions whatever about men of letters, *ah non!*'.[41])

'To begin with, who is Victor Serge?' Paz asked rhetorically, picking up the story from the time Victor Kibalchich, the future Victor Serge, became politically active. Between the ages of seventeen and twenty Serge worked as a printer in Paris, 'a fiery and convinced anarchist'. Convicted, falsely Paz emphasized, of contributing to an anarchist plot to rob a bank that claimed several lives, Serge spent the next five years, 1912–1917, in solitary confinement. In 1917, barely at liberty, he took part in a failed workers' uprising in Barcelona led by anarchists. (It was there that Victor-Napoléon Kibalchich became Victor Serge.) Inspired by the outbreak of the Russian Revolution, Serge abandoned anarchism and tied his political future to Communism. Determined to help the beleaguered Soviet Union get on its feet, he arrived there in February 1919, just in time to pick up a gun in defence of Petrograd. Having been admitted to the Communist Party, he assumed the task of coordinating the struggles of the international proletariat. His devotion to the cause was beyond reproach. Articles and books poured forth from his pen. Excellent comrade, he won over many a sceptic.

In the drawn-out power struggle that ensued upon Lenin's death in 1924, Serge took Trotsky's side and, let's face it, Paz acknowledged, 'in his heart, he is a Trotskyist, but only in private conversation'. Exiled to Orenburg, deprived of books and newspapers, it is a life punctuated by hardship: his wife loses her reason, Serge is hospitalized and near death, Vlady practically an orphan. None of this, Paz underscored, was meant to evoke pity; the Congress was not the place for that; the Congress was there to uphold the principle that thought enjoins 'inalienable rights', including the freedom to write as one pleases. Serge's only 'crime' was to commit his thoughts in letters to friends abroad. As the first country to make a proletarian revolution, the Soviet Union should be the last to deprive individuals of the right to speak.

Toward the end of her long speech, Paz cited the three pillars Serge considered indispensable to the orderly functioning of any healthy society, but none more so than the socialist: the defence of man ('It must never be forgotten that a human being is a human being'); defence of truth ('I hold truth to be a precondition of intellectual and moral health'); and defence of thought ('respect for man implies his right to know everything and freedom to think'.). Throwing down the gauntlet, Paz appealed to the Congress of writers, 'the conscience of the people, ardent champions of dignity', to move beyond the empty phrases, 'oratorical jousting, the silence of libraries, the abstractions of the ivory tower' and rally to the defence of writers victimized for speaking their mind, no matter where. 'Let us be revolutionaries to the extent — and it is immense — writers ought to be'.

— 3 —

With Malraux, Gide, and the majority of writers and the gallery on its side, the Soviet delegation could easily have dismissed the charge of the pro-Serge surge as a tempest in a teacup and, with some twenty-four hours to go, let the Congress run its course. Challenged, the Soviets mounted a response. The response took the form of a debate, threaded, like the evening before, around the theme of the problem of creativity and the dignity of the word. Ilya Ehrenburg, Nikolai Tikhonov, Vladimir Kirshon, and Anna Seghers comprised the Soviet team. Speaking up for Serge were Magdeleine Paz and Belgian novelist Charles Plisnier. André Gide moderated.

Anna Seghers was the only non-Russian on the Soviet side. Those familiar with Seghers's work cannot help but be somewhat puzzled by the decision to gang up on Victor Serge, for in novels such as *Aufstand der Fischer von St. Barbara* *(Revolt of the Fishermen of Santa Barbara)*; *Der Kopflohn: Roman aus einem deutschen Dorf im Spätsommer 1932 (A Price on His Head)*, and *Das siebte Kreuz (The Seventh Cross)* she consistently championed the cause of the underdog and the hunted. The first-mentioned novel netted Germany's prestigious Kleist Prize. *The Seventh Cross*, published in the United States in 1942, became a Book-of the-Month Club selection and a Hollywood movie starring Spencer Tracy. By all accounts, Seghers was difficult to fathom; in interviews she gave nothing away. After the war, Seghers occupied important posts in East Germany's literary establishment. For staying the Stalinist course, she was awarded the DDR's gold-plated National Prize and the International Stalin Prize for Strengthening Peace Among Peoples, both in 1951. 'Ulbricht's Anna' died in 1983, aged 82.

Nikolai Tikhonov teed off. In his principal speech, delivered the previous evening, the Soviet poet and novelist, the son of a barber and a dressmaker, portrayed life in the Soviet Union as an earthly paradise in which Hobbes's war of all against all had at last been laid to rest. The fate of Victor Serge, Tikhonov argued, rested on a misunderstanding, or, possibly, a deliberate error. Seeing that he became a Soviet citizen of his own accord, the Soviets did not consider Serge a French writer: 'he ate our bread, knowingly submitted to the laws adopted by the entire working population of the USSR'. As a functionary of the state, Kibalchich took an active part in the counter-revolutionary activities of the Trotskyists that led to the assassination of Kirov. (Tikhonov deliberately referred to Serge's given name to reinforce his Russianness.) A legal decision taken by the Soviet government led to the writer's exile to Orenburg, 'where he lives and is employed by the translation bureau'. The noises about his hardships were false. 'We believe our government can freely dispose and refuse the right of departure to a political adversary. As an unpolitical author, I say in all honesty: among the enemies of the USSR, there is no one more dangerous than oppositionist Trotskyists on the left like Kibalchich.'

Magdeleine Paz responded that nothing that had been advanced against Victor Serge was true and accused the Soviet delegation of committing outright fraud, detracting from its prestige. 'These were fresh accusations that were pulled out from the suitcase of the delegate's bag of tricks. Why had they waited three years to articulate them?' It was a shame, Paz went on, that at a Congress 'dedicated to the "Defence of Thought"', Soviet writers would invoke reason of state to justify gagging a writer's voice'. A writer accused of transgressing the law, she said in closing, should be allowed to defend his beliefs in the full glare of public light.

Substituting Revolution for State, Ilya Ehrenburg argued future needs over present-day niceties. The Soviet captain acknowledged that the Revolution had injured some, even those who had formerly served it. On the other hand, the Revolution had the right to defend itself again those who wished it harm. 'There is one law, and that law requires that the individual subordinate himself before the future of the whole.' What was the freedom Paz had in mind? 'You come here with information. What the Soviet delegates bring from the Soviet Union, they carry in Soviet trunks. From which trunks do you pull your material?'

Charles Plisnier contended, like Paz before him, that the Congress would betray its very purpose if it failed to respond to these ridiculous charges. The specious distinction between Serge and Kibalchich did not fool anyone. The Belgian Marxist refuted the assertion that Serge was gainfully employed, as well as the 'stupid and odious' charge that had been involved in the Kirov murder: Serge had been deported two years before the assassination and was thousands of kilometres away.

Anna Seghers feared prolonging the discussion on a case she acknowledged required close attention, 'but not at this place'. Throwing the ball back into the opponents' court, Seghers wanted to know what the supposed fighters of fascism and defenders of the USSR had done 'for Carl von Ossietzky, or Ludwig Renn, or Erich Mühsam, whose fingers were cut off so he could not write to his parents before being executed?'[42]

The playwright Vladimir Kirshon injected a touch of the theatrical. When the Soviet writers speak, he declared, hundreds of thousands of combatants rise up behind them, prepared to lay down their lives for the USSR. These were the true defenders of culture. Let us not forget, Kirshon pointed out, that words directed against the Soviet Union had a way of turning into bullets. No one was entitled to deprive Soviet power of the right to turn those bullets against its enemies. The Soviet people stood foursquare behind its government.

The Soviets also had the support of André Gide, whose irrepressible habit of temporizing seemed to be taking a breather. Serge's case differed from the Dreyfus Affair, Gide noted, in that the latter entailed opposing reactionary forces embracing openly pre-fascist methods, and that, Gide said, deserved our hatred. Serge's trouble, on the other hand, concerned the Soviet Union, 'toward which goes our love and our admiration. The success of the Soviet Union comes first. In a case like this our faith is the greatest proof of love we can give the USSR'.

A few days later Gide spoke to the Soviet ambassador, who promised to forward a letter from Gide to Stalin. In it, Gide acknowledged that the Soviet Union undoubtedly had reason to pronounce Serge guilty, yet had been unconvinced by the arguments of the Russian speakers and done his utmost to avoid the discussion altogether.[43] Ten months later Stalin ordered Victor Serge's release.

— 4 —

*Victor Serge: Coda.*[44]

In June 1935 an 'International Congress of Writers for the Defence of Culture' took place in Paris, formally upon the initiative of such left-wingers as Alain, Barbusse, Romain Rolland, Élie Faure, André Gide, André Malraux, and Victor Margueritte. The actual initiative came from certain Communist back rooms that specialized in organizing congresses of this kind; their objective was to arouse a pro-Stalinist movement among the French intelligentsia and buy over a number of famous consciences. My friends decided to attend the Congress and demand to be heard. Some of them got themselves ejected by the stewards. Aragon and Ehrenburg manipulated the assembly in accordance with secret directives. Barbusse, Malraux, and Gide presided with some embarrassment. [...] Salvemini caused a scene by condemning 'all the oppressions' and mentioning my name. Gide, amazed to find that fierce efforts were being made to hush up the dispute, insisted on the ventilation of the matter, and Malraux, who was chairing the session, finally allowed Magdeleine Paz to speak: she spoke harshly, in fighting terms.

[...]

The delegation from the Soviet writers included two men with whom I had been on friendly terms, the poets Boris Pasternak and Nikolai Tikhonov, and also a person in the innermost circle of Party confidence, whom I had met in Moscow, the official journalist Mikhail Koltsov, a man as remarkable for his talent as for his pliant docility. Besides these there were the successful playwright Kirshon and the hack agitator-novelist Ehrenburg. Pasternak, who is at once the Mallarmé and Apollinaire of Russian poetry, a truly great writer and a victim of semi-persecution besides, kept in the background. The other four fulfilled instructions and declared without a blink that they knew nothing of the writer Victor Serge — these, my good colleagues of the Soviet Writers' Union! All they knew of was a 'Soviet citizen, a confessed counter-revolutionary, who had been a member of the conspiracy which had ended in the murder of Kirov.' As he declaimed this from the platform, Koltsov did not suspect that in 1939 he himself would disappear, in complete obscurity, into the G.P.U. prisons. Kirshon did not suspect that two years later, he would disappear himself, dubbed a 'terrorist-Trotskyist' — he whose pen had never been anything than strictly conformist. Ehrenburg forgot his flight from Russia, his banned novels, his accusation against Bolshevism of 'crucifying Russia'. Tikhonov forgot his hymns to Courage, in those splendid epic ballads of his that I had translated into French. Nobody there could foresee the grim tumbrils of the Moscow Trials, but they knew of the 127 executions of innocents; these had been publicly announced the day after Nikolayev's deed [Kirov's assassin] and, according to the Soviet press, were even stoutly approved by humanists such as Jean-Richard Bloch and Romain Rolland. The shameless statement that justified my captivity by a murder committed two years after my arrest sent a shiver down more than one spine. André Gide went to see the Soviet Ambassador, who could give him no enlightenment at all.

## III. André Breton

René Crevel's sacrifice, if we may call it that, had not been in vain. Breton was to have his say after all. His speech was to be read by fellow Surrealist Paul Éluard, the closing act to a tumultuous day.

Breton was not the type to stop blowing the Surrealist horn and check it in the lobby of the Mutualité as if it were an umbrella; he was, in Dalí's words, a 'man of integrity and straight as a St Andrew's cross'.[45] By the time Éluard took the stage, however, it was already after midnight — 'when the hall was already emptying out and the lights were being switched off', bitterly recalled Breton years later.[46] There was more than one way to administer a slap.

The speech read by Éluard made short work of the Soviet game plan. 'Breton' took aim at the 'defence of culture' rallying cry, arguing that writers on France's extreme right could claim no less without batting an eye; better to start out defining the precise nature of the threat. From there, Breton went on to skewer Moscow's sharp turn to the right, soft-pedalling revolution. He did not buy the argument from 'harsh necessity' — Hitler's recent decision to introduce the draft and to begin rearming. Overnight French workers were supposed to have a dog in France's cultural heritage, and defend it at all cost. France did not become any less imperialist for being allied with the Soviet Union. The new line had nothing to do with securing the peace, as claimed. Rather, it would speed up the arms race and make war more likely. To Breton none of it made sense.

As for a rapprochement on the cultural front, there was nothing in it for intellectuals, Breton declared. 'Surrealists', he said, taking aim at socialist realism, 'are against every regressive idea that sacrifices content to form.'

Trotsky, too, believed the Popular Front was a huge mistake, a mote in the eye of world revolution. In 1938, Breton visited the Soviet pariah in Mexico. By now, the show trials were history, and so was the image of the Soviet Union as a light unto the nations no one could deny. In the course of this visit, Breton and Trotsky hammered out a manifesto for the arts that also bore the signature of Diego Rivera, another artist with a slap in his portfolio.

The manifesto, like Breton's speech at the Mutualité, assailed the Soviet 'Thermidorian reaction' and the deadly vice of totalitarian control. Fascism was not a hair better, of course, while the 'conservative and frightened' bourgeois democracies seemed intent on 'clinging to the tattered remnants of the "democratic" past'. The Trotsky-Breton document made the case for unfettered freedom of thought and art, even as it recognized the right of the revolutionary state 'to defend itself against the counterattack of the bourgeoisie' as a 'temporary measure'. 'We believe that the supreme task of art in our epoch is to take part actively and consciously in the preparation of the revolution.' Two concluding phrases captured the manifesto's gist: 'The independence of art — for the revolution!' 'The revolution — for the complete liberation of art!'

## IV. Jef Last

'Make sure you mention Last's speech, or else he'll think we're
trying to annoy him.'
Eddy du Perron to Menno ter Braak, June 1935.[47]

— *1* —

It was on a visit to Morocco with André Gide in 1935 that Jef Last discovered that it was possible to give birth to children based on the friendship between two men: children of the spirit. Last's trip to Morocco, his first, was an epiphany, a 'literary turning point'. He had never been happier. For the first time in his life he felt totally free, as though a 'heavy rock' had been lifted from his shoulders.

> To happen upon a society where the problem of homosexuality with its ever-present threat of scandal, of blackmail and snooping morality police simply do not exist; where you are less likely to encounter pronounced hetero and homosexuals as you are exclusively bisexuals; where sensuality has no more, but also no less, significance than a flower one plucks along the side of the road and carelessly discards soon after having enjoyed its smell. What a relief![48]

Last came from a solidly bourgeois family. His father had been a colonial officer in the Dutch East Indies. In midlife he befriended André Gide. Last, like Gide and Klaus Mann, was a pioneer in putting homosexuality on a novelistic footing; Gide with *Corydon* (1924); Mann with *Der fromme Tanz* (1926), 'a manifesto for gay youth'; Last with *Zuiderzee* (1934), a proletarian novel set against the backdrop of the construction of a dyke enclosing Holland's Zuiderzee. The home page of the website devoted to Last describes him as a writer, poet, socialist, Communist, sinologist, film pioneer, adventurer, avant-gardist, gay rights activist, sailor, miner and, finally, a Provo (Dutch anti-establishment group founded in the 1960s). Last also fought on the Republican side in the Spanish Civil War. Upon his return to Holland, he was deprived of his Dutch citizenship and briefly incarcerated. A photograph taken in the mid-thirties depicts the revolutionary from the lowlands arrayed in meticulously pressed trousers, hip-length stylish leather jacket, topped off by a rakish flat cap. A photograph of Last at fifty brings to mind Fred Astaire around the same age.

Last's novels and poetry of the interwar years are fictionalized adaptations of *The Communist Manifesto*. A typical Last product of the thirties was *Een huis zonder vensters* [A House without Windows]. Last's 'house without windows' was the mansion of 'bourgeois insanity' whose windows wanted smashing, revealing a glorious vista of the Communist future.

> 'A house without windows — indeed that was not only your family, that is every bourgeois family in which the only interests are those of the family members; that is the nature of the bourgeois fixated on his own kind, and only his own kind, as if one can stay safely at home when the house of his neighbour is on fire.'

'A lunatic asylum?'

'Isn't the whole world a lunatic asylum? When grain is burnt and coffee thrown into the sea? When rubber plants are uprooted? When gas bombs and tanks are deployed to civilize Africa? And when children in Paris schools are underfed?'[49]

Last's presence at the Moscow writers' Congress marked his third visit to the Soviet Union. He did not speak but took notes. Upon his return to the Netherlands, Last submitted his findings, typewritten and stencilled, to the Workers' Film and Theatre Association, a vehicle designed to stimulate proletarian interest in all things cultural. Last's report, 'The Proletarian Writers' Congress', glowed like a falling star. Five-year-olds, he wrote, were asked how they imagined the Congress. 'All writers', they answered, 'sat in a circle and Alexei Maximowitz arrives in a plane named "Gorky" and tells them how to write, meaning, the way things really are or as in a fairy tale.'

From there it was but a small step to Gorky's opening speech, where 'the father of proletarian literature' shared some of his insights into the hidden meanings of fables, folklore, songs and myths. Looked at through proletarian lenses, they revealed hitherto unsuspected possibilities. The seven-league boots Tom Thumb straps on to escape from the giant symbolized 'the primitive yearning for the express train'. This, Last clarified, served as an example of literature rooted in material conditions. Icarus prefigured Lindbergh; toiling nocturnal gnomes, robots. The gods were idealized forms of humanity, inspiring young people to work for the betterment of society. Not the rich stepdaughters wind up marrying the prince but Cinderella. This Gorky equated with the ultimate victory of the proletariat. As for socialist realism, its chief characteristic was action, not contemplation, action on behalf of 'recasting the world in a socialist spirit.'

'Two things stood out that would have had to impress anyone, "friend and foe"', concluded Last: 'the enormous interest of the great mass of farmers in this Congress,' and 'the bold criticism', regardless of the target, adding that no one dissented from Gorky's views.[50]

A number of attendees from the West gave the speech a failing grade, or at best a mere pass. Last gave it 10 out of 10.

There were delegates whose critical faculties showed signs of sagging like a fifteen-year-old mattress under the weight of banquets, liquor and snack-laden trays backed up like rush hour traffic in the big city. Not Last. Not then at least. Thirteen years later the Dutchman sang a different tune, singling out the Moscow Congress as 'one of the worst spiritual crises in my life'. Between 1934 and two of his earlier visits, in 1931 and 1932, much had changed, he said. In 1934, he saw homeless kids wandering the streets with nowhere to go while Congress attendees ate and drank themselves into a stupor and Muscovites danced, zombie-like, to jazz. To Last, these were symptoms of an embourgeoisement he hadn't seen before. The speeches of Bukharin and Radek were like a 'death sentence'. He left Moscow, Last asserted, sick to the stomach, sick with disappointment.[51]

(In the course of the Paris Congress *Pravda* published a short piece by Last headlined 'Fascism Is Barbarism', in which Last stated that the difference between

1934 and 1935 was that in 1934 it was a question of constructing, in 1935 one of defending, culture.[52])

When Last raised the Soviet slide into the bourgeois mode with Gide, the latter brushed it off as a reaction to the deprivation of bygone years and likely to pass. He felt the same about socialist realism, a breakthrough into 'a healthier opinion of art'. Gide counselled a wait-and-see attitude.[53]

Another development affected both Last and Gide personally: the persecution of homosexuals. Criminalized by Stalin in 1933, homosexuals faced up to five years of hard prison labour. The threat of incarceration did not, however, seem to have dampened the spirit of the former cook in the Russian navy Last had in his sights in the course of his fourth, and final, visit to the Soviet Union in 1936, demonstrating, once and for all, that Russia's Man of Steel was a man for all seasons. Last:

> I made the acquaintance of a pleasant young cook who had served for some time in the Russian navy. I said: 'You must have looked terrific in your sailor's suit!' The following evening, the last before our departure, he suddenly materialized in his sailor's outfit in the lobby. I asked if he felt like going for a little walk. I never would have thought that this farewell stroll we took that night on the grounds of the hotel would assume such a nightmarish, lugubrious character. In the course of this walk he granted me a glimpse into his soul, and I still think of it [1966] as a journey into Dante's inferno. Never before or after did I come across someone capable of making love with almost animal passion while his mouth, whenever it wasn't engaged, kept up a lengthy and extremely dull patter. He continued to talk at the point of the highest ecstasy; continued to talk while he straightened his clothes, and he was still talking about the politics of the Communist youth movement when we re-entered the doorway to the hotel. While he threw himself unconsciously into his long suppressed desire, he tried to convince me, consciously, of the correctness of the party line.[54]

— 2 —

Last's speech at the Paris Congress centred on fascism's appeal to young people, specifically graduating high school students in Germany. Youth without job prospects was an easy target. This youth, he said, was raw meat for fascist rhetoric, prone to develop a mentality altogether different from their proletarian coevals. The latter, intuitively allied to culture, respected thought, perceived as 'a treasure of which they will have need tomorrow', whereas the former tended to develop an 'ardent love of anarchic liberty, nature, eroticism, and above all, the desire to fight.' These were the young men who filled the ranks of Germany's Brownshirts. Young people craving idealism were everywhere, yet writers had failed to reach out to them. Rationalism, pacifism and liberalism were not likely to inspire young people questing after heroism and meaning in life. In Last's view, defence of culture meant joining the battle for the soul of youth in danger of going over to the other side, for only the proletariat and its offspring were capable of defending the creativity and dignity of thought. In this struggle, literature was the weapon of choice.

As Last spoke, Nico Rost must have been squirming in his seat. Attending the proceedings as an observer, Rost was aghast at his compatriot's grim assessment. Especially the reference to youth's vulnerability to the Nazi Siren stuck in his craw.

The thirty-nine-year-old Rost knew Germany like the back of his hand. He had spent a good deal of his adult life in Berlin, earning a living as a translator and a journalist. As a member of the German Communist Party, he was rounded up soon after Hitler came to power and briefly interned in Oranienburg concentration camp. In 1944, 'the man who loved Germany' wound up in Dachau.[55] His best-known work, *Goethe in Dachau*, was based on the diaries he kept there until his liberation in 1945.

Toward the end of 1938, with the Republicans in the Spanish Civil War heading for defeat, Rost launched a brutal assault on his comrade and fellow Dutchman that left nothing standing. Germany's young people were neither desperate nor psychologically unhinged, Rost affirmed, but a vibrant force, 'the best part' of which was committed to carrying on the struggle against Nazism with every means at their disposal, legal and illegal.

Last's erroneous perception of Germany's youth was the least of it. Wielding the broad brush of Trotskyism, Rost turned Last inside out: a 'literary adventurer' latching on to Communism to advance his career; Franco's accomplice, a double agent secretly working for Trotsky; betrayer of the Soviet Union for failing to condemn Gide's anti-Soviet books; a defeatist of 'unlimited vanity' and political immaturity more interested in pederasty than the Moroccan class struggle. Under the 'poisonous influence' of André Gide, Last had embarked on a course openly criticizing Soviet policy toward homosexuals. 'The Soviet Union believes', Rost clarified,

> that pederasty necessarily leads to the formation of factions, to cliques whose discipline is other than that required for the construction of socialism. Doesn't Jef realize that such cliques quickly become a point of attraction for all kinds of political riffraff and underworld types [...]?[56]

— 3 —

Last spent his final years in an old people's home undergoing treatment for cancer. Toward the end of 1971 a popular Amsterdam columnist looked him up in the hospital. Last was in a bad way, angry at the world. No one was paying any attention to him. Magazines kept returning his contributions. Fellow patients accused him of having betrayed the revolution. Nobody was buying his books. The treatment in the hospital was terrible. 'They won't even give you a pair of underpants.' He died soon thereafter.[57]

## V. Louis Aragon

— 1 —

In 1931, Louis Aragon was indicted for 'inciting the military to disobedience and provocation to murder as a goal of anarchist propaganda', a charge that carried a five-year prison sentence. The culprit was Aragon's poem 'Front Rouge' calling for the assassination of the socialist leader Léon Blum and other 'social fascists'.

The indictable lines went as follows:

> [...]
> Fire on Léon Blum
> Fire on Boncour Frossard Déat
> Fire on the dancing bears of social democracy [...]
> Fire fire [...].[58]

'If bloodshed is a criterion of Communism', observed Stephen Spender as though atoning for his fleeting adhesion to Communism, 'Hitler is as much a Communist as Mr. Aragon, and his rhetoric is even more effective. The intellectual capacity of Hitler and this poet seems about the same. Readers of the poem should compare it with any speech by Hitler.'[59]

Aragon got away with a suspended sentence. Aragon had clout, friends in high places.

Aragon joined the French Communist Party in the same year as Breton: 1927. A year later, Aragon visited the Soviet Union and fell under the spell of Vladimir Mayakovsky — and that of his sister-in-law, Elsa Triolet, whom he subsequently married. The son of a forest ranger, Mayakovsky was a luminous specimen in the early phase of Communist experimentation in the arts. Roots in the working class supplied the necessary credentials to go forth and shine. Upon his suicide in 1930, Mayakovsky reaped the highest possible praise from the highest possible authority. Mayakovsky, declared Stalin, was 'the best and the most talented poet of our Soviet era'. A few lines of Mayakovsky put Lenin to sleep. Not Stalin, evidently.

'Front Rouge' channelled Mayakovsky in significant ways. Spender noted its 'effective cinematographic technique'. Aragon himself dubbed the stylistic hybrid 'Communist Futurism'.

The firestorm triggered by Aragon's poem took its time dying down. In effect, it spread into an area that had been smouldering for some time: the relationship between Surrealism and Communism (culminating, as we have seen, in Breton's ousting from the Congress). Despite a shared interest in épater le bourgeois, each after its own fashion, there was no genuine feeling of kinship. Surrealists, as was noted by Klaus Mann among others, provoked scandals as ends in themselves, not as steps toward a radical transformation of society envisioned by Communism. That Surrealists were a privileged caste that delighted in biting the hand that fed them — Ehrenburg's 'spoiled brats' — is of scant importance; many a Communist, foremost the intellectuals, sprang from the lap of the bourgeoisie. Breton was well-off; Crevel never seemed to want for money for drugs, liquor, and taxis; Aragon spoke perfect English with a touch of an Oxford accent. The Surrealist's métier was énerver rather than épater the bourgeois. The Surrealist, observed Jean-Paul Sartre, is someone who revolts — a révolté — but not a revolutionary. Surrealists, he said, had no readers among the proletariat, their approach to the Communism abstract and utopian.[60]

L'affaire Aragon blew the lid off Surrealists' Communist pretensions. Charles Plisnier, Victor Serge's advocate at the Paris Congress, excoriated Surrealism as

> a secret malady in the brain of the bourgeoisie, a haunting preoccupation with
> suicide, a taint of madness, the anguish of the general paralytic who believes

that he is achieving the acme of lucidity but who cannot tell you if tomorrow he will have a new and astonishing revelation or be riding around in a wheel-chair.[61]

Entering the fray, *L'Humanité* condemned Aragon's indictment as 'ridiculous and odious', even as it accused Surrealists with exploiting the affair 'to call attention to themselves'. Surrealists only bother to protest when it concerns a poem, asserted the paper. These 'pretentious intellectuals' shut up when suppression hits the workers but move 'heaven and earth when it as much scratches their own precious persons'.

> They demand political impunity for poets and only for poets. [...] Their revo-lutionism is only verbal. [...] The bourgeoisie, in its oppression of the proletariat, sometimes strikes those who attach themselves by chance to the working class movement. That is the significance of 'l'affaire Aragon'.[62]

Surrealists responded to Aragon's indictment with a petition and two pamphlets. The petition circulated among France's intelligentsia (Gide and Rolland refused to sign it). Breton followed up with 'La Misère de la poésie: L'Affaire Aragon devant l'opinion publique', a lengthy pamphlet defending Aragon and attacking the Communist daily. On 10 March 1932, *L'Humanité* carried a brief item conveying 'comrade' Aragon's unconditional disapproval of Breton's sally: 'every Communist has to condemn the attacks contained in this pamphlet as incompatible with the class struggle and thus objectively counter-revolutionary'.[63] Breton, in turn, responded with a second pamphlet calling Aragon a 'clown'. Signatories included Salvador Dalí, Max Ernst, Tristan Tzara and René Crevel.[64] Across the Atlantic, adding insult to injury, America's John Reed Clubs in 1932 turned down Aragon's nomination as an honorary member 'on the grounds that he had openly pleaded poetic license to save himself from a five-year jail sentence for writing a poem in the *Magazine of Revolutionary Literature*'.[65]

Aragon's 'career as a Communist', observed Arthur Koestler, 'was rather in the Surrealist tradition'. In the Spanish Civil War '[h]e toured the Spanish front in a loudspeaker-van dispensing poetry to the militiamen at the time when Malraux organized the International Squadron of the Republican Air Force [...]'.[66]

With fascism in the ascendant, Aragon argued two months prior to the Paris antifascist Congress, there now could only be one criterion for assessing writers: how did their ideas hold up

> in the face of certain very elemental facts: that workers are staring down the barrels of cannons aimed at them by the police, that war is threatening, and that fascism is already enthroned. [...] It behooves a man, for the sake of his dignity, to submit his ideas to these facts, and not to bend these facts, by some conjuring trick, to his ideas, however ingenious.[67]

— 2 —

Congress' final session led off with Aragon's discourse 'Le retour à la réalité' — The Return to Reality. The Mutualité was packed to the rafters and steaming hot; the day's temperature had soared to 31°C. Facing the podium, and well within shooting range, was Léon Blum, Front politics having taken him off the endangered species list.

Aragon, too, addressed The Problems of Creation and the Dignity of Thought. As Aragon saw it, there wasn't much of a problem at all. As long as writers took care to place realism squarely at the centre of their work, all would be well, he said. *Je réclame ici le retour à la réalité!* — I hereby demand a return to reality! — Aragon kept repeating, as though trying to wake up from a bad dream. What, he asked, can we salvage from the literary movements that have preceded us? The trick, he said, was to strip away the 'haze of mysticism and lies' and appropriate their realistic content, their 'light'. Aragon turned out to be a master stripper, lustily scraping away at past literary movements to expose their recyclable parts. In his view, Romanticism, Naturalism, Symbolism, and all subsequent poetic and literary movements contained some 'light'. Hugo, for example, introduced argot into language. Zola was doing just fine until he started preaching social peace. Rimbaud, the equal of Shakespeare and Dante, inserted everyday objects into his poetry. Nor did Aragon spare himself. Dadaism, Cubism, Surrealism, the poet's prior incarnations, received short shrift. Cubism, a 'brake on all thought', turned out to be an 'abominable can of sardines' he was proud to have helped kick down the road. The same held for that 'explosion négative' known as Dadaism. Surrealism, the latest ism to land on the chopping block, Aragon saw as a 'desperate attempt to overcome the Dadaist negation' by constructing a new reality. For all their lip service to Marxism, Surrealists did not take reality as their point of departure and never became serious materialists.

Stripped of its intellectual bark, the point Aragon was trying to make was simple enough. With the entry of the working class on the historical stage 'the clouds had parted and the new hero was neither a Charlemagne or le Cid, but the worker of Belleville'. This was the new reality Aragon had made his own, a foot soldier in the 'march of progress' that was bringing 'socialist Realism and revolutionary Romanticism', 'two big words [that] make us dream', from East to West. Time to stop playing fast and loose with language and to return to basics; the torture chambers of the SA called for nothing less. Referencing Mayakovsky, Aragon reminded the Congress that the Russian poet had started out on a path similar to that travelled by the Futurist Marinetti. But unlike Marinetti — 'stupid Marinetti' — Mayakovsky had seen the light and entered 'the red stream of history'.

The proletariat, 'rich in all human truth' was the class, Aragon prophesied, whose miracles would not be found etched in church windows 'but in the street and in the countryside, in the hands of living human beings, the workers'. Aragon terminated his discourse invoking the last of Marx's *Eleven Theses on Feuerbach*: 'The philosophers have only interpreted the world. The point is to change it.'

## VI. Mike Gold

'An historic document of our time'

— 1 —

Establishing his bona fides as a true son of the proletariat, the American delegate Michael Gold informed the Congress that he had started out working in a factory at the age of twelve and had known every humiliation attendant upon poverty. 'I have always worked for my keep, for my education, for my right to live and to think. Like the masses, I've given more to America than she's given me.' Yet he said he loved his country, despite its leeches and lynchers, gangsters, crooked politicians, shady lawyers and exploiters — the entire 'crowd of parasites'.

As an up-and-coming working-class author Gold 'affected dirty shirts, a big, black, uncleaned Stetson with the brim of a sombrero; smoked stinking, twisted, Italian three-cent cigars, and spat frequently and vigorously on the floor. [...] These "proletarian" props were as much a costume as the bohemian sideburns and opera cape. They enhanced Gold's lovable qualities.'[68] In the mid-1920s Gold joined half a dozen editors of *The New Masses*, the revolutionary magazine dedicated to the American working class. 'I am an internationalist', he told a gathering of its editors in 1926.

> I will not deny that Soviet Russia and its revolutionary culture form the spiritual core around which thousands of the younger writers in every land are building their creative lives... What I deny is that I, or anyone else, demands of young American writers that they take their 'spiritual' commands from Moscow. [...] Moscow could not have created John Reed, Upton Sinclair, Jack London... American life created them.[69]

— 2 —

In Paris, too, Gold defined himself as an internationalist, first and foremost, and urged all 'intellectuals, writers and thinkers [...] to love their own country more profoundly and openly.

> They will make it their business to immerse themselves in the life of the masses. There is no other way to launch the struggle against the fake nationalism of the fascists except through a profound knowledge of the lives of the masses.

For, as Gold pointed out elsewhere in his speech (he spoke in the evening of 24 June): 'Those who love culture must recognize that only the working class is capable of maintaining and developing it. That's the lesson of the Russian revolution.'

Gold's article in *The New Masses* summarizing the Congress was vintage Gold: combative, passionate.[70] 'The Writers Meet in Paris' paid fulsome tribute to the Congress — somewhat of a rarity among Western participants — conveyed in a spirit of unbounded, well-nigh boyish enthusiasm. In it, Gold played up the United Front and its fight against French fascists like Colonel de La Roque and their tie-ins with the agents of the French ruling class (police, generals, industries and bankers) killing workers, attacking 'foreigners and open raids into workers' districts'.

> It was like Hitler in Germany — except for the one immortal difference. The working-class and the middle-class republicans had formed a United Front. When the fascists threatened to visit a workers' town, all the church bells were rung, the fire engines rushed through the streets, the Mayor put on his sash and thousands of miners and textile workers and tradesmen answered the summons of bells and sirens and gathered in the public square. [...] [E]veryone in France knows that only the United Front can save France from being Hitlerized.

Gold next supplied a who's who of the Congress, 'a galaxy of distinguished authors that any American publisher would give his eye teeth to have in his catalogue (that is, if the bankers have left him a solitary molar) [...].' Gold commended Gide especially for having 'hewed his path through the confusing jungle of contemporary thought, to a clearing where a new sun was shining', in step with the likes of 'Alexei Tolstoy and Michael Koltzov, two of the Soviet writers who are leading humanity into a new world'.

> Do not think, however, this was a Congress of writers in defense of Communism. It was a Congress built on the united front; it was a Congress possible only because there is a raw, grinning young sadist in Nazi uniform, who shrieks with cannibal joy at the bonfire he has made of the modern books. There were Socialists, Communists, Protestants, Zionists, liberals and democrats at this Congress. There were 'skeptics' like Aldous Huxley, 'Olympians' like Julien Benda and Catholics like Lenormand. There were enemies of Communism like the Italian professor, Salvemini and the Trotzkyite, Magdalene [sic] Paz.

Gold came down hard on 'the Trotzkyite lady' ... [who] created the only disruptive event at the Congress.

> To a noisy claque that came in with her, this fat, flabby fool with the marcelled hair delivered a slanderous speech full of the usual clichés against the Soviet Union, because a Trotzkyite named Victor Serge was in prison there. To her mind, and those who applauded her, this Congress was a 'fraud' unless it went on record equally against fascism and the Soviet Union. These people can see no difference between a Nazi concentration camp and a Soviet collective farm. [...] Such are the little Trotzkyites everywhere, pathalogues living in a self-centered world and helpful only to the enemy.

Their 'little raid had not even the effect of a mosquito's sting', Gold reassured the readers back home.

> [E]very night from two to five thousand intellectuals and workers paid their way into the meetings. They listened intently, they cheered, applauded, made notes. Our Hemingways have reported to us only the cheap and nasty tourist side of Paris; but here was the heart of it, the Paris of Revolution and thought, the Paris of Diderot and Vaillant-Couturier. The speeches would fill a volume of several thousand pages [...] an historic document of our time.[71]

Not surprisingly, Gold focused on the writers who had no quarrel with Communism, unlike Julien Benda, 'to whom Communism and Humanism seemed enemies'. But the fight against fascism was something on which all men of good will and not predisposed to write off the Soviet Union could take part. One such was 'the mystic Zionist author, Max Brod'. 'As for me', Gold quoted from Brod's lengthy speech,

> I remain in my original thought: The Dream belongs to the Individual and his profound soul: Reason, clear, luminous and without myths, belongs to society. There two factors should not destroy each other, but on the contrary, should be bound together by the most enigmatic word in the language... by this supreme and magic word, 'AND!'. Dream and reason; night and day, profound belief in God and collaboration, rational and active, with the Soviet Five-Year Plan. Perhaps the romantic Heine, who threw off the cowl, could tell us how to realize the supreme union of these contradictions, not easily, indeed, but after great internal struggle.

On several occasions Gold connected the issues raised inside the Mutualité with the American experience.

> The fascists have made the national tradition of each country their chief point of demagogy. As in America, where Daniel Boone and the tradition of landless, hungry pioneers is used by capitalists and their intellectual valets as a club against the hungry proletariat of today. We have learned in America, how to answer these parasites. We are beginning to unmask their false claims and to reconquer the revolutionary traditions of our land.

Gold next returned to deal with the Trotskyists, laying into Breton/Éluard for opposing 'the Franco-Soviet pact and all cultural traffic between the two lands'.

> But other former Surrealists answered him. Among them Louis Aragon, one of the half-dozen great poets in the world today and one of the organizers of the Congress. Tristan Tzara, the father of Dada also answered Eluard, when he confessed, 'Formerly, I believed that salvation lay through literature and the written word; now I know that only social forces such as that released by the Soviets can give us the palaces of a new and beautiful life.'

Gold presented a picture of the Congress that was at odds with the overall assessment by participating Western writers. Few would have agreed with the American delegate that 'the authors of Germany, France and the Soviet Union discovered a common cultural tradition that they would defend against fascism', or that the proletariat was 'the heir of all the culture which the decline of the bourgeois regime is threatening'.[72]

Gold wrote in a muscular, macho vein. 'Writers', he concluded, wrapping up his report,

> under capitalism have become effete. They have abandoned their comfort in the famous ivory tower which to my eyes always resembled the boudoir of a spoiled chorus blonde whom a millionaire was keeping. Or with the best of the writers, individualism was often a monk's cell, where in melancholy self-abuse they wasted their manhood on the follies of metaphysics. Fascism wakes them from their vanity and dreaming. It is a glorious thing to see writers accepting the challenge and taking their place among the leaders of humanity. Writers are, as Stalin said in his oft-quoted speech, 'the engineers of the human soul'. [...] [W]riters are like other men and in solidarity they find courage for the battle.

This was precisely the point Gold made in a statement conveying his greetings on behalf of to the Soviet Union that appeared under his byline in *Pravda* on 24 June. Captioned 'Let's Build a New World', the Congress representing diverse countries, Gold asserted, had helped strength the ability to fight fascism. The articled ended expressing gratitude to the Soviet Union for contributing its great strength toward laying the foundations of a new culture.[73]

# VII. H.-R. Lenormand

### 'Falsifiers of genius'

— 1 —

25 June, evening. The final session of the writers' Congress in defence of culture crackled with nervous tension. The afternoon's brouhaha precipitated by *l'affaire Serge* was still percolating. Writers whose speeches had been axed because the clock was running out were fuming in the wings, poised to seize the microphone and have their say. Gatekeeper Malraux had his hands full keeping the snubbed delegates from storming the stage.

With twelve other speakers and closing ceremonies on tap, a long session loomed, freighted with resolutions and similar initiatives designed to send the participants and public home with a sense of achievement. On several occasions, *L'Humanité* reported, the audience rose to rock the hall with sustained cries of 'Rot Front', the underground paramilitary organization of the German Communist Party, and vociferous renderings of *The Internationale*. Fist-pumping detachments of boys and girls entered carrying banners and emblems 'sworn to defend culture.' It was, *L'Humanité* reported, 'an unforgettable session'.[74]

The year before, in Moscow, such outbreaks of popular fervour had been the order of the day, with Malraux looking on as a guest. There, cameramen had been on hand to capture several of these exuberant displays. A film clip captioned 'The reader meets the writer' featured Red Army soldiers marching into the hall and down the aisles onto the stage, intoning 'Brothers in arms in the struggle for the working class! From the Red Army soldiers, officers, commanders and political workers of the Moscow garrison to the First All-Soviet Congress of Soviet Writers: Long live [...]!' A worker held up a model aeroplane. A gangly young girl identified as a member of the Camp of the Pug-Noses shouted 'We want to learn! We want to know a lot, so we can be good Komsomols. Give us books, which we can show the whole world. [...] Help us grow! [...] Comrade grown-up writers: Be prepared!' Thunderous applause.[75]

But this was Paris, not Moscow. Yet Congress's co-chairman knew better than to clamp down on these unrestrained Soviet-style eruptions; reining them in was a good deal trickier than keeping unknown speakers at arm's length, or acceding to the expulsion of the pro-Serge troublemakers of the night before. The overwhelmingly working-class audience would not have stood for it.

The evening's second speaker was Vladimir Kirshon. Fresh from that afternoon's debate drubbing Victor Serge, the playwright recapped the state of the theatre in the Soviet Union. It was in full flower, he reported, performing classical as well as Soviet plays. Participation in non-professional theatre stood at 1,200,000; choirs, musical, fine arts and dance companies, at 5,000,000. Theatres filled to capacity, and there was a lively dialogue between actors and the public, critical but affectionate. Post-performance discussion groups assessed the play's merit, the staging and the acting, in big cities like Moscow no less than in the provinces. A sixty-four-year-old illiterate woman dictated a play 'to a young peasant of the new kolkhoz generation' that had found its way to the stage. New plays were cast in the mould of socialist realism. Socialist realism, the Soviet thespian explained, was a unique and universal method capable of 'coordinating the world of contemporary ideas and to subordinate them to a single dominant idea'. Through it, the artist 'renders a truthful reflection of the world, people and events in the light of socialist perspectives of which it has become conscious'.

To Henri-René Lenormand, Kirshon's numbers must have sounded like something out of a fairy tale. The French playwright and director was up next and the things he had to say about the state of his country's theatre packed all the comfort of a cold shower. He and Malraux had gone over the speech beforehand, with the latter suggesting several cuts, cuts to which the playwright had acceded. Theatre in France was in bad shape, Lenormand declared. An indifferent state doled out less and less money to fewer and fewer authors writing for the theatre, with the lion's share going to playwrights catering to petty bourgeois tastes: operettas, light comedies, 'made to measure theatre'. Serious theatre had been hit hard, to say nothing about the state of provincial theatre. Employing Marxist jargon, painting with a broad brush, Lenormand declared that in the West 'exchange values' had been riding roughshod over spiritual values.

> In our time and in this country, the theatre no longer responds to the needs of the soul but is looked upon as a diversion. It is no longer considered a vital need, but an ornament of the bourgeois life. Of all spiritual nourishment, this is the one whose disappearance would be the most easily borne. [...] It is because the French public can live without theatre that it does nothing to compel their leaders to save the theatre. Here the indifference of governments reflects that of the masses, the so-called elites and the politicians that represent them.

In other words, indifference was two-way: lack of interest on the part of the public let the state off the hook. By blaming the public and pausing at the right places for dramatic effect, drawing on every register of the 'miserable glibness of rhetoric', Lenormand was able to win over the audience, prompting applause at several artfully plotted junctures.

The audience could be forgiven for understanding the burden of Lenormand's talk to be the shrinking fortunes of the French theatre. The actual message Lenormand was trying to drive home was neither the state's indifference nor the theatrical fluff on tap. 'What makes it so difficult', he went on,

> in this country to create an art and a theatre that are truly proletarian is that when it comes to dramatic fare the taste of the workers is, in sum, bourgeois. The bourgeois theatre, with its tinselled insipidity, its hypocritically erotic

shows put on by masterful directors and often performed by admirable actors, this total mix of technical perfection and intellectual flabbiness, of visual splendour and base morality; this hybrid art that revolts the spirit while charming the senses, does not merely give satisfaction to the middle classes: it also reflects [...] the secret desires of working people. And how could it be otherwise?

What's more, Lenormand added, the conflation of bourgeois and proletarian taste was a major reason why populist theatre had never been able to strike more than superficial roots in French soil.

H.-R. Lenormand had a dramatist's nose for sensing when a play does or does not go down well with the public. Laying the ultimate blame for theatre's deplorable condition and bleak prospects at the feet of the proletariat had Lenormand worried. And indeed, as his speech wore on he detected a palpable rise in tension, silent but hostile. Speaking ill of the proletariat, however mild, was not *comme il faut*, not at this gathering. Being a dramatist put him at a decisive advantage over the audience, however, for the discourse had been drafted in such a way as to blunt the message; the emphasis on the condemnation of the bourgeois theatre, a known crowd-pleaser, overriding the pairing of petty bourgeois and proletarian taste — and was rather ashamed of it all. 'The accusation struck home, but it did not provoke a reaction because the listener was still flush with excitement for having had the pleasure of hearing a hated social class thoroughly condemned.'[76]

Even so, Lenormand fully expected to be booed for uttering such unconscionably heretical views. He wasn't. His friends congratulated him on his courage. The Soviet delegation was *enchanté*. No wonder. How pitiful the Frenchman's lament compared to Kirshon's paean.

— 2 —

On 14 July, a great crowd gathered in Paris's Parc des Princes, the starting point of the march announced by the Communist Party at the time of the anti-Hitler rally at the park of Montreuil three weeks earlier. Orator after orator fired up the masses, promising to put paid to capitalism once and for all. H.-R. Lenormand:

> The *Internationale*, roared countless times in the meetings, erupted like thunder. The forgotten *Marseillaise* emerged slowly from throats and memory. Thousands of voices haltingly repeated the old revolutionary hymn. For us it was the message of one revolution to the other and the solemn affirmation of the national character with which we wanted to endow it. We were convinced that we were present at something as important at the Tennis Court Oath or the Night of 4 August 1789.
> [...]
> As we passed, the crowd that filled the sidewalks burst into loud cheering. There was a constant *Long live the intellectuals! Long Live Science! Long live Malraux!* One shout touched us deeply, because of its naïvete: *Long live the teachers! Would that they never die! May they never die!* [...] Clara Malraux walked alongside her husband, bare feet in sandals that stuck to the pavement. All of a sudden he lifted her up to show her the sea of red flags that fluttered in the wind behind us for kilometres on end. [...] Hope, incoherence, madness and

the enthusiasm of revolutions took hold of the movement's non-intellectual elements. 'The Masses,' Malraux said to me, 'are not hostile to intellectuals. But the cadres, yes.' [...]

All in all, a disorganized crowd jostled one another under the illusion that they were replicating one of those typical parades depicted in Soviet films. Only the Young Communists gave the impression of disciplined troops, with their signs, their blue shirts striated with thunderbolts and their military appearance. The slogans hammered out by each of the groups revealed the obsession with the Bolshevik Revolution: Les Soviets-partout! — The Soviets Everywhere! — Marxisme é-tu-diez! — Marxism stu-dy! — As-sas-sins-fa-scistes! — Fas-cist as-sas-sins!

Eighteen years down the road, Lenormand said he looked upon it all with mixed emotions.

It wasn't because I believed deeply in the triumph of the new gospel that I went to the Parc des Princes [...] but as a witness to events that I expected to be confusing and, further, to observe for myself, a self that I knew to be too emotional, always in search of tragedies in the making.

— 3 —

In August 1935 Lenormand, accompanied by his wife, paid a visit to the Soviet Union, 'a tourist of the human soul'. What Lenormand found was one gigantic will to make whole again. In the course of his sojourn, he visited Bolshevo, the town populated with 'reforged' prisoners, as well as a facility known as the Prophylact-orium. Prophylactorium was home to three hundred 'reforging' prostitutes. The Frenchman noted the presence of musical instruments in their rooms: trumpets, saxophones, cornets and such. A guide explained: 'Many of these girls are musicians. We encourage musical studies. When night falls, they are sometimes overcome by the nostalgia for the street, adventure, for the unknown man. Hence we make them play the saxophone. This calms them down and turns them away from temptation.'

As well, the French playwright was in a position to put to the test Kirshon's seemingly outrageous claims. It did not take him long to ascertain that the Soviet author had been on the level. 'In Moscow, the life of the theatre throbbed with elemental violence', Lenormand recalled years later. The theatre, completely integrated into the social life, 'had become the spiritual bread of innumerable multitudes'. The state's largess knew no bounds, spreading beyond the capital and major cities into the provinces and the Republics, where it funded national theatres. Nor were minorities left out; there was a Jewish as well as a Gypsy State Theatre. Thousands of new jobs were created, with workers solidly represented across the spectrum, from apprenticeships in stagecraft to actors and directors. Kirshon's contention about the interaction between playwright, actor, and crowd, the theatrical equivalent of the rapport between writer and public, likewise passed with flying colours.

Contacts made in Paris opened doors in the Soviet Union. There were face-to-face meetings with some of the world's greatest living directors, men like Meyerhold and Stanislavsky, and playwrights like Vladimir Kirshon and Mikhail

Pogodin. The latter struck Lenormand as a robust little chap with a fiery disposition and a 'marvellously sympathetic' face, 'soft and severe at the same time', coalescing into a harmonious whole when the author of *Aristocrats* was deep in his cups. Pogodin's friend, the director Nikolai Okhlopkov, took the idea of interaction between audience and actors to new heights by seating the spectators on the stage around the actors, as in his production of *Aristocrats*. Pogodin's play was having a run in Moscow and Lenormand went to see it. The staging was a marvel to behold. 'Okhlopkov', Lenormand wrote in a lengthy appraisal,

> has at his disposal a theatrical space consisting of two platforms connected by a passage way. It is on this Cross of Lorraine that each scene is acted out. A flash of light from a projector; thirty seconds of acting; darkness. The actors re-emerge on another platform. The entire work unfolds to this rhythm, without sets. As in Chinese theatre, the props are positioned by presumably invisible stagehands. And we very quickly cease to be aware of them. [...] To our eyes they remain impersonal agents of the production and much less of a nuisance than the buzz around the edges of the stage. On the contrary, the absence of scenery, the forests of the extreme north, the whiteness of the empty spaces, begin materializing before our eyes. And when props do cause an interruption, hurling white confetti at the heads of the actors, the snowstorm suffocates and terrifies us. There is a drowning scene performed by means of a black twill cloth pierced with holes and shaken sideways by two men. We watch the head of the actor emerge from the holes and his hands stirring beneath the cloth. The fury of the waves, the struggling individual, and his complete immersion are fiercely conveyed. The emotion of the performance spills over into the public situated in closed ranks around the platforms. At the conclusion, cries erupt: the actors and the crowd greet one another and shake hands. Okhlopkov, with his theatre that isn't; Pogodin, with his play that isn't, has established new relationships, or re-established traditional ones, between spectator and performer.

With theatre as a teaching tool, Soviet directors managed to transform the most banal drawing room into a critique of capitalism. Yet, though Lenormand found much to admire in their staging, in the end he slapped a rather dubious epithet on their collective effort: 'falsifiers of genius'.

Lenormand also attended a play by Kirshon. The staging impressed him as superior to anything he had seen in Europe. The two had met at the Paris Congress and got along well, so much so that the playwright hosted Lenormand and wife at his dacha in the countryside. Kirshon radiated health and *joie de vivre*. The dacha, made of wood in the peasant style, was 'set amidst a flourishing vegetable garden' and filled with 'the smell of dried apples'; huge meadows separated the house from distant pine forests. This is where Kirshon did his writing during the summer. He was the proud papa of two adorable little boys, one of whom was always laughing. Servants prepared a traditional Russian dinner. At the end of their visit, Kirshon drove the Lenormands back to Moscow and saw them off at the station prior to their departure for Tiflis. He would have liked to accompany them, he said, but the government was sending him to Kiev with instructions to write a play about the manoeuvres of the Red Army.

Lenormand: 'A play about the manoeuvres of the Red Army [...] that's not very exciting ....'
Kirshon: 'But it is, it is! A very beautiful subject, the Red Army!'

— 4 —

Confusion and conflict obtruded throughout the month-long stay. 'Scruples and doubts' interfered with his sleep. How to keep an open mind when reality and the all-pervasive gospel of optimism were light-years apart? What was a beggar doing at a station when the official line decreed that beggars were non-existent? Ditto signs of famine. At times such as these Lenormand was overcome by a 'repugnant pettiness', rooted in 'class prejudices and bourgeois conformity', that kept him from seeing the big picture. He sincerely wanted to believe in the Soviet Union, the new Arcadia and the new Adam. 'The reaction of a single individual in the face of movements that transports the world to new destinies has no more importance than a dog barking at a passing convoy.' In order to 'give a definite yes or no to the tableau presented by the revolution, the defenders of an exhausted civilization would have to smash all preconceived notions, the inhibitors of duality, of rational evaluation, this curse of for and against [...]'. To be sure, the works of Russian authors were 'tendentious'. Yet it could not be otherwise. 'With my insistence on universality, my Cartesian scruples, I resembled an inhabitant of a dead star, judging with suspicion the torrential élan of a cosmos in formation.'

Lenormand showed no such crippling hesitancy in his post-war assessment of the Paris writers' Congress. The playwright devoted a significant portion of the final chapter, 'The Revolutionary Mirage', to its appraisal. 'The misfortune of this Congress', Lenormand writes there, 'was to defend humanism and culture by relying on Bolshevism', a 'vast trap' designed to 'snare the world's intelligentsia'. The Molotov-Ribbentrop Non-Aggression Pact demonstrated, if any more proof was needed, 'with tragic irony the feeble perspicacity, the lack of political intuition and prescience of the foremost intellectuals'.

> But we were in full flower of the Popular Front and prey to the noblest of illusions. Not always that noble, in other respects. For how many among us did not view being affiliated with a mass party as an opportunity to expand their readership, and to descend, at last, from their ivory tower, where they were dying of virtue, solitude and boredom? There, I fear, lies the unacknowledged reason behind many a conversion of participants whose exalted thought and inaccessibility of style translated into weak sales figures. The 3000 spectators at the Palais de la Mutualité were not only the representatives of 'the great living masses we were obliged to enlighten', they were also potential readers to be won over.

At times, Lenormand observed, the talks went over the heads of the spectators. Malraux's 'obscure and glacial incantations' were greeted 'in profound silence'; seconds passed before the hall resounded with feverish applause. After Malraux, 'the grandest intellects of the century, a Gide, a Huxley, resembled professors tripping over their own words'. Euro-centric snobbism seeded with condescension and racism revealed an astonishing lack of worldliness: Lenormand's.

Difficult to appease the representatives of cultures of countries without culture! Even more difficult to understand why a good-natured chap given the opportunity to speak holds forth in atrocious, barbaric French. [...] Animated with an enormous confidence in the destiny of humanity, a pure flame of love, faith in the importance and efficacy of the resolutions of our Congress, the enthusiasm of the representatives from small American republics and the steppes of Eastern Europe was generally free from posturing; that much must be said. We will never know why the Chinese delegate showed up 'swaddled', nor why a brown-skinned woman draped in a Hindu Sari speaking on behalf of her 'oppressed sisters', tendering a salute with two clasped hands raised above her head, was applauded. Turns out she was an American journalist whose tan had been acquired on the beaches of California.

[...]

Barbusse, very much applauded when he appeared, gradually lost his audience to the buffet. Merely to see the writer of *Le Feu* get up behind the microphone, wearily gathering up his papers; merely to listen to him drone on through loudspeakers transmitting a constant buzz of words; given all that, they reckoned they had more than enough time to enjoy their break. When it became obvious, from the acceleration of the flow, that the speechifying was about to end, everyone regained their seats; knowing that they had satisfied the condition of attendance while overcoming its drawbacks, the crowd's enthusiasm could not have been more sincere. They were pleased with their chief, whom they applauded, and with themselves, for having 'cut the long-winded speech'.

Apparently Menno ter Braak was not the only one to lose his audience to the treats on offer in the corridors.

'The weapons available to the defenders of culture', Lenormand concluded,

were of no greater use than the machine guns of the war of 1914. [...] But, at the time, both duped and dupers joined hands in the spirit of trust, perpetuating the illusions democracy retained until its temporary collapse. Culture and freedom of thought, considered as a bulwark of a liberal social order with revolutionary proclivities, was a mirage we were unable to dispel. Unforgivably. It is a fact that if anyone among us had mounted the stage and declared that he did not believe in the power of the intellect and that he considered it incapable of transforming political events, that person not only would not have been able to make himself heard but would have been expelled as a traitor and agent of fascism.

The resolutions passed by the Congress added a final layer of self-deception.

It is without irony, but from the awareness of the impotence of intellectuals, henceforth unshakable, that I report these resolutions history would very soon prove to be completely and cruelly ineffective. Should we be touched or shocked by the power of illusion that took possession of us?

### Notes to Chapter 3

1. Lion Feuchtwanger, *Moscow 1937, My Visit Described for My Friends,* trans. by Irene Josephy (New York: Viking Press, 1937), p. viii.
2. Lion Feuchtwanger papers, Box A4a/folder 43, Collection no. 0204, Feuchtwanger Memorial Library, Special Collections, USC Libraries, University of Southern California.

3. Feuchtwanger papers, Box A4a/folder 31.
4. For the recipe, see Feuchtwanger papers Box A4a/folder 39.
5. Marcuse, *Jahrhundert*, p. 279.
6. 'An meine Sowjetleser', *Das Wort, Literarische Monatschrift*, 7 (1938), 82–85 (83).
7. Feuchtwanger papers, Box A4a/folder 24.
8. Lion Feuchtwanger, *The Devil in France, My Encounter with Him in the Summer of 1940* (Los Angeles: Figueroa Press, n.d.), p. 20.
9. Marcus G. Patka, *Zu nahe der Sonne: Deutsche Schriftsteller im Exil in Mexico* (Berlin: Aufbau, 1999), p. 144.
10. *The House of Desdemona or the Laurels and Limitations of Historical Fiction*, trans. by Harold A. Basilius (Detroit: Wayne State University Press, 1963).
11. Julien Luchaire, 'Confession d'un Français moyen', II (Florence: Olschki, 1965). Feuchtwanger papers, Box A3a/folder 39.
12. *Devil*, pp. 20, 30.
13. *Jahrhundert*, pp. 184–85.
14. *Devil*, p. 20.
15. Diary entry 23 June, Feuchtwanger papers, Box A19-b/folder 16, Diary transcriptions 1906–1940.
16. *Jahrhundert*, p. 279.
17. *Paris Gazette*, trans. by Willa and Edwin Muir (New York: Viking Press, 1940), p. 169. The original German, *Exil*, came out in Amsterdam the previous year.
18. Diary entry, 25 June, Feuchtwanger papers, Box A 19-b/folder 16.
19. *Jahrhundert*, p. 219.
20. 'Lion Feuchtwanger in der UdSSR', *Das Wort, Literarische Monatschrift*, 1 (1937), 101. The piece included a tally of Feuchtwanger's publications in the Soviet Union in Russian translation, along with numbers. The latter added up to 216,900. *Das Wort* ceased publishing in April 1939.
21. Stern, *Western Intellectuals*, pp. 162–74.
22. 'Fashizm i Germanskaia intelligentsiia', p. 6.
23. 'Estet o Sovetskom Soiuze', p. 3. The article also appeared in the original German in *Das Wort*, 2 (1937) 86–88.
24. Hartmut Boehm, *Porträt Lion Feuchtwanger*, Teil 3/4, <https://www.youtube.com/results?search_query=lion+feuchtwanger> [accessed 17 October 2014].
25. Diary, Feuchtwanger papers, Box A 19-b/folder 16.
26. 29 January 1937. Feuchtwanger papers, Box A 19 b/folder 16.
27. 'Pervye vpechtlenniai ob etom protsesse', p. 4.
28. 7 February 1937. Feuchtwanger papers, Box A-19-b/Folder 16.
29. *Moscow*, p. viii.
30. *Moscow*, pp. 150–51.
31. *Jahrhundert*, p. 279.
32. Boehm, *Porträt*, Teil 2/4 <https://www.youtube.com/watch?v=th2ZjNoGHho> [accessed 17 October 2014].
33. 'Het Schrijverspalet', *Verzameld Werk*, III, pp. 406–08; 410.
34. Lion Feuchtwanger, *Die Wartesaal Trilogie*, <http://www.weltbild.de/3/17763316-1/dvd/lion-feuchtwanger-die-wartesaal-trilogie.html> [accessed 20 October 2014].
35. *Briefwisseling*, p. 226.
36. Lenormand, *Confessions*, II, p. 344.
37. Trotsky, though, was not very keen on Paz. 'Magdeleine Paz has fought for your freedom; it is the only praiseworthy thing she has done in her life'. Letter to Victor Serge, 29 April 1936. Cited in *Writings of Leon Trotsky: Supplement (1934–40)* (New York: Pathfinder Press, 1979), p. 660. <https://rosswolfe.files.wordpress.com/2015/05/leon-trotskii-collected-writings-supplement-1934–1940.pdf> [accessed 28 November 2015].
38. Letter to Marcel Martinet, 20 March1933, cited in Nicole Racine, 'Victor Serge. Correspondance d'URSS, 1920–1936', *Mil neuf cent*, 8, 86–87.
39. Cited in Jean-Guy Rens, *Vlady: De la Revolución al Renacimiento*, trans. by Tessa Brisac (Mexico: Siglo XXI, 2005), p. 55. See also Susan Weissman, *Victor Serge: The Course Is Set on Hope*

(London and New York: Verso, 2001), pp. 161–64. Victor Serge's autobiography, *Memoirs of a Revolutionary,* trans. by Peter Sedgwick (New York: Society Writers and Readers Publishing, 1984), pp. 316–20.

40. Rens, *Vlady,* p. 55.
41. Letter to Trotsky, 21 August 1936. *La Lutte contre le stalinisme. Textes 1936–1939,* ed. by Michel Dreyfus (Paris: François Maspero, 1977), p. 146.
42. Erich Mühsam, a leading figure in the short-lived Bavarian Soviet Republic, hanged himself in Oranienburg concentration camp in 1934.
43. Vegesack, p. 167.
44. *Memoirs,* 317–18.
45. *La Mort difficile,* p. 9.
46. *Conversations,* p. 139.
47. *Briefwisseling,* p. 227.
48. Gillesse, p. 69.
49. Cited in Gillesse, p. 75.
50. Jef Last, 'Het proletarisch schrijverscongres 1934' (Amsterdam: A.f.t.b., 1934).
51. Gillesse, pp. 67–68. A month after the Congress, Last 'confessed' to Du Perron that he no longer knew what to think. Du Perron, *Grootse tijd,* p. 18.
52. 'Fashizm — eto Varvarstvo', *Pravda,* 24 June 1935, p.5.
53. Gillesse, p. 68, note 189.
54. Gillesse, p. 229.
55. '[T]he Man who Loved Germany' refers to the title of Hans Olink's biography of Nico Rost, *Nico Rost: De man die van Duitsland hield* (Amsterdam: Nijgh & Van Ditmar, 1997).
56. Nico Rost, 'Het geval Jef Last: over Fascisme en Trotzkisme' (Amsterdam: Pegasus, 1938), 39 pp. (p. 13). Rost had in mind Gide's *Retouches à mon 'Retour de l'U.R.S.S.',* which appeared one year after his *Retour de l'U.R.S.S.* Rost also was part of the Dutch delegation but did not speak.
57. Simon Carmiggelt, *Met de neus in de boeken* (Amsterdam: De Arbeiderspers, 1983), p. 86.
58. Feu sur Léon Blum/Feu sur Boncour Frossard Déat/Feu sur les ours savants de la social-démocratie/Feu feu [...]. Joseph Paul-Boncour, André Frossard, and Marcel Déat were French politicians in Aragon's bad books, i.e. 'social fascists'.
59. Spender, 'Louis Aragon's *The Red Front',* in *Thirties and After,* pp. 30–31 (p. 31).
60. Jean-Paul Sartre, *Qu'est-ce que la littérature?* (Paris: Gallimard, 1948), pp. 168, 233.
61. Cited in Putnam, p. 187.
62. 'L'inculpation d'Aragon', *L'Humanité,* 9 February 1932, p. 2.
63. 'Mise au point communiqué par l'Asociation des Ecrivains Revolutionaires.'
64. Putnam, p. 188.
65. Aaron, p. 241.
66. Arthur Koestler, 'Meanderings', in *The Yogi and the Commissar,* p. 23.
67. Cited in Benjamin, *Arcades Project,* p. 464.
68. Aaron, p. 104, citing Max Eastman and Joseph Freeman.
69. Cited in Joseph Freeman, *An American Testament: A Narrative of Rebels and Romantics* (London: Gollancz, 1938), p. 343.
70. *The New Masses,* 30 July 1935, 9–11.
71. The speeches take up roughly 500 of roughly 665 pages in Teroni and Klein, *Pour la défense de la culture.*
72. Quoted from Russian delegate Ivan Luppol's speech.
73. 'Postroim Novy Mir', *Pravda,* 24 June 1935, p. 3.
74. 'La dernière journée du congrès des écrivains', *L'Humanité,* 26 June 1935, p. 1.
75. Ceremonial Opening of the Soviet Writers' Congress (1934), <https://www.youtube.com/watch?v=HZUelR9jZik> [accessed 12 December 2014].
76. Lenormand, *Confessions,* II. Citations and material in this segment are drawn from 'Le Mirage révolutionnaire', the final chapter, pp. 336–79.

# CHAPTER 4

❖

# Epilogue

## I. Anna Seghers

— 1 —

You are a doctor posted to a military field hospital on the Western front and things are far from quiet. One of your patients is a despicable human being. You are inclined to withhold treatment. But you are a doctor, a specialist in mental and nervous disorders, not a restaurant owner with the right to refuse service to anyone. The choice is not yours to make.

Your patient is a lance corporal blinded by gas (subsequently diagnosed as hysterical blindness). From dawn to dusk, and deep into the night, the 'blinded' soldier spits out hatred like gobs of phlegm: hatred of the English, hatred of the French, hatred of everything 'un-German' and, most obsessively, hatred of the Jews. Jews are the scum of the earth and must die. Yet this monster of unfeeling, perversely charismatic, succeeds in surrounding himself with a small band of disciples who hang on to his every word.

The lance corporal, of course, is Adolf Hitler.

To the doctor, A. H. embodied the ultimate legacy of the war: the debasement of life, the extinction of human essence.

In the end, professional pride and curiosity trump bafflement and loathing. Psychiatry and history teach that the urge to dominate and to destroy is deeply embedded in the human psyche. The psychiatrist knows this. He also knows he can make this madman see again and restore a semblance of normality, but that only God could expunge the dark matter buried in his soul.

The psychiatrist succeeds in curing A.H.'s 'blindness' through hypnotic suggestion. On the loose, A.H. turned out to be no mean hypnotist himself, a crafty manipulator of a defeated, traumatized nation's hysterical blindness. In power, Hitler at once ordered the arrest of his wartime therapist, lest he go public with the record.

The physician wrestling, like Hamlet, with a grave matter of conscience is the narrator of *Der Augenzeuge* (*The Eyewitness*), a novel by Ernst Weiss.[1] Weiss's novel ponders one of those what-ifs in history. What if Cleopatra's nose had been stuck on her face like a potato? (No cinemascope Hollywood blockbuster.) What if the Turks had not been stopped before Vienna? (No croissants.) What if the wartime

FIG. 6. Writers' Congress for the Defence of Culture. Anna Seghers.
(David Seymour/Magnum Photos)

psychiatrist had committed Hitler to a mental institution instead of playing enabler to his insanity? (No Holocaust.)

*The Eyewitness* was Weiss's entry in a competition for the best novel by a German émigré. The incentive was a small cash prize from the contest's sponsor, the American Guild for Cultural Freedom, and, more importantly, publication by the New York publishing house of Little, Brown & Company. The contest attracted 177 entries. The prize went to one Arnold Bender for *Es ist später denn ihr wisst*. At this point, Little Brown reneged on the deal, contending that Bender's book failed to live up to the contractual obligation of finding 'a fair-sized reading public in America'.[2]

Ernst Weiss epitomized the straitened author in exile. 'The times are hungry and bitter', he wrote to his publisher from Prague in November 1933, and nine days later: 'we really have no idea how we are supposed to find our readers'.[3]

*The Eyewitness* is fiction. Weiss's fate is not. With Hitler's accession to power, the Czech-born long-time Berlin resident fled to Switzerland. 1934 saw him in Paris. Penniless, lonely and depressed, he found no peace there. On 14 June 1940, German troops entered the French capital. That same day Weiss took poison in a hotel room.

— 2 —

In Anna Seghers's novel *Transit*, Weiss is Weidel, the personification of the hapless fugitive scrambling for scraps of paper stamped with the promise of life. Few works capture the ordeal of exile, of life squirming at the end of a hook, with greater penetration. Like Weiss, Weidel commits suicide in a Paris hotel room. Among his meagre belongings is a small suitcase containing an unfinished manuscript. By and by, Weidel's suitcase winds up in the hands of another fugitive from Nazi Germany, *Transit*'s unnamed narrator; let's call him X. A suitcase is an apt metaphor for the life of the stateless writer on the run; Anna Seghers embraced it to jump-start *Transit*.

Oddly enough, X showed not the slightest interest in the Weidel manuscript. For X considered reading books an inauthentic substitute for life, the printed page of little use in fixing the wrongs of the world, and boasted of never having read a book from cover to cover. But now there was this suitcase with a 300-page manuscript, beckoning, testing his resolve. At long last, bowing to boredom and curiosity, X opened the suitcase, pulled out the manuscript, started reading — and couldn't put it down.

> And as I read line after line, I also felt that *this* was my own language, my mother tongue, and it flowed into me like milk into a baby. It didn't rasp and grate like the language that came from the throats of the Nazis, their murderous commands and objectionable insistence on obedience, their disgusting boasts. — *This* was a serious, calm, and still.
> I felt as if I were alone again with my own family. I came across words my mother had used to soothe me when I was angry and horrible words she had used to admonish me when I had lied or been in a fight. [...] The whole thing was a fairly complicated story with some complicated characters. One of whom, I thought, resembled me.[4]

Seghers began *Transit* en route to Mexico, where she would spend the war years. With the ordeal of the German invasion, flight and the visa merry-go-round, her own and that of others, fresh in mind, a good deal of personal history found its way into the novel, circumscribing a universal fate. A brief spell in a Nazi jail preceded exile in Switzerland, then France. In May 1940, László Radványi, Seghers's husband, was interned as an enemy alien in Le Vernet concentration camp. Conditions there resembled the German prototype. When Germany invaded, Seghers set out for the camp in the foothills of the Pyrenees, children in tow, resolved to bring about her husband's release. 'The roads were impassable', she told John Stuart of *The New Masses* in 1943. 'We were bombed and machine-gunned. The children were terrified. [...] I could make no headway along the jammed roads. [...] We ran into Nazi soldiers — young fanatics.'[5]

X's experience paralleled that of Anna Seghers. He, too, was living in Paris when Hitler invaded, and he, too, made his way south on roads clogged with throngs of the uprooted swept along by fear. In Marseille, X joined legions of refugees like himself frantic to ship out. The key was lining up the necessary papers. But lining up the necessary papers was the stuff of nightmares, for the line-up kept changing, a revolving door of residency permits, passports, safe conducts, exit and transit visas, a paper chain whose weakest link was unpredictability. Typical was the case of the conductor from Prague. The maestro had signed a contract with a prominent orchestra in Caracas, Venezuela, on the strength of which he had been granted a visa: by the time the exit visa arrived, the original visa had expired and the contract was rescinded. Catch-22 *avant la lettre*.

Marseille was awash with uniforms on the lookout for undocumented refugees; Vichy interned paperless strangers under dehumanizing conditions. But the first glimpse of Marseille's harbour, sparkling white poised on the lip of the blue Mediterranean, made the case for life with irrefutable clarity. There, rejoiced X, 'I felt at last, after so much absurdity, madness and misery, the one genuine happiness that is available to everyone at any time: the joy of being alive.' (35)

An escapee from two camps, one German, the other French, X's will to live was strong. Enduring is clearing hurdles and jumping through hoops until the ship weighs anchor and her bow is pointing west. Days are filled marking time, making contacts, pursuing leads, removing roadblocks; cooling one's heels inside and outside consular offices for hours on end; of minutes ticking away like a time bomb, unless you are a consul whose understanding of 'recent' may mean several months whereas to a visa hunter clinging to life several months loom as an eternity. A chance encounter with Weidel's widow brings the visa quagmire to an abrupt end: assuming the dead husband's identity yields American exit visas for himself and the widow.

But then X does the unexpected: he dumps the visa and goes into hiding instead. Europe needed him more than America. The fight was here and now.

X's disclaimers notwithstanding, perfect strangers sniffed out the writer in him. 'No! Not a chance!' X shot back when asked, as though responding to an insult. Questioned by an American consular official about his future plans, X replied that he was thinking of learning a trade. Taking him for Weidel, the official expressed surprise:

> 'How come? Aren't you going to write another book?'
> Then under that severe gaze of his that demanded the full truth, it just burst
> out of me. 'I? No. Let me tell you why. As a little boy I often went on school
> trips. The trips were a lot of fun, but then the next day our teacher assigned
> us a composition on the subject, 'Our school trip', And when we came back
> from summer vacations we always had to write a composition: 'How I spent my
> vacation'. And even after Christmas, there was a composition: 'Christmas'. And
> in the end it seemed to me that I experienced the school trips, Christmas, the
> vacations, only so that I could write a composition about them. And all those
> writers who were in the concentration camp with me, who escaped with me, it
> seems to me that we lived through these most terrible stretches in our lives just
> so we could write about them: the camps, the war, escape, and flight.'
> [...]
> He made a note and said with a glimmer of kindness, 'This is a grave
> confession for a man like yourself. What kind of trade would you like to take
> up?'
> 'I have a talent for precision mechanics.'
> Then he said, 'You're still young. You can still make changes in your life. I
> wish you good luck.' (213–14)

## II. *Le Capitaine Paul-Lemerle*

— 1 —

The *Capitaine Paul-Lemerle* wasn't pretty. Freighters rarely are. They are not meant
to carry anything but timber, grain, or some such bulky substance, and since 1921
*Le Capitaine Paul Lemerle* had gone about her business doing just that, dutifully
shuttling back and forth between France and South America on behalf of her
owners, the Compagnie des Transports Maritimes. With the outbreak of war and
fewer seas to ply, the *Paul-Lemerle* was converted into a troop carrier, bunks in the
hold and cannons on the gangway. Of the troops submerged in the hold, stacked up
like pieces of cord-wood, there is no record.

By every measure, the *Paul-Lemerle* appeared destined to share the fate of this
Unknown Soldier, confined to a page of history never to be written or, at best,
relegated to a footnote in the storied annals of French maritime history. But a
single voyage, a crossing between Marseille and Martinique, decreed otherwise.
The *Paul-Lemerle* left Marseille on 25 March 1941, and arrived in Martinique in late
May, dipping in and out of ports along the way, presumably to drop off or take on
contraband.

What set the *Le Capitaine Paul-Lemerle* apart from kindred freighters was the
composition of her cargo: neither wood, cement, nor instruments of war, but
hundreds of passengers at risk, 'contraband' by another name. The passenger list
included André Breton; the Cuban artist Wifredo Lam; the Rumanian cartoonist
and illustrator Saul Steinberg; Austria's 'racing reporter' Egon Kisch; Anna Seghers;
the anthropologist Claude Lévi-Strauss; Victor Serge and his now twenty-year-

old son Vlady. This cargo of 'misfits' lifted an ordinary freighter with a single smokestack from obscurity, besting counterparts with multiple smokestacks and far greater capacity. A French maritime historian likened *Le Capitaine Paul-Lemerle* to men who lack every outward sign of distinction yet go on to achieve great things, for having had 'the dubious privilege' of transporting some of the finest flower of Europe's intelligentsia.[6]

No, she wasn't pretty. Checking her out at the dockside the day before departure, Victor Serge compared the *Capitaine* to a 'sardine can in which someone has extinguished his cigarette'.[7]

Conditions on board resembled the slave ships of the Middle Passage. 'About 350 people', recalled Claude Lévi-Strauss in *Tristes Tropiques*,

> were crammed on to a small steamer which [...] boasted only two cabins with, in all, seven bunks [...]. But the most disagreeable feature was what is referred to in the army as the sanitary arrangements [...] the crew had erected two pairs of wooden huts, with neither windows nor ventilation; one contained a few shower sprinklers which worked only in the morning; the other was provided with a long wooden trough crudely lined with zinc and leading directly into the sea [...] the unventilated huts were made of unseasoned, resinous pine which, after being impregnated with dirty water, urine and sea air, began to ferment in the sun and give off a warmish, sweet and nauseous odour; this, added to other smells, very soon became intolerable, especially when there was a swell.[8]

Prior acquaintance with the captain secured Lévi-Strauss a private berth.

Food was rationed and nauseating. The toilets were on deck: in turbulent seas, the excrement spilt into the hold. 'When we complained about the food', recalled a passenger, 'the steward warned that malcontents would be shipped back to Casablanca and turned over to the Nazis. We were *sales étrangers* — "dirty foreigners" — with no right to complain.'[9] A month into the voyage and at the first sight of land, the Fort de France lighthouse at the entrance of Martinique, the ship's peculiar cargo gathered on deck, driven by a single thought:

> Instead of the call 'Land! Land!' as in traditional sea stories, 'A bath, at last a bath tomorrow!' could be heard on every side [...][10]

Lévi-Strauss was one of only three passengers given permission to land. The rest were interned in an old leper colony.

There would be no baths.

Compared to Martinique, the *Paul-Lemerle* resembled a luxury liner. Harassed and robbed at every turn, compelled to pay for their own 'maintenance'; plagued by bedbugs, flies and mosquitoes, the passengers had every reason to believe that they had landed in 'the power of gangsters'.[11]

Martinique — 'the flower of French colonial rule at work' (Anna Seghers) — waffled a good deal before allowing the *sales étrangers* to resume their journey in the direction ordained by their visas. A chapter had ended but not the ordeal. There was no shortage of human depravity on the final leg of the outbound journey. Further internments, delays and plain human nastiness loomed on the horizon.

— 2 —

If *Tristes Tropiques* was Lévi-Strauss's search for 'a human society reduced to its most basic expression', the structural anthropologist had to look no further than the phenomenon of scores of *beaux esprits* casting all intellectual baggage overboard to clamour for a place in the tub. To Lévi-Strauss, the European was no less exotic than, say, the Caduveo of Brazil, riff-raff no more so than the cream of the European intelligentsia. But while Lévi-Strauss left a fairly detailed account of the horrendous living conditions aboard ship, the trailblazing anthropologist paid surprisingly little attention to his fellow outcasts, singling out only André Breton and Victor Serge for fleeting appraisals. With the former he carried on a lively correspondence and discussion concerning the 'the relationships between aesthetic beauty and absolute originality'. Tracking Breton's demeanour, Lévi-Strauss observed that the Surrealist 'was very much out of place *dans cette galère*, [striding] up and down the few empty spaces left on deck; wrapped in his thick nap overcoat, he looked like a blue bear'.

Lévi-Strauss was less impressed with Victor Serge:

> I was intimidated by his status as a former companion of Lenin, at the same time as I had the greatest difficulty in identifying him with his physical presence, which was rather like that of a prim and elderly spinster. The clean-shaven, delicate-featured face, the clear voice accompanied by a stilted and wary manner, had an almost asexual quality, which I was later to find among Buddhist monks along the Burmese frontier, and which is very far removed from the virile and superabundant vitality commonly associated in France with what are called subversive activities. The explanation is that cultural types which occur in very similar forms in every society, because they are constructed around very simple polarities, are used to fulfil different social functions in different communities. Serge's type had been able to realize itself in a revolutionary career in Russia, but elsewhere it might have played some other part.[12]

Men and women slept in separate quarters. Anna Seghers and Victor Serge could not have cared less. Nocturnal separation diminished the likelihood of running into each other by some eight hours. No doubt they gave each other a wide berth in broad daylight as well. Inscrutable fate had placed both, prosecutor and prosecuted, on and in the same boat.

Europe's exiles were divided between those resolved never to set foot in Europe again and others equally resolved to return as soon as the coast was clear. For the latter, departing was like leaving home for the hospital and not knowing whether you would ever be back. Victor Serge, for one, felt the loss like a phantom pain following the removal of a body part. 'So here we are, my son and I', Serge wrote in his *Memoirs*,

> on a cargo boat converted into an ersatz concentration-camp of the sea, the *Capitaine Paul-Lemerle*. I feel no joy at going. I would a thousand times rather have stayed, if that had been possible: but before liberation of some kind comes its way, the chances are ninety-nine out of a hundred that I shall have perished in some filthy prison. Europe, with its bullet-ridden Russia, its crushed and trampled Germanies, its invaded nations, its gutted France — how one clings to it. We are parting only to return.[13]

Lévi-Strauss reached New York in the second half of May, having been detained in Puerto Rico on suspicion of being a 'Jewish International Communist'; Breton arrived in July, likewise suspected of Communist sympathies. Wifredo Lam entered Cuba in midsummer; Victor Serge and Vlady disembarked in Mexico in September; Egon Kisch followed suit in October; Anna Seghers the month thereafter. Among them, only Victor Serge would never again see Europe.

— *3* —

The Biblioteca Miguel Lerdo de Tejada is a hyper-modern facility located in the heart of Mexico City in what used to be a church. The pews have yielded to two vertical rows of twenty desks, each with a computer positioned on the right-hand side, separated by ten vertical rows of low-slung bookcases filled with four centuries' worth of philosophy, religion, history, law, literature, and the sciences, a Mondrianesque dissection of floor space surrounded by swirling rhythms of paint that cover every centimetre of the library's 2,000 square-metre interior walls.

*La Revolución y sus elementos*, the mural's title, is the creation of Russo-Mexican artist Vlady (he went by a single name), who died in 2005. *La Revolución* is Vlady's homage to his father, Victor Serge. The dedication, set within the mural itself, reads: *A La Probidad Intelectual de Victor Serge (To the Intellectual Honesty of Victor Serge)*. Upon entering, just above the arched doorway, cascading above and around the entrance, are books, open and shut, spinning and tumbling like wet clothes in a drier. Obstructing their path is a monster, half-human, half-reptile, with multiple claw-like hands. Further down skulk two goons with beaky, bird-like profiles, boots planted amid books and papers gored and streaked with blood. One book in particular commands attention. Suspended in the air like a bird in flight and awash in a halo of muted red flames, this is a book with a pair of shoes wedged inside the pages, soles pointed outward, with a hole in each like a pair of eyes. They are the shoes Victor Serge wore on the day he died, 17 November 1947, of a massive heart attack, on his way home in a taxi from Mexico City's main post office. He was found dead sprawled across its back seat with the soles of his shoes facing outward, as in Vlady's mural.

Vlady's homage to his father features a skeletal horse, inserted like a sidebar in a textbook. Captioned *The Structural Sketch of a Skeleton of Obsolete Politics*, the list of indicted politics, wrapped like labels around the skeleton — upright, frisky, doltish — is a long one: the Conquest; colonialism; apathy; foreign intervention; poverty; misery; corruption; injustice; enslavement of women; ideological poverty; illiteracy; torture; stupidity; egoism of the rich, and, strangely, football madness, 'Etc, Etc, Etc....' Vlady had had it with politics, 'the major source of our misfortunes' and 'a waste of time'. 'I don't want to talk about politics or social questions', he informed participants in a round-table discussion. 'I only want to talk about how a blue mixes with green'.[14]

# Notes to Chapter 4

1. Ernst Weiss, *Der Augenzeuge* (Frankfurt a.M.: Suhrkamp, 2000). Ernst Weiss, *The Eyewitness*, trans. by Ella R. W. McKee (Boston: Houghton Mifflin, 1977). Quotations herein are from the English version.
2. Volkmar Zühlsdorf, *Hitler's Exiles: The German Cultural Resistance in America and Europe* (London and New York: Continuum, 2004), p. 149.
3. Hermann Kesten, ed., *Deutsche Literatur im Exil: Briefe Europäischer Autoren, 1933–1949* (Vienna: Kurt Desch, 1964), pp. 63–64.
4. Anna Seghers, *Transit*, trans. by Margot Bettauer Dembo (New York: New York Review of Books, 2013), p. 21
5. John Stuart, 'Anna Seghers', *The New Masses,* 16 February 1943, 22–23.
6. 'Capitaine Paul-Lemerle', <http://maitres-du-vent.blogspot.com/2008/05/capitaine-paul-lemerle.html> [accessed 20 February 2012]
7. Rosemary Sullivan, *Villa Air-Bel: World War II, Escape, and a House in Marseille* (New York: Harper Perennial, 2006), p. 326. In Seghers's *Transit* the ship is mentioned several times by name, though never without denigrating modifiers: 'hideous', 'ramshackle'.
8. Claude Lévi-Strauss, *Tristes Tropiques,* trans. by John and Doreen Weightman (New York: Penguin Books, 1992), pp. 24–26.
9. Martin Ruppel, 'Hell-Hole in Martinique', *The New Masses*, 26 August 1941, 14.
10. Lévi-Strauss, p. 26.
11. Ruppel, 14.
12. Lévi-Strauss, p. 25
13. Serge, *Memoirs*, p. 366.
14. Cited in Arnold Belkin, 'Contra la amnesia. Para comprender a Vlady', in Rens, *Vlady*, p. 214.

# CONCLUSION

❖

— *1* —

On the day the Congress wrapped up its business, the house was packed, despite temperatures that hovered around 30°C. Arguably 'the largest and most ambitious mobilisation of its kind' was drawing to a close.[1] Malraux and Barbusse supplied the final touches. The former totted up the pluses and minuses and came up with a positive differential. Barbusse had the last word. 'For my part', he said, encapsulating the Communist view of the role of the writer: 'I've often said that the writer is a public person, that the book is a public act. What we say gets spread around; what we write, we sow in this inchoate mass that is public opinion.' Barbusse further extolled socialist realism as 'a splendid enrichment of literature and art' and defused talk of 'brigade' literature by reminding the public and writers present that 'one does not give up one's freedom by rallying behind a correct point of view'.

On 25 June, *L'Humanité* observed that it was still too early to draw up a balance sheet. Sticking to generalities, it asserted that everyone agreed that culture was threatened by fascism and that all more or less agreed that in the Soviet Union 'freedom of thought and the spirit of inquiry, far from being manipulated, as contended by fascist countries, offered the greatest possibilities for human advancement'. Everyone came out ahead, there were no losers.[2]

Two days later *L'Humanité* explained the meaning of it all. Workers, it said, needed writers who spoke the unvarnished truth. The working class and writers were allies, as in the Soviet Union, and, like Barbusse, its author dismissed charges regarding the straitjacketing of culture. 'The best minds acknowledge that Marxism does not constitute a rupture with the cultural tradition, but that what is best in that tradition is fertilized and augmented by Marxism and at last put within the reach of all men.' To this end, socialist realism was proving its worth in the Soviet Union.[3]

*L'Humanité's* assessment was par for the course. From the point of view of international Communism (read: Comintern) the Congress had done the job: it struck a blow for Front politics in the cultural realm and paid off handsomely as a forum in which to talk up the joys of socialist realism as the continuation of the political struggle by other means.

*L'Humanité* took its cue from the mother ship *Pravda*. *Pravda's* elaborate two-week coverage registered not a single false note. The writers' Congress had the ear of Stalin, as befitted 'The Greatest Event in the History of Culture', comparable to the collaboration of the Encyclopedists of the eighteenth century.[4] There was much talk of fascist barbarism, degenerate capitalism, Communist solidarity, the new man, socialist humanism, and similar fill-in-the-blanks copy. A quick look at the headlines capture the essence of the coverage: 'Fascism Leads to the Degeneration of Mankind — Proletariat — Bearer of Culture'; 'Only Communism Can Save

Civilization': 'Only in the Soviet Union Can Man Be of Value'. There was a long piece expounding the tenets of Soviet humanism. 'Powerful Demonstration Against Fascism' headlined the piece reporting the termination of the Congress. *Pravda* editors cherry-picked the speeches to cite or paraphrase, avoiding mention of any and all criticism of the Soviet Union, however mild, and altogether ignored naysayers like Salvemini and Paz. A good deal of the proceedings was transmitted by telephone, primarily by Koltsov, in time for next day's edition, as though covering a crucial political summit. Needless to say, the Victor Serge intermezzo was banished to the print version of the Gulag. Johannes Becher summarized the results of the Congress in a letter to the International Association of Revolutionary Writers (MORP) in Moscow as follows: 'The Congress was a great and partly unexpected success. [...] Approaching the issues as we did in Paris will enable us to couple the best forces of literature to the workers' movement.'[5]

The internal reports submitted to Moscow were not uniformly glowing, however. Gustav Regler was hauled over the coals for exhorting the faithful to join him in singing *The Internationale*, feeding the impression that the Congress was a Communist creation. The Congress had gone too far to the left. There had been too much chatter about 'the destiny of man' and emphasis on Marxism as humanism.[6]

— 2 —

From Gide and Malraux to Ter Braak, Lenormand and Klaus Mann — Western delegates may have had their doubts and conflicting emotions, though not all felt comfortable to express them openly at the time, or only did so years after the event. As noted, the American Michael Gold had no such reservations, giving the Congress an unqualified thumbs-up. Writing years after the event, another American man of letters (not a participant) gave the Congress an equally unqualified thumbs-down. 'The Congress was one of the most thoroughly rigged and steamrollered assemblages ever perpetrated on the face of Western literature in the name of culture and freedom', declared Roger Shattuck. 'That estimate', Shattuck continued, 'does not diminish but rather amplifies its significance as a historical and intellectual event. [...] There sat some of Europe's most distinguished men that systematically swept into a corner any dissent from the prevailing opinion that the true revolutionary spirit belonged to the Soviet government.'[7]

Elsewhere, Shattuck writes:

> What then was this 1935 Writers' Congress that we should pick over it for so long? Wasn't it purely and simply a flop? It could be painted very easily as a monstrous machine for grinding out worthless copy. It had no effect on history or policy, and the principal side effects worked to the benefit of a militant party subservient to a terroristic foreign state. [...] Since it really had no terms, the Paris Congress neither succeeded nor failed.[8]

The essay in which Shattuck raised the 'terrorist' banner bore the title 'Having Congress: The Shame of the Thirties'. Oblivious to the unprecedented political and economic conditions that produced it, Shattuck pilloried Western participants for assuming the woman's place in the missionary sex position, as though the most shameful act in that baleful decade was a group of writers indulging in an extended gabfest.

With a nod to Benda of *La Trahison des clercs*, British historian Frances Stonor Saunders advised intellectuals to leave politics alone. 'In the 1930s,' she writes, 'the real world was worrying itself through a prolonged political and economic crisis that threw intellectuals into a state of tension sometimes verging on panic' — and into the Soviet camp.[9]

> The fatal compromise made by intellectuals in the Thirties was to abandon the search for an alternative, a 'neither/nor', and to sign up instead to the Manichaean 'either/or'. As a result, good intentions and real moral courage (of the kind that took many writers and artists into the trenches of the Spanish Civil War) were sacrificed to an impossible bargain.[10]

— 3 —

'In 1935, the knowledge and the judgments of our day', writes Wolfgang Klein in the epilogue to *Pour la défense de la culture*, 'if they already existed, constituted the minority. There were other experiences and hopes that dominated the conversation.' Even Julien Benda, the champion of 'eternal values', conceded: 'In sum much good will, much heart, much faith, most often of the good kind.' On the whole, then, contemporaries did not feel that they had been taken for a ride. The Congress, Klein writes, made short work of a number of prevailing myths: that the Congress was organized by outside elements; that the delegates were mere puppets; that International Communism Soviets bankrolled the Congress. Finally, the German scholar posits a number of positive outcomes. To Magdeleine Paz's subsequent characterization of the Congress as a 'shining assembly of the princes of the pen', Klein counters that the Congress marked the apogee of political influence: 'it is the public attention produced by their action at the Mutualité that goes directly to the rare denial of Soviet power'; the intervention of Paz and company helped spring Serge from the Gulag.

The Association of Writers for the Defence of Culture, likewise an offshoot of Congress, also gets honourable mention. Designed to maintain and broaden contacts made at the Congress and headquartered in Paris, its twelve-member presidium included Malraux, Gide, Thomas Mann, Gorky, Sinclair Lewis, Shaw, Selma Lagerlöf, Ramón del Valle-Inclán, Aldous Huxley and E. M. Forster. The presidium met sporadically but fizzled out for lack of funds and interest. Huxley and Forster, for example, had been deeply disappointed in the Congress and seemed in no hurry to lend their names to the arrangements constituted in its name.

Yet between the time of its creation and the onset of war, the Association accomplished not a little. Among its achievements, Klein remarks spin-offs of both the Association and similar congresses in other countries. Until developments in Spain swept all before it, the Paris-based Association organized demonstrations, meetings, cultural events, and helped organize writers' congresses at home and abroad. The final act was a committee, founded in 1939, to assist Spanish intellectuals interned in concentration camps in southern France after the defeat of Republican Spain and to enable them to make a living afterwards.[11]

And even that great scoffer and slayer of the Tuis, Bertolt Brecht, did not think the Congress had been such a fiasco after all; at least that is what he told Johannes Becher, most likely for Soviet consumption. Writing in July 1935, he impressed upon the exiled poet in the USSR to build upon the things achieved at the Congress:

> A publicistic infrastructure must be ready for the grave times ahead. A book (or pamphlets) is a more reliable instrument than appeals to the press. (As the Congress seems to have shown, the latter are usually unsuccessful.) I regard a periodical as less effective, because only mediocrities contribute regularly. A process of *communication among writers* [emphasis in the original] must be created. The Congress was undoubtedly a beginning. But only a beginning. [...] To sum up: On the whole I regard the Congress as a success, indeed what with the limited funds available and the short period of preparation, as an outstanding success, but I believe it will take hard work to exploit this success.[12]

Unlike their Soviet counterparts, Western writers suffered no long-term damage to their careers. A number who sought refuge in the United States subsequently became targets of a witch hunt in the form of the House Un-American Activities; Lion Feuchtwanger, for example, was never able to get American citizenship and thus could not risking leaving the United States for fear of not being able to return. But these were mere bagatelles compared to the fate suffered by Soviet delegates. Here, ultimately, resided the real victims. Examples abound. Kirshon and Koltsov perished in the Gulag. Luppol, arrested in 1940, died in 1943; Babel, arrested in 1939, disappeared in a camp and was not heard from again. Pasternak was forced to say no to the 1985 Nobel Prize in Literature.

At the 1938 International Writers' Association for the Defence of Culture, a special conference summoned to discuss the tasks of writers in the face of increased fascist aggression, Aragon spoke of the changes that had taken place since the meeting in Paris three years earlier. While in 1935, he wrote in his introductory remarks summarizing the conference, the discussion centred on the writer's social role, the principal concern in 1938 was to define *'the task of the writer in the world'* (emphasis in the original). That task today, he asserted, centred on action, effective action, wherever and whenever.[13]

— 4 —

Slovenia's Marxist philosopher Slavoj Žižek: 'We need intellectuals — not to make decisions, but to make clear what the issues are about.'[14] If this is the criterion, and it is not a bad one, then the Congress has nothing to be ashamed of or apologize for, and doubly so when we factor in the Victor Serge eruption. By exposing the Serge charade the advocates of freedom of speech had the last word. The affair clearly underscored the limits of Front politics in the literary realm by breaking the 'silence' around the issues that had brought the delegates together to begin with. The alleged politicization of Western authors may be viewed as a function of the cultural politics of despair, although in 1935 'despair' may be too harsh a term. Those who remained *au-dessus de la bataille* ultimately were no less affected than those who entered the fray. The Cold War greatly muddied the picture. Like the Pope, writers have no legions, and far less moral authority. Or, to put it in the words of the Congress's chief engineer Ilya Ehrenburg: 'A revolver and a pen are entirely different things, and a revolver carries with it no shame.'[15]

## Notes to the Conclusion

1. Frances Stonor Saunders, 'What have intellectuals ever done for the world?', *The Observer,* 28 November 2004, <http://observer.theguardian.com/comment/story/0,6903,1361235,00.html> 2004 [Accessed 15 September 2015]

2. 'Les débats du congrès des écrivains ont porté hier sur les rapports entre la nation et la culture', pp. 1–2.

3. 'Ce que signifie le premier congrès international des écrivains. Une prise de conscience des dangers qui menacent la culture, du rôle de l'écrivain dans la société, de la conception socialiste de l'humanisme', p. 4.

4. 'Krupneishchee sobytie v istorii kul'tury', *Pravda,* 25 June 1935, p. 2.

5. Cited in Vegesack, p. 171.

6. Teroni and Klein, *Pour la défense de la culture,* Épilogue, pp. 573–78.

7. Roger Shattuck, 'Letter to the Editor', *PMLA,* 108. 5 (October 1993), pp. 1168–69.

8. Shattuck, 'Having Congress: The Shame of the Thirties', in *The Innocent Eye,* pp. 29–30.

9. The Spanish Civil war caused Benda to have a change of heart. See Vegesack, p. 183.

10. Saunders.

11. Teroni and Klein, pp. 569–70 (pp. 567, 569–70, 581).

12. Brecht, *Letters, 1913–1956,* pp. 208–09.

13. 'Zum Kongress', *Das Wort,* 9 (1938), 109–27 (p. 113). The article also contains contributions by Thomas Mann, Jean Cassou, Ernst Toller and Anna Seghers.

14. Cited in Saunders.

15. *Second Day,* p. 222.

# BIBLIOGRAPHY

❖

AARON, DANIEL, *Writers on the Left* (New York: Avon Books, 1961)

*André Gide-Jef Last: Correspondance 1934–1950* (Lyon: Presses Universitaires de Lyon, 1985)

ANDRINGA, ELS, *Deutsche Exilliteratur im niederländisch-deutschen Beziehungsgeflecht: Eine Geschichte der Kommunikation und Rezeption 1933–2013* (Berlin: de Gruyter, 2014)

ANT TER BRAAK-FABER, <http://www.mennoterbraak.nl/tekst/braa002brie11_01/braa002 brie11_01_0204.php> [accessed 9 December 2014]

BELKIN, ARNOLD, 'Contra la amnesia. Para comprender a Vlady', in *Vlady: De la Revolución al Renacimiento*, trans. by Tessa Brisac (Mexico: Siglo XXI, 2005)

BENDA, JULIEN, *The Betrayal of the Intellectuals*, trans. by Richard Aldington (Boston: Beacon Press, 1955)

BENJAMIN, WALTER, *The Arcades Project*, trans. by Howard Eiland and Kevin McLaughlin (Cambridge, MA, and London: Bellknap Press of Harvard University Press, 1999)

——*Reflections: Essays, Aphorism, Autobiographical Writings*, ed. by Peter Demetz (New York: Harcourt Brace Jovanovich, 1978)

BLOCH, JEAN-RICHARD, 'Parmi les leçons d'un congrès', *Europe,* 37 (1935), 98–108 (pp. 99–100) <http://gallica.bnf.fr/ark:/12148/bpt6k6282358r/f119.item.zoom> [accessed 15 November 2015]

BRAAK, MENNO TER, 'Emigranten-Literatur', in *De artikelen over emigrantenliteratuur 1933–1940.* Selected and introduced by Francis Bulhof (The Hague: Uitgeverij BZZTôH, 1988)

——'Fascistische gelijkheid', in *Verzameld Werk*, III

——'Het national-socialisme als rancuneleer', *Verzameld Werk*, 2nd edn, 7 vols, III, (Amsterdam: van Oorschot, 1980), pp. 575–94

——'Het Schrijverspalet', in *Verzameld Werk*, III, pp. 400–18

——*Briefwisseling Menno ter Braak/ Eddy du Perron* (Amsterdam: van Oorschot, 1965)

——*Briefwisseling Menno ter Braak/Jan Greshoff*, 1926–1940 <http://www.mennoterbraak. nl/brieven/lijst.php?id=gres002> [accessed 9 December 2014]

BRECHT, BERTOLT, *Briefe*, ed. by Günther Glaeser, (Frankfurt a.M.: Suhrkamp, 1981)

——*Journals*, ed. by John Willett, trans. by Hugh Rorrison (New York: Routledge, 1993)

——*Letters 1913–1956*, ed. by John Willett and trans. by Ralph Mannheim (New York: Routledge, 1990)

——'Speech at the Second International Writers' Congress for the Defense of Culture' <https://www.marxists.org/subject/art/lit_crit/works/brecht/fascism-culture.htm> [accessed 9 February 2016]

——*Der Tui-Roman. Fragment* (Frankfurt a.M.: Suhrkamp, 1973)

——*Bertolt Brecht Werke*, Prosa 2, Roman Fragmente und Romanentwürfe, ed. by Werner Hecht and others, 30 vols (Frankfurt a.M.: Suhrkamp, 1989), XVII

BRETON, ANDRÉ, *Nadja,* trans. by Richard Howard (New York: Grove Press, 1960)

——*Manifestoes of Surrealism*, trans. by Richard Seaver and Helen R. Land (Ann Arbor: University of Michigan Press, 1969)

——*Conversations: The Autobiography of Surrealism*, with André Parinaud and others, trans. by Mark Polizzotti (New York: Marlowe & Co., 1993)

CARLISLE, OLGA, 'The Art of Fiction', in *The Paris Review* 26 (1961) <http://www.

theparisreview.org/interviews/4636/the-art-of-fiction-no-26-ilya-ehrenburg [accessed 5 October 2012]

CARMIGGELT, SIMON, *Met de neus in de boeken* (Amsterdam: De Arbeiderspers, 1983)

CATE, CURTIS, *André Malraux: A Biography* (New York: Fromm International, 1995)

COWLEY, MALCOLM, *And I Worked at the Writer's Trade, Chapters in Literary History: 1918–1978* (New York: Viking Press, 1978)

CREVEL, RENÉ, *La Mort difficile* (Paris: Pauvert, 1979)

—— 'Le Suicide est-il une solution?', in *La Révolution Surréaliste*, 1, 15 January 1925, pp. 8–15 (p. 8) <http://gallica.bnf.fr/ark:/12148/bpt6k58450811/f1.item.r=Crevel> [accessed 14 February 2016]

—— 'Mais si la mort n'était qu'un mot', *Le Disque Vert*, 1 (1925) <http://www.psychanalyse-paris.com/908-Mais-si-la-mort-n-etait-qu-un.html> [accessed 21 April 2012]

——*Putting My Foot in It*, trans. by Thomas Buckley, with a foreword by Ezra Pound (Normal, IL: Dalkey Archive Press, 1992)

DALÍ, SALVADOR, preface to *La Mort difficile* (Paris: Pauvert, 1979)

DREYFUS, MICHEL, ed., *La Lutte contre le stalinisme. Textes 1936–1939* (Paris: François Maspero, 1977)

EASTMAN, MAX, *Artists in Uniform: A Study of Literature and Bureaucratism* (London: Allen & Unwin, 1934)

EHRENBURG, ILYA, *Memoirs: 1921–1941*, trans. by Tatania Shebunina and Yvonne Kapp (New York: Grosset & Dunlap, 1963)

——*Chekhov, Stendhal, and Other Essays* (New York: Knopf, 1963)

—— *The Second Day*, trans. by Liv Tudge (Moscow: Raduga, 1984)

FEUCHTWANGER, LION, Feuchtwanger papers, Collection no. 0204, Feuchtwanger Memorial Library, Special Collections, University of Southern California

—— *The Devil in France, My Encounter with Him in the Summer of 1940* (Los Angeles: Figueroa Press, n.d.)

—— *The House of Desdemona or the Laurels and Limitations of Historical Fiction*, trans. by Harold A. Basilius (Detroit: Wayne State University Press, 1963)

—— 'An meine Sowjetleser', *Das Wort*, 7 (1938)

—— 'Lion Feuchtwanger in der UdSSR', *Das Wort*, 1 (1937)

——*Moscow 1937, My Visit Described for My Friends*, trans. by Irene Josephy (New York: Viking Press, 1937)

——*Paris Gazette*, trans. by Willa and Edwin Muir (New York: Viking Press, 1940)

FLANNER, JANET, *Paris Was Yesterday, 1925–1939*, ed. by Irving Druttman (New York: Penguin Books, 1979)

FONTIJN, JAN, FRANK LIGTVOET, and CAREL PEETERS, EDS, 'Menno ter Braak, Politiek en Cultuur: 3 Generaties, 3 Forums' (Amsterdam: Stichting Literaire Aktiviteiten, 1982)

FREEMAN, JOSEPH, *An American Testament: A Narrative of Rebels and Romantics* (London: Gollancz, 1938)

GALLANT, MAVIS, 'Speck's Idea', in *Paris Stories* (New York: New York Review of Books, 2002)

GIDE, ANDRÉ, *Journals 1889–1949*, trans. by Justin O'Brien (Harmondsworth: Penguin Books, 1967)

——*Si le grain ne meurt* (Paris: Gallimard, 1955)

——*Return from the U.S.S.R.*, trans. by Dorothy Bussy (New York: Knopf, 1937)

GILLESSE, ROBÈRT, *De Tijd der Idealisten: Jef Last in de jaren dertig* (unpublished doctoral thesis, Rijksuniversiteit Leiden, 1994)

GOLD, MICHAEL, 'Notes from Kharkov', *The New Masses* (March 1931). (Note: With some exceptions, editions of *The New Masses* can be found at <http://www.unz.org/Pub/NewMasses/?Period=1935>)

—— 'The Writers Meet in Paris', *The New Masses* (30 July 1935)

GOLDBERG, ANATOL, *Ilya Ehrenburg, Revolutionary, Novelist, Poet, War Correspondent, Propagandist: The Extraordinary Epic of a Russian Survivor* (New York: Viking Press, 1984)

GORKY, MAXIM, and OTHERS, eds, *Belomor: An Account of the Construction of the New Canal Between the White Sea and the Baltic Sea*, trans. by Amabel Williams-Ellis (London: John Lane, 1935)

GREEN, JULIAN, *Diary 1928–1957*, trans. by Anne Green (New York: Caroll & Graff, 1985)

GROSSMAN, RICHARD, ed., *The God that Failed*, (New York: Bantam Matrix, 1965)

HANSSEN, LÉON, *Menno ter Braak 1902–1940: Leven en werk van een polemist*, 2 vols (Amsterdam: Balans, 2001)

HARRIS, FREDERICK JOHN, *André Gide and Romain Rolland: Two Men Divided* (New Brunswick, NJ: Rutgers University Press, 1973)

HERMSDORF, KLAUS, HUGO FETTING, and SILVIA SCHLENSTEDT, *Exil in den Niederlanden und in Spanien* (Leipzig: Reclam, 1981)

ISHERWOOD, CHRISTOPHER, *My Guru and His Disciple* (New York: Farrar Straus & Giroux, 1980)

——*Christopher and His Kind* (Minneapolis: University of Minnesota Press, 2001)

KESTEN, HERMANN, ed., *Deutsche Literatur im Exil: Briefe Europäischer Autoren, 1933–1949* (Vienna: Kurt Desch, 1964)

——*Lauter Literaten. Porträts. Erinnerungen* (Vienna: Kurt Desch, 1963)

KIŠ, DANILO, *A Tomb for Boris Davidovich*, trans. by Duška Mikić-Mitchell (New York: Penguin Books: 1980)

KOESTLER, ARTHUR, *The Yogi and the Commissar and Other Essays* (London: Jonathan Cape, 1964)

LAST, JEF, *De persoonlijkheid van André Gide*, AO — Reeks Boekje 1287 (Amsterdam: Stichting IVIO, 1969)

——*Het proletarisch schrijverscongres 1934'*, Cycloboekje, 2 (Amsterdam: A.f.t.b., 1934)

LENIN, VLADIMIR, 'Letter to Anatoly Lunacharsky', 6 May 1922, in *Lénine, Sur l'art et la littérature*, selected and presented by Jean-Michel Palmier, 3 vols (Paris: Union Générale d'Éditions, 1975), III

LENORMAND, H.-R., *Les Confessions d'un auteur dramatique*, vol. 2 (Paris: Albin Michel, 1953)

LÉVI-STRAUSS, CLAUDE, *Tristes Tropiques*, trans. by John and Doreen Weightman (New York: Penguin Books, 1992)

LEWIS, WYNDHAM, *Rude Assignment: An Intellectual Autobiography* (Santa Barbara, CA: Black Sparrow Press, 1984)

LITTLEJOHN, DAVID, ed., *The André Gide Reader*, (New York: Knopf, 1971)

LUCHAIRE, JULIEN, 'Confession d'un Français moyen', II (Florence: Olschki, 1965). Box A3a/folder 39. Lion Feuchtwanger papers, University of Southern California.

LUTKER, SHANA, 'Some fistfights of the Surrealists', *Material*, 3 (Los Angeles: Materialpress, 2012)

MALRAUX, ANDRÉ, *Anti-Memoirs*, trans. by Terence Kilmartin (New York: Holt, Rinehart and Winston, 1968)

——*Days of Wrath*, trans. by Haakon M. Chevalier (New York: Random House, 1936)

MANDELSTAM, NADEZHDA, *Hope Abandoned*, trans. by Max Hayward (New York: Atheneum, 1974)

MANN, ERIKA and KLAUS, *Escape to Life: Deutsche Kultur im Exil* (Munich: Spangenberg, 1991)

MANN, KLAUS, *André Gide and the Crisis of Modern Thought* (New York: Creative Age Press, 1943)

——Diary, <http://monacensia-dev.visuallibrary.de/content/pageview/12190> [accessed 13 January 2014]

——ed., *Die Sammlung, Literarische Monatschrift unter dem Patronat von André Gide, Aldous Huxley, Heinrich Mann* (Amsterdam: Querido, 1933–35)

——*Heute und Morgen: Schriften zur Zeit*, ed. by Martin Gregor-Dellin (Munich: Nymphenburger Verlagshandlung, 1969)

——*Het keerpunt: een autobiograpfie,* trans. by Willem van Toorn (Amsterdam: Arbeiderspers, 1987)

——*Kind dieser Zeit* (Hamburg: Rowohlt, 1967)

——'Notizen in Moskau', *Die Sammlung*, 6 (1934), 72–83.

——*The Turning Point: Thirty-Five Years in This Century* (New York: Fischer, 1942)

——*Der Vulkan. Roman unter Emigranten* (Amsterdam: Querido, 1939)

MANN, THOMAS, 'In Memoriam Menno ter Braak', in *Over Menno ter Braak* (Amsterdam: van Oorschot, 1949)

MARCUSE, LUDWIG, 'De Duitse strijd tegen het Duitse idealisme', in *Die Sammlung: Een bloemlezing uit het emigranten-maandblad*, ed. by Gerda Meijerink (Amsterdam: Querido, 1983)

——'Gespräch mit meinen Freunden', *Die Neue Weltbühne*, 21 (1937), 655–58

——'Ein volles Leben', *Die Westküste. A Fortnightly Publication of 'Aufbau' for California, Oregon and Washington*, 10.29. Box A3a/folder 52, Lion Feuchtwanger papers, Collection no. 0204, Feuchtwanger Memorial Library, Special Collections, USC Libraries, University of Southern California

——'Zur Debatte über die Emigranten-Literatur', in *De artikelen over emigrantenliteratuur, 1933–1940*, selected and introd. by Francis Bulhof (The Hague: Uitgeverij BZZTôH, 1988)

——*Mein 20. Jahrhundert. Auf dem Weg zu einer Autobiographie* (Munich: List, 1960)

MARXIST INTERNET ARCHIVE <https://www.marxists.org/subject/art/lit_crit/sovietwriter congress/index.htm> [accessed 1 June 2012]

MECHANICUS, PHILIP, *Van sikkel en hamer* (Amsterdam: Blitz, 1932)

*Menno ter Braak. Schrijversprentenboek 5*, 2nd printing (The Hague: Nederlands Letterkundig Museum en Documentatie Centrum, 1980)

OLINK, HANS, *Nico Rost: De man die van Duitsland hield* (Amsterdam: Nijgh & Van Ditmar, 1997)

ORWELL, GEORGE, *An Age Like This 1920–1940. The Collected Essays, Journalism and Letters*, ed. by Sonia Orwell and Ian Angus, 4 vols (Boston: Nonpareil Books, 2000)

PATKA, MARCUS G., *Zu nahe der Sonne: Deutsche Schriftsteller im Exil in Mexico* (Berlin: Aufbau, 1999)

PERRON, EDDY DU, *In deze grootse tijd* (The Hague: Stols Uitgever, 1946)

——*Het land van Herkomst* (Amsterdam: van Oorschot, 1989)

——*De smalle mens* (Amsterdam: Querido, 1934)

POGODIN, NIKOLAI, *Aristocrats, A Comedy in Four Acts*, trans. by Anthony Wixley and Robert S. Carr (London: Lawrence and Wishart Ltd., n.d.)

PRYCE-JONES, DAVID, 'André Malraux: Politicizing literature, fictionalizing politics', in *The New Criterion*, March 2005. <http://www.newcriterion.com/articles.cfm/andre-malraux-politicizing-literature-fictionalizing-politics-1287> [accessed 12 June 2013]

PUTNAM, SAMUEL, *Paris Was Our Mistress: Memoirs of a Lost & Found Generation* (Carbondale: Southern Illinois University Press, 1947)

RACINE, NICOLE, 'Victor Serge. Correspondance d'URSS, 1920–1936', *Mil neuf cent*, 8, 86–87

RADEK, KARL, 'Contemporary World Literature and the Tasks of Proletarian Art,' <www.marxists.org/archive/Radek> [accessed 12 January 2012]

RENS, JEAN-GUY, *Vlady: De la Revolución al Renacimiento*, trans. by Tessa Brisac (Mexico: Siglo XXI, 2005)

RENSEN, MARLEEN, *Lijden aan de tijd: Franse intellectuelen in het interbellum* (Soesterberg: Aspekt, 2009)

ROST, NICO, *Goethe in Dachau: Literatuur en werkelijkheid,* 3rd edn (The Hague: Kruseman, 1984)

——'Het geval Jef Last: over Fascisme en Trotzkisme' (Amsterdam: Pegasus, 1938)

ROTH, JOSEPH, *Right and Left,* trans. by Michael Hofmann (Woodstock and New York: Overlook Press, 1992)

RUPPEL, MARTIN, 'Hell-Hole in Martinique', *The New Masses,* 26 August 1941

SACHS, MAURICE, *Heksensabbat, verslag van een ondraaglijk leven* (Amsterdam: Arbeiderspers, 1967)

SARTRE, JEAN-PAUL, *Qu'est-ce que la littérature?* (Paris: Gallimard, 1948)

SAUNDERS, FRANCES STONOR, 'What have intellectuals ever done for the world?', *Observer,* 28 November 2004. <http://observer.theguardian.com/comment/story/0,6903,1361235,00. html. 2004>

SCHOLEM, GERSHOM and THEODOR W. ADORNO, eds., *The Correspondence of Walter Benjamin, 1910–1940,* ed. and trans. by R. Jacobson and Evelyn M. Jacobson (Chicago and London: University of Chicago Press, 1994

SCHWARZSCHILD, LEOPOLD, 'Autobiographical Notes', Leopold Schwarzschild Collection; AR 7043 / MF 571; box 1; folder 1; Leo Baeck Institute, New York

——*Tagebuch' 1933–1940,* ed. by Valerie Schwarzschild. Mit einem Vorwort von Kurt Sontheimer (Hamburg: Christian Wegner, 1965)

SCOTT, JOHN, *Behind the Urals: An American Worker in Russia's City of Steel* (Bloomington: Indiana University Press, 1973)

SEGHERS, ANNA, *Transit,* trans. by Margot Bettauer Dembo (New York: New York Review of Books, 2013)

SERGE, VICTOR, *Memoirs of a Revolutionary,* trans. by Peter Sedgwick (New York: Society Writers and Readers Publishing, 1984)

SHATTUCK, ROGER, *The Innocent Eye: On Modern Literature & the Arts* (New York: Farrar, Straus, Giroux, 1984)

——'Letter to the Editor', *PMLA,* 108.5 (October 1993), 1168–69

SPENDER, STEPHEN, *The 30's and After: Poetry, Politics, People, 1930's–1970's* (New York: Random House, 1978)

——*World Within World: The Autobiography of Stephen Spender* (New York: St Martin's Press, 1994)

SPERBER, MANÈS, *Until My Eyes Are Closed with Shards* (New York: Holmes & Meier, 1994)

STENDHAL, *Rome, Naples et Florence,* trans. and foreword by Richard N. Coe (London: John Calder, 1959)

STERN, LUDMILLA, *Western Intellectuals and the Soviet Union, 1920–40. From Red Square to the Left Bank* (London and New York: Routledge, 2007)

STUART, JOHN, 'Anna Seghers', *The New Masses,* 16 February 1943

SULLIVAN, ROSEMARY, *Villa Air-Bel: World War II, Escape, and a House in Marseille* (New York: Harper Perennial, 2006)

TANNERY, CLAUDE, *Malraux, the Absolute Agnostic, or, Metamorphosis as Universal Law* (Chicago: University of Chicago Press, 1991)

TERONI, SANDRA and WOLFGANG KLEIN, *Pour la défense de la culture. Les textes du Congrès International des écrivains, Paris, juin 1935* (Paris: Éditions Universitaires de Dijon, 2005)

TRETYAKOV, SERGEI, 'Bert Brecht', in *Brecht as They Knew Him,* ed. by Hubert Witt, trans. by John Peet (New York: International Publishers, 1974)

VEGESACK, THOMAS VON, '*De Intellectuelen: Een geschiedenis van het literaire engagement 1898– 1968,* trans. by Petra Broomans and Wiveca Jongeneel (Amsterdam: Meulenhoff, 1989)

VESTDIJK, SIMON, *Gestalten tegenover mij. Persoonlijke herinneringen* (Amsterdam: De Bezige Bij, 1992)

——'Ter Braak na de oorlog', in *Over Menno ter Braak* (Amsterdam: Oorschot, 1949)

VIERTEL, BERTHOLD, 'Brecht, Robbed of Citizenship', in *Brecht as They Knew Him*, ed. by Hubert Witt and trans. by John Peet (New York: International Publishers, 1974

WEISS, ERNST, *Der Augenzeuge* (Frankfurt a.M.: Suhrkamp, 2000)

——*The Eyewitness*, trans. by Ella R. W. McKee (Boston: Houghton Mifflin, 1977)

WEISSMAN, SUSAN, *Victor Serge: The Course Is Set on Hope* (London and New York: Verso, 2001)

WESTERMAN, FRANK, *Ingenieurs van de ziel*, (Amsterdam: Atlas, 2002) (*Engineers of the Soul* (New York: Vintage, 2011))

WITT, HUBERT, ed., *Brecht as They Knew Him,* trans. by John Peet (New York: International Publishers, 1974)

TROTSKY, LEON, *Writings of Leon Trotsky: Supplement (1934–40)*, ed. by George Breitman (New York: Pathfinder Press, 1979), p. 660. https://rosswolfe.files.wordpress.com/2015/05/leon-trotskii-collected-writings-supplement-1934–1940.pdf [accessed 28 November 2015]

ZÜHLSDORF, VOLKMAR, *Hitler's Exiles: The German Cultural Resistance in America and Europe* (London and New York: Continuum, 2004)

## Newspapers

### *L'HUMANITÉ*

ARTICLES FROM *L'Humanité* are available from the digital library of the Bibliothèque nationale de France, <http://gallica.bnf.fr/>

'L'inculpation d'Aragon', *L'Humanité*, 9 February 1932

NIZAN, PAUL, 'Hugo et nous', *L'Humanité*, 2 June 1935

'L'écrivain révolutionaire René Crevel est mort', *L'Humanité,* 21 June 1935

'Travailleurs et écrivains ont rendu à Victor Hugo un magnifique hommage', *L'Humanité*, 21 June 1935

'Les débats du congrès des écrivains ont porté hier sur les rapports entre la nation et la culture', *L'Humanité*, 25 June 1935

'La dernière journée du congrès des écrivains', *L'Humanité*, 26 June 1935

'Ce que signifie le premier congrès international des écrivains. Une prise de conscience des dangers qui menacent la culture, du rôle de l'écrivain dans la société, de la conception socialiste de l'humanisme', *L'Humanité,* 27 June 1935

'Ris et larmes d'André Gide,' *L'Humanité*, 18 December 1936

### *PRAVDA*

GOLD, MICHAEL, 'Postroim Novy Mir', *Pravda*, 24 June 1935

LAST, JEF, 'Fashizm — eto Varvarstvo' ('Fascism is Barbarism'), *Pravda*, 24 June 1935

'Krupneishchee sobytie v istorii kul'tury', *Pravda*, 25 June 1935

FEUCHTWANGER, LION, 'Estet o Sovetskom Soiuze', *Pravda*, 30 December 1936

——'Fashizm i Germanskaia intelligentsiia', *Pravda*, 28 January 1937

——'Pervye vpechtlenniai ob etom protsesse', Pravda, 30 January 1937

### *HET VADERLAND*

ARTICLES FROM *Het Vaderland* can be found at the website devoted to Menno ter Braak: <http://www.mennoterbraak.nl/> The website is part of the Digitale bibliotheek voor de Nederlandse letteren, <http://www.dbnl.org/>

BRAAK, MENNO TER, 'Schrijverscongres te Parijs', *Het Vaderland*, Kunst en Letteren, 24 June 1935

——'Het probleem van het individualisme ontbreekt', *Het Vaderland,* Kunst en Letteren, 25 June 1935

——'King Christina. De emigranten vluchten in de geschiedenis. Barok en hysterie', *Het Vaderland*, Kunst en Letteren, 29 September 1935


## Multimedia

BOEHM, HARTMUT, 'Porträt Lion Feuchtwanger' (parts 2 and 3 of 4) <https://www.youtube.com/results?search_query=lion+feuchtwanger> [accessed 10 November 2014]

*Capitaine Paul-Lemerle*, <http://maitres-du-vent.blogspot.com/2008/05/capitaine-paul-lemerle.html> [accessed 20 February 2012]

CEREMONIAL OPENING OF THE SOVIET WRITERS' Congress (1934) <https://www.youtube.com/watch?v=HZUelR9jZik> [accessed 12 December 2014)

FEUCHTWANGER, LION, *Die Wartesaal Trilogie* <http://www.weltbild.de/3/17763316–1/dvd/lion-feuchtwanger-die-wartesaal-trilogie.html> [accessed 20 October 2014]

SMIT, JAN PIETER, DIR., *L'ami hollandais. Jef Last & André Gide* (The Netherlands: SNG Film, 2005)

——SMIT, JAN PIETER, DIR., *Magnitogorsk — Forging the new man*, (The Netherlands: 1966)

# INDEX

❖

www.ingramcontent.com/pod-product-compliance
Lightning Source LLC
Chambersburg PA
CBHW080017280326
41934CB00015B/3379